CASINO
CONQUEST
Beat the Casinos
at Their Own Games!

Frank Scoblete

TRIUMPH
BOOKS

Library of Congress Cataloging-in-Publication Data

Scoblete, Frank.
  Casino conquest : beat the casinos at their own games! / Frank Scoblete.
      p. cm.
  ISBN 978-1-60078-708-9 — ISBN 1-60078-708-8
1. Gambling—Handbooks, manuals, etc. I. Title.
  GV1301.S384 2012
  795—dc23

                               2012025111

This book is available in quantity at special discounts for your group or organization. For further information, contact:

Triumph Books
814 North Franklin Street
Chicago, Illinois 60610
(312) 337-0747
www.triumphbooks.com

Printed in U.S.A.
ISBN: 978-1-60078-708-9
Design by Patricia Frey

Images courtesy of Frank Scoblete

To my teammates on the Five Horsemen:
Dominator
Jerry "Stickman"
Nick@Night
John "Skinny"

And to my good friends:
Marilyn "the Goddess"
and
Charlie "Sandtrap"

Contents

Introduction

This year I am writing my opuses on casino gambling: a two-book treatment of what I consider to be the major games one can play in the casinos—and how to play them properly.

I want players to learn how to beat those games that are beatable, which include craps (with dice control); blackjack (with card counting); Pai Gow poker (with hand-play and betting strategies); video poker; and traditional poker-room games, such as Texas Hold'em and Omaha Hi-Lo.

I will also cover games in which players cannot get an edge, such as roulette; baccarat; and the carnival games, such as Let It Ride, Four-Card Poker, Three-Card Poker, and others. For these I will provide the best possible strategies to keep the house edge as low as it can go and also betting methods to reduce the overall hit on your bankroll.

The first book, the one you are reading now, will give you everything you need to know about the casinos, my experiences in the casinos, and strategies for the following games: baccarat, blackjack, Spanish 21, craps, roulette, slots, casino war, Sic Bo, the Big Wheel, keno, and the lotteries.

The second book, titled *Poker Conquest*, will give advantage-play methods for Pai Gow poker; video poker; and traditional poker-room games, such as Texas Hold'em and Omaha Hi-Lo. It will also give the strongest possible strategies and playing methods for other casino poker games, such as Caribbean Stud, Let It Ride, Three-Card Poker, Four-Card Poker, and others.

These two books should appeal to new players and to those veterans looking to reverse their playing fortunes.

I have not included all games that can be found in all casinos, as many such games come for a short while and go away forever. I've stuck with the games that have a strong hold on the casino-playing landscape.

The more a player knows about the games, the better off that player will be. Keep in mind, luck tends to favor the well prepared.

PART 1:
A Heads-Up on Casino Gambling

CHAPTER 1

Relax: Casino Gambling Is Easy

I f you have never before played a casino game, no need to fear. The games were not developed for geniuses; otherwise very, very few people would play them. Indeed, I wouldn't be able to play any of them, as I am certainly not in the Einstein category.

There are a few simple facts to know before you read about and/or learn any game. I will cover these facts in this chapter, and then you will be off and running.

Playing with Chips

Casinos want players to bet with casino chips—sometimes called "checks" or "cheques"—rather than with cash, although some venues sometimes allow cash play. Dealers will call out, "Money plays!" for a player betting cash.

To convert your cash to casino chips, wait until the dealer completes the round of play in progress, then place your cash on the layout *in front* of your betting spot in card games or on the layout in front of you in games such as craps and roulette. The dealer will exchange your cash for an equivalent amount in casino chips, which you then use for betting.

When you are finished playing, you put your chips in front of you and say, "Cashing out," "Coloring up," or something to the effect of "I'm done." The dealer will then take the chips, count them, give you

1

larger denominations (if that can be done), and you can then go to the cashier, also called a "cage," where the cashier will give you money for your chips.

Chip Denominations

Chips have denominations imprinted on them and are also color-coded. The most common chip colors and denominations are:

Blue or White = $1
Pink = $2.50
Red = $5
Green = $25
Black = $100
Purple = $500
Burgundy or Orange = $1,000
Silver or Gold = $2,000
Brown = $5,000

Some casinos might have even higher-limit chips, and others might even allow play with quarters, meaning 25¢, but the above are representative of most casinos.

Protect Your Chips

It is bad enough to lose your chips to the casino, but it is far worse to lose your chips to a thief, also known as a "crossroader." You must protect your chips. At games such as craps, where there are chip rails, put the highest-denomination chips in the middle, put the second-highest-denomination chips next to those on both sides, and so on down to the lowest-denomination chips that you have.

In games such as blackjack and table games, where the chips are just stacked in front of you, do not make your stacks based on one denomination. Put the highest denomination at the bottom of the stacks, the second highest next, and so on. Most chip stealers are not looking to take handfuls of chips; they just want to scoop up a few of the highest denomination. You stand a much better chance of thwarting them by making it difficult to get to your highest-denomination chips.

Just notice what the casinos do in protecting their chips in the chip racks. The highest denominations are in the middle, and the lowest are at the ends. Even though casinos are generally safe places, they are not perfectly safe—so always be aware.

Count your chips before you color up and hand them in to the dealer. Before you lay down your chips to color up after your play, make sure you know exactly how much money you have there. Divide your chips by color, and hand them in this way. There is no rush in coloring up, so do it methodically and correctly. If you know exactly how much you have, you can correct any mistakes. Never take your eyes off your chips as a floor person, box person, or dealer is counting them. The casino personnel are not looking to cheat you, but mistakes are occasionally made... so be watchful.

If someone spills a drink while you are playing, you can dry off your clothes later; grab your chips or hold your hands over your chip rack or stacks! One of the oldest scams in the book is to drop a drink, and as everyone is leaping out of the way, the drink spiller scoops up some of a player's chips. When a drink spills over the layout, everyone looks at the event, including the dealers and the players. It is a great time for the crossroader to snatch a few chips from the rail.

The Eye in the Sky

Take a look at the ceiling when you are in a casino, and you'll notice black globes attached to it. These are spread throughout the property over all the gaming and nongaming areas, with the exception of the bathrooms. The black globes are collectively called "the eye in the sky," and in them are cameras keeping track of everything taking place. These eyes are hooked into monitors that the security personnel watch to make sure no cheating or other criminal activity is taking place in the casino or other areas.

Betting Limits

Before you sit down at a game, make sure you know what the table's betting limits are. There is a small display on each table that states the table's minimum and maximum bets, and it usually also lists the rules of the game.

A table with a $10 *minimum* betting requirement means that a player must wager at least $10 on each hand or wagering opportunity. If a table has a $1,000 *maximum*, this means a player is not allowed to make a wager greater than $1,000. In some games, such as craps and roulette, a player is able to make more than one bet at a time, but in other games each player can only make one bet at a time.

If you are not sure of what to do or what you are allowed to do, the best advice I can give is—just ask. The dealers and floor people will be happy to answer any questions you have; after all, they want your action at the table. Slot machines are somewhat different—just about everything you need to know is printed on the machine. In fact, there really isn't too much you need to know!

Sometimes It's "Units" Wagered

Sometimes gambling writers use the term "units" when discussing amounts wagered. The player decides what his unit will be. If you are a green-chip player and your minimum bet is $25, then your minimum unit is $25. That's one unit. If the most you bet is $100, then your maximum is four units. However, if you are a $5 bettor whose minimum unit is $5 and whose maximum bet is $100, that maximum is a 20-unit bet.

The reason for the "unit" terminology is that it allows players not to have to waste wordage going through all the various amounts a person can bet. I tend to go back and forth between units and money.

The Personnel of Table Games

Table games are played in a "pit," and the person in charge of the pit is called (creatively) the "pit boss." Under the pit boss is the "floor person" or, as some casinos call them, the floor man or floor woman. This individual is in charge of rating the players' action (how much you bet and for how long you play) and resolving any disputes that might occur. If a dispute cannot be resolved by the floor person, the pit boss will be called in.

Yes, there are people above the pit boss, as casinos have redundancy in abundance. There is the casino table-games manager, who is in charge of all the pits, and the casino shift manager, who is in charge of the entire casino during a given eight-hour shift.

The last line in the table-game hierarchy—I refuse to call it the "lowest" line, because these are the most important people the player deals with almost all the time—are the dealers. Good dealers make the casino experience enjoyable; bad dealers make it crummy.

Playing and Betting Advice

There are three types of casino players:

- The *advantage players,* who have actually turned the tables or machines in their favor and have the edge over the casino. These players bet smart and know the games they play perfectly, and they beat those games.
- The *smart players,* who do not have an edge but play the very best bets and strategies at their favorite games.
- The *ploppies,* who plop down at a table or machine, play stupidly using poor strategies, believe in silly gambling myths, and make the casinos enough money to build empires.

Comparison of Players

Item	Ploppy Players	Smart Players	Advantage Players
Chips	Chips are not money, just chips.	Chips are another form of money and are thought of as such.	Think of chips as money but will never play so many chips that this will interfere with their game.
Money management	Will go to the ATM machine if they run out of cash so they can buy in and get more chips.	Players will never buy in for more chips than they can afford.	Have large bankroll and make small bets, so losing does not throw them into a tailspin.
Bankroll	Do not have a bankroll but will use their "house money" to play the games.	Players will also have a 401(g), a separate bank account, for their gambling money.	Players keep separate 401(g) gambling account.

Item	Ploppy Players	Smart Players	Advantage Players
Gaming knowledge	Believe in superstitious nonsense such as the "gambler's fallacy" that when something hasn't happened it is due to happen, trend-betting at random games, inspiration and intuition, and that the short run allows stupid bets that the long-run wouldn't allow.	Understand the meaning of the math and how casinos make their money off them and other players. Recognizes that the speed of games will have a huge impact on the results of those games, even if the game has relatively low house edges. Eschews all ploppy ideas.	Know the math of the games over which they have edges and know how to bet into those edges, giving them the strongest possible attack against the casino. Understand what games can be beaten and how they can be beaten. Do not play a game in which they can't get an edge.
Strategy	Catch as catch can! Have no idea of what works and what doesn't work. They go with the flow even when no flow exists in the random games they play. Players like to play fast, drink, and bet on their instincts.	Make the lowest house-edge bets and try to slow down the games to reduce the number of decisions. In games where proper play lowers the house edge, such as blackjack, they play properly. Players drink in moderation and trust in math, not instinct.	Card-count at blackjack, use dice control at craps while only making bets they are mathematically capable of beating, play at a maximum speed where they will not make mistakes but will capitalize on their skills. Players don't drink before or during play.
Comps	Feel like big shots when they get a comp and go after them even if it means betting more than they can afford to bet.	Take whatever comps are given to them but don't hustle for them and never play for more money to get them.	Take whatever is given them but often don't bother with going after comps or letting the casino know who they are.
Results	Big-time losers.	Small-time losers.	Winners.

CHAPTER 2

Why We Gamble

Why do we gamble? I know this question has been asked a million times, and there have been a million answers. Make that one million and one, as I am going to give it a shot.

Certainly in life we all have to gamble, as life is one long contest with luck, circumstance, and our eventual big loss. Life has a house edge to it, certainly, that grinds away at us, and even those who have had the best of times cannot escape the worst of times when they must say sayonara to the world. Of course, those who have had rotten lives because of chance or circumstance might look upon the fateful last moment as a blessing: *I am so happy to be out of here!*

I think real life is a combination of the fated and the decided. You are fated to die. The generation that will never die has not yet been born. You are fated to get old despite wrinkle creams and face lifts that often cause people to look as if someone is trying to rip the skin right off their skulls. I look in the mirror, and I see a guy with gray hair who is closer to 70 than to 40. Is that really *me* now?

The other day in the bagel shop the girl behind the counter asked me if I got the senior citizen discount. My wife was asked, that very night, in our small village theater if she got the senior discount for the movies. We both said no as if that would mean that fate was not hastening us toward seniorville—the place from which no one returns!

Oh yes, we can fight fate, scream at fate, and maybe even delay the ultimate fate, but we can't change fate. In the ancient societies, fate was often called "nemesis," which does not bode well for us.

Most of life—at least in America, for just about all Americans—has to do with the decisions we make and the aftermath of those decisions. Not every decision is going to be a good one. Some of them explode in our faces, and we have to make more decisions to handle the poor decisions that went *ka-boom*. Even little kids make decisions that have real and long-term consequences. That first-grader goofing off when the teacher is instructing in math doesn't realize that his fun today will limit what he can do with his tomorrows. If he goofs off throughout his school career, his prospects will be severely limited, and rail as he might against the "system," or "society," this person has created his dismal situation, and only he can uncreate it.

The rule of life is biblical—*as you sow so shall you reap*—and that rule starts as soon as we start crawling around the house looking for stuff to chew on and electrical sockets in which to stick our little fingers. You can bank on that.

We gamble in life because we must gamble—there is no other choice. Not gambling in life is actually gambling that doing nothing will have a better outcome than doing something. We have to decide what schools to go to or whether to go to school at all; whether we should study or forget about studies; whom we should marry or whether to marry at all. Each and every decision opens some doors and closes other doors. No decision is without some consequence.

And that is exactly what we do in the casinos, admittedly in a more rarified, more symbolic, but still very real way. We engage in the life struggle. We face the fate of the ever-grinding house edge and what that means for our future prospects. We devise plans for how to handle early defeats at our favorite game in order to come back into the black. Some players will increase their bets, figuring something good has to happen and they can make it all the way back with just a few wins. Other players bet smaller amounts after a dismal start, figuring bad times are the norm in the casino, so they want to ride it out.

When we face real life, there are just too many factors to fathom in each and every moment. The complexity of life makes it somewhat messy and hard to fully grasp. Our decisions are usually made with too little information. You love Jane; Jane loves you. Pretty simple, right? Will the marriage work out? Who the heck knows? That's just too complicated a question, requiring an insight into the future none of us has.

But the casino games are not like that at all. Even experts at casino gambling must admit—it isn't all that complicated. The games are relatively simple and have to be in order to attract the largest crowds to play them.

Let's say we know, for example, that the $1 slot machines pay back 92 percent of all the money put in them. We know if we were to play those $1 machines forever that we'd be behind by about 8 percent of all the money we put through the machine. Our gamble, a very simple gamble, is that the machine does not pay back the money smoothly. It is volatile. It is cold more often than hot, but when it gets hot you can hit some big money. Our gamble is that it will hit for us in the short time we are playing it.

Still, most of the time it won't. We accept that fate. But we have decided that the gamble is worth the intermittent thrill of a big win—or any win—because that win goes against long-term fate. We know we are bucking the house edge. We know the casino will win in the end—against almost every single casino gambler out there. But we gamble we can change that fate, at least for ourselves, at least for tonight. And sometimes it happens.

And that is the big thrill. Casino gambling is the war against fate—a war almost everyone must lose but occasionally some of us will win.

> **Helpful Hint:** *My mentor, the late Captain of craps, whose ideas I will discuss in the craps section of this book, called casino gambling a "manageable thrill," because the risks a typical casino gambler takes will not destroy him but will get that adrenaline flowing.*

It doesn't have the interminable "unknowables" of whether you and Jane will be married happily ever after. It isn't like the war against fate in real life, in which we have no possibility of winning and we all know it. The war against fate in the casino gives us a lot more power than we have in real life because occasionally we do indeed cheat death.

And that's why 26 percent of the adult population in America loves to gamble!

CHAPTER 3

How Much Should You Bet?

he late Captain of craps, the legendary Atlantic City player I have written about in many of my books, once explained to me his theory on how much a person should bet at whatever game he wishes to play in order to experience a high degree of thrill with a low chance of having a heart attack and an even lower chance of being totally bored.

Casino gambling for the recreational player should be a "manageable thrill." The Captain stated that a typical casino blackjack player playing for matchsticks or pennies would get bored rather quickly, because no hand really means that much to him—losing has no sting, and winning has no adrenaline jolt. But if he bets $500 per hand, he might find himself sweating profusely as he sees his rent money or food money going out the window on a sustained series of losses. He might, quite literally, drop dead from anxiety. In the case of the $500 bettor, the emotions would range from dread at losing to relief at not losing. Where's the fun in that?

The Captain's theory of a manageable thrill comes down to a simple formula: the bets you make have to be large enough to make it worth wanting to win but small enough to make losing them not cause you to think of all the things you could have bought had you not lost. That is your "thrill zone"—the range of betting that has meaning, win or lose, but is not really hurtful to your emotional or economic life.

Often players will bet a certain amount when they first start a game but gradually increase their bets until they hit the "sweat zone," as the

Captain called it. The sweat zone is the place where the bet becomes uncomfortable to think about. Many craps players hit the sweat zone after several presses of their bets. Worse, a controlled shooter who is having a good roll will sometimes start to think more about the money at risk than about shooting the dice in a relaxed and careful manner. This makes shooting the dice no longer a thrilling exercise for the player, but an agony. *What if I roll a seven? What if I lose? Look at all that money!*

There's no doubt the average casino player is a thrill seeker. Going up against Lady Luck is a roller-coaster ride on which your money and your emotions go up and down, up and down. For many people, going on roller coasters is a delight—but it isn't a delight if you've had a big meal and become sick to your stomach. Betting too much at a casino game is the equivalent of going on a roller coaster with a full, gurgling belly. It could become a sickening experience for you and for others watching you. Then again, going on the kiddie boats that go around and around, with those little kids ringing the bells, might not be thrilling enough for you.

Interestingly enough, I have also noticed similar phenomenon among some card counters. They may start their betting at $25, but when the count calls for it, they have to move that bet up, sometimes by a lot. At a certain point, and even with that edge over the casino to boot, these card counters will begin to sweat their action. The escalation of their bets gets their hearts pounding, and they enter the sweat zone. Losing such large amounts, amounts actually measured in emotions and not cash, has made what up to that point had been a pleasant pastime into an emotionally wrenching moment.

I once entered the sweat zone in the early 1990s when I found myself betting several thousand on two hands that I had split, resplit, and doubled down on those resplits. The sweat literally poured out of me, and one drop went right down my nose and landed on my cards as the dealer turned over a 16, hit it with a 5, and wiped me off the board. Plop, drop, and I was monetarily and emotionally soaked and stunned.

The fact is, no amount of rationalizing can really stop a person from entering the sweat zone, because the dimensions of that sweat zone are deeply rooted in the subconscious mind. Many of us have no control over where the sweat zone starts—it's just there! I knew a skilled blackjack player, worth millions in his businesses, who just couldn't handle a bet higher than $50. He used to talk about the fact that he should be able to bet 10 times that amount, especially when the count favored him, but for some reason, $50 was his emotional limit. Over that, and he became anxiety ridden.

Gaming writers love to talk about strategies, house edges, and bankroll requirements, but rarely do we discuss the emotional bankroll that a person must have to bet at this or that level. A red-chip player might wish he could play at the green level, might even be able to objectively afford it, but he just can't bring himself to do it. His hands start to tremble as he pushes out the chips. If this happens to you at a certain betting level, don't make the bet! If you know this fact, then be content to bet within your thrill zone and don't attempt to push the envelope. It isn't worth the consternation, second-guessing, and self-flagellation such an action would cause you.

The Captain had, from years of experience, learned that some bets just aren't worth making—even bets where you might have an edge—if the fear of loss becomes so overwhelming that the act of making the bet becomes an act of anguish.

Some philosophers have speculated that man is composed of three parts: mind, body, and spirit. To enjoy casino gambling, all three of those components should be utilized. Your mind should tell you which are the best bets to make, your spirit should enjoy the contest, and your body will let you know when you've gone overboard, because it will start sweating!

CHAPTER 4

Scratch a Gambler, Get a System

After you read this book, you will be able to go into any casino and win a million dollars or more any time you want. You'll be able to buy an island paradise where you will live a life of luxury few people have ever experienced. You'll live in a mansion bigger than any palace any king or emperor has ever constructed. You'll have cars and airplanes and servants. The pleasures of the world await you within the pages of this book.

And to top it off, I have a bridge you can buy that links Brooklyn and Manhattan. Right now it is called the Brooklyn Bridge, but you can name it after yourself once you own it.

Obviously the above paragraphs are total baloney, the kind of baloney systems-sellers hawk to unwary casino gamblers. So ignore them and come down to earth with the rest of us.

I can tell you this without any of the baloney: *Casino Conquest* is just what its name clearly states. It is a book that will give you mathematically proven methods to actually beat certain games; it will give you ideas on how to lower the house hit at games in which you can't get a mathematical edge. It will also reveal methods for getting more comps for less risk, and I will discuss some advantage methods that can bring you more money from comps than you actually lose in the games (*don't tell the casinos this*).

Can you make millions of dollars every time you play? That is doubtful—highly doubtful—unless you have a lot of money to bet. Millions of dollars are probably not in your gambling future. But you can be the smartest, strongest, and savviest player you can possibly be.

Okay, let's do it!

There used to be a television commercial where pretty twins debated the merits of a tasty mint. It went something like this:

Pretty Twin One: Certs is a breath mint.
Pretty Twin Two: Certs is a candy mint.
Pretty Twin One: No, Certs is a breath mint.
Pretty Twin Two: No, Certs is a candy mint.
Deep-Voiced Narrator: Stop, stop!
The pretty twins stop, and their pretty faces look really confused.
Deep-Voiced Narrator: You're both right!
The pretty twins are happy because they are both right.

In the world of casino gambling, myriad arguments also rage among many players. These arguments tend to be just like this:

Player One: No systems can beat the games.
Player Two: Betting systems can beat the games.
Player Three: Trend systems can beat the games.
Player Four: Money management can beat the games.
Player Five: Hedge-betting systems can beat the games.
Good-Looking Frank Scoblete: Stop, stop, you're all wrong...well, mostly.

Why Player One Is Too Cynical

Some games can be beaten by some systems—if we define *system* merely as an organized, mathematically valid, advantage-play approach to a specific game—such as card counting at blackjack, dice control at craps, 100 percent–return video poker machines, advantage-play slot machines, etc. These kinds of systems have been shown to turn the edge in favor of the player. These systems are not the wishing or hoping or relying on anecdotal evidence type of systems. They are real; they work, and they are not difficult to learn.

Sadly, most casino players have little interest in learning these advantage-play systems, so such skilled players are rare indeed, although the casinos are often paranoid about them. Considering that there are approximately 54 million casino gamblers in the United States alone, advantage players do not even make up one-fiftieth of a percent, in my estimation.

Many card counters do not like to call what they do at blackjack a "system" because the word *system* has a bad connotation. They think of what they do as an advantage-play "method"—meaning the player has the advantage over the casinos. Dice controllers do not like to call what they do a "system" either, because in their world so many other (losing) systems exist that it taints their achievements. They will often refer to what they do as a "technique" of advantage-play.

Needless to say, an advantage-play "system" is a "method" is a "technique" or whatever you prefer to call it—in short, a way to play with an edge. Choose whichever of these words you like, or create one of your own; the bottom line is that some games can indeed be legitimately beaten.

Player Two's Betting Systems Resemble Sewer Systems

The typical betting systems, such as doubling up after one's previous loss—known as the Martingale system—or searching out trends that you bet with or against or only allowing yourself three, four, or however many consecutive losses before switching tables or some such are all losers. Such betting systems cannot overcome the house edges despite the fact that many (losing) gamblers swear by such systems. If these systems could overcome the house edges, there would be no casinos, because the bulk of regular players use these systems in their play. Probably more than half of all casino players use these betting systems with ultimately fruitless results.

Betting systems do not require knowledge of what cards remain in the shoe, as advantage-blackjack betting does. Betting systems do not require the skill to influence the outcome of a dice throw. Betting systems are simply hopeful expressions of a gambler's hopelessness, because such systems will invariably fail, as they are all based on nothing more than faith and hope. Unfortunately, the casinos don't care about gamblers' faith and hope, and they give no charity when clobbering players who use such betting systems.

Such betting systems are often sold to the unwary, hopeful, hapless gamblers as surefire winners ("Win a Million Every Time You Play!"). They aren't surefire winners; they are losers. But gamblers keep buying and using them.

Player Three Is on the Wrong Trend Too

Trend betting is the most appealing system of play for almost all casino gamblers. A trend bettor sees red show up at roulette five times in a row and thinks, *Red is hot; I am going to bet red!* Or the trend bettor thinks, *Black has to show now with so many reds appearing. Black is due! I'm betting black.*

Trend betting can actually be called "bi-bet-u-ality," because a wager can be made that the trend will continue, or a wager can be made that the trend won't continue.

So why can't trend betting work? Because it is and it ain't, to coin someone else's phrase. There are two sides to the trend-betting proposition; one side wins and one side loses, and thus you then might think that the bets cancel each other out. They don't. In fact, the casinos just grind away at both sides, because the winning bets are usually not paid off at the proper odds. So even the winning bets are losing the winning player some money.

If you are confused, just watch how this scheme works:

Pauline bets one dollar on number 17 at roulette. It hits. She is paid $35 for the dollar she wagered. Wow! That is some big score. But is it? On a wheel that has two green zeros, there are 37 ways Pauline can lose and only one way (that 17!) for her to win.

In a game with no house advantage, when she won she would be paid $37 for her dollar wager. She would lose $37 on all the other numbers but win $37 on her number, and the game would be even; this is called a "fair game." But the casino can't make money on a fair game, so it pays the winning bet less than fair odds. Poor Pauline only gets $35 instead of $37, and the casino keeps two dollars for itself. Think of it this way: Pauline is a sole proprietor when she loses, but she has a partner when she wins: Mister Casino.

In roulette again, Jim bets on red; it wins. He is paid even money. Hey, how could the house be taking money from Jim? He wins even money; he loses even money. There you have it—a fair game! Sorry, that is mere illusion; *maya*, as the Hindus might say.

The fact is that Jim only has 18 chances to win on red but has 20 chances to lose on black and green! So as Jim plays red into the sunset, the house will win 20 times, and Jim will win 18 times, and...Jim loses in the long run. Certainly not a fair game. If Jim's wife, Charlene, decides to show Jim how silly he is by betting red, she will bet black. Oops, she also wins only 18 times, and she also loses 20 times—no better, no worse than Jim. It doesn't matter how they bet. I'm guessing they are still going to argue into the night concerning who knows more about gambling.

Trend systems cannot buck these facts, no matter what the trend bettors believe or how they structure their trend-betting attacks. The bottom line is simple and sad: trend bettors lose the entire bet when they lose, and they lose some of the bet when they win—just like all other bettors not using trends. There are no useful trends when it comes to trend betting.

A Closer Look at Streaks

Every casino gambler, from the best of them to the worst of them, knows that all casino contests are streaky. You win some, you lose some. You win a few in a row, you lose a few in a row. You have good days, you have bad days.

Streaks and gambling go together like a horse and a carriage, love and marriage, Belvedere and a martini. We all know this for a fact.

However, some gambling pundits pontificate that the good and bad streaks even out in the games—which is *not* the case in almost all casino games. Indeed, if you are a betting man or woman (and who else would be reading this book?), wager your money on the fact that the casino will have more "good" streaks for them (*good* meaning they win more decisions) than "bad" streaks against them. The players will face just the opposite situation. They will have more bad streaks and fewer good streaks.

The reason for this is in the nature of the games, which usually means the math of the games. Let's take a look at the casino players' favorite table game, blackjack. It is no secret that blackjack is a very close contest between the player and the casino—if (and this is a big *if*) the player knows the correct basic strategy, the computer-derived best play of each player hand against every dealer's up-card.

In most traditional blackjack games, the player using correct basic strategy will face an approximately 0.5 percent house edge, which means a loss of approximately 50¢ for every $100 the player wagers. That's a good game, pretty close.

However, blackjack is not the equivalent of flipping a coin, where the player and the casino win half the hands and lose half the hands respectively. Absolutely not. The house will win approximately 48 percent of the hands, the player will win approximately 44 percent of the hands, and approximately 8 percent of the hands will be pushes (ties).

Clearly the house will have longer winning streaks and shorter losing streaks than the player because of these percentages. If there were no other betting options in a blackjack game, the player would lose $4 for every $100 he bet. Yet the player does not lose this much; in fact, the player loses much less because blackjack has certain playing options that allow the player to get more money on the table in certain hands: he can double down on two cards, he can split pairs, he can sometimes double down on his split hands, and he might even be able to surrender his poor hands. A big benefit for the blackjack player is getting that 3-to-2 payout for a blackjack—with blackjacks appearing in about 5 percent of the hands.

These playing options bring the *monetary* edge of the casino down to that approximate 0.5 percent, but the casino is still the favorite to have the longer winning streaks. Casinos that have instituted the 6-to-5 payout for blackjacks have therefore seriously hurt the players' chances of winning at the game by drastically increasing the house edge.

Craps puts the house in a favorable streaking situation on its most popular bet, the Pass Line. The house wins 251 decisions, while the player wins 244 decisions on this wager. While this makes it a very close contest, you can see the house will have slightly longer winning streaks than losing streaks.

As with roulette's straight-up wagers, the proposition bets at craps are all long shots that pay less than their true odds. Take a bet such as the 12, known as boxcars, which has a 1-in-36 chance of appearing. Obviously, the player who bets the 12 each and every roll will find himself in enormous negative streaks. However, when he hits this number, the house doesn't pay the win off at 1-to-1, as only the truly insane would then make such a bet. Instead, the house usually pays off at 30-to-1—much less than the true odds of 35-to-1 but far better than 1-to-1. The house edge on this bet comes in at almost 14 percent—a huge edge, nevertheless. You only have to be somewhat crazy to make this particular bet.

So what is the bottom of the bottom line? Anyone who tells you to chart tables and players in a random game is telling you to jump off the Empire State Building because, "Don't worry, you will go up, not down."

Player Four Has an Inkling of an Idea

Money management—defined as how you handle your gambling money, how much you bet, and when you stop playing—cannot overcome house edges. Still, money management is an important ingredient in all gambling, whether you are a player who doesn't have an edge or whether you are a player who does have an edge. Cautious management of one's money is always best, as I will show you.

I will give you the best money-management principles for each game. But I repeat: money management alone cannot give you an edge over the casino.

Player Five Has Obviously Never Done Any Gardening

You cut your hedges, and what do they do? They grow back to annoy you and also your loud, complaining neighbors. That annoying fact explains why there is no way to cut the house edge by hedging one's bets—you just lose more money because you are adding more bets of the high-house-edge variety. In your garden, if you don't want the annoyance factor of hedges, don't grow any; same with casino gambling.

So what is a hedge bet? It is using one bet to offset the house edge of another bet. Sounds interesting and intelligent, yes? Except it doesn't work to lessen the house advantage over the player—it usually gives the casino a higher house edge.

Let's take a quick look at hedging a bet in blackjack. The biggest hedge bet that many blackjack players make is the one called "insurance," sometimes called the "even-money" bet if a player has a blackjack. From my book *Beat Blackjack Now!*, here is the description of the insurance and even-money bet:

When the dealer's up-card is an ace, the dealer will ask players if they want to make the insurance wager. Insurance is a side bet where players are betting that the dealer's hole card will be a 10-value card. Players can make an insurance bet equal to one half of their initial bet made on the hand. To make the insurance bet, you simply place your chips on the insurance line, which is located right above the player betting spot. You win your insurance bet if the dealer has a 10-value card in the hole. A winning insurance bet pays off at 2-to-1 odds.

When the player has a blackjack hand and the dealer has an ace showing, the dealer will ask the player if he wants "even money." Even money means the dealer will automatically give you a 1-to-1 (or even-money) payoff on your bet before he checks his down-card for a potential blackjack. Taking even money yields the same result as making an insurance bet on your blackjack hand.

That would seem like a good hedge, especially if you have a hand of 20 or, even better, a blackjack. Unfortunately, the normal house edge for a player using the computerized version of "basic strategy" gives the house an approximate 0.5 percent advantage over the player—and that is a very close contest. But what if you take insurance to hedge your bets? The house now takes between 5 and 8 percent from that insurance bet. That's some hedge, isn't it? You bet more money and lose much more money on the extra bet.

Gambling hedges are usually using bets with high house edges to protect bets with low house edges. Not a good exchange. But some players and even some gambling writers think these bets are the cat's meow, the wolf's howl, and the lion's roar, but they are more like the Titanic's iceberg. They will sink you rather quickly.

The game with the most and most varied hedges is craps—you can hedge like crazy, especially if you *are* crazy. Indeed the hedge bets in craps have been called "Crazy Crapper" bets by my late mentor, the Captain, the world's greatest craps player.

I'll tackle hedging at craps in the section on craps. For now, just trust me—hedging is a bad idea. It's like cutting poison ivy using your bare hands.

CHAPTER 5

All About Comps: Getting What You Deserve, Getting What You Don't Deserve, and Maybe Getting the Edge!

By now everyone going to casinos will know something about comps. Table-game players dutifully hand in their cards to the floor person, who either swipes them in the computer or records the players' names on a piece of paper. When these players are finished with their play, they either ask that floor person or pit boss for a comp or wait until their trip is over to see what the casino can do for them.

In slot machines it is even easier. Just put your card in the machine, and when you want a comp, you go to the players' club and see what they will give you or—as the casino says—"what you have earned." Naturally "what you have earned" is based on how the casinos see your potential losses. Ah, yes, in casinoland, you get by giving!

Casinos have elaborate comping formulas, and while all casinos are a little or a lot different in their formulas, everyone gets what he or she deserves based on each casino's particular analysis of each customer's playing worth. Getting what you deserve is just fine and dandy, and I'm all for it, to a degree. But getting what you *don't deserve*—in fact, getting a *lot more* than what you deserve—is a heck of a lot more fun and can, when added into one's gambling equation, actually give the savvy comp commander what I call the "monetary edge" over the casino.

Getting What You Deserve

Before you are deserving of entering the world of the undeserving, you must first understand what kind of general formula the casinos use to rate your play. By way of cliché, you must first learn to walk before you can run. So let me walk you through the composite of what comping formulas most casinos will use to judge your play at this or that game.

Here's the general formula: *average bet* multiplied by the *number of decisions per hour* multiplied by *number of hours you play* multiplied by *house edge* equals your *theoretical loss* multiplied by *whatever percent of your theoretical loss the casinos will give back,* which (finally, thank God!) equals *how much the casino will give you in comps.*

Simple?

I'll plug in some numbers to see how this works. And don't worry; I'm not a mathlete either.

Let's say your game is blackjack. You play $25 per hand because you've decided that the heart operation you need can be delayed. Most casinos figure you to play between 60 and 80 hands per hour at blackjack, so let's say 70 hands (or decisions) per hour for you. So you play $25 per hand for 70 hands; that's $1,750 per hour that you wager. Let's say you play for four hours, the usual length of time casinos like for players to play in order to get a full range of comps (that translates into half a workday), which brings your day's wagers to $7,000.

Most casinos will rate blackjack players as playing against a house edge of between 1 and 2 percent. So let's split the difference and say that the casino you're playing in figures you to lose at a rate of 1.5 percent of all your action. So your theoretical loss is established by taking the $7,000 you wagered and multiplying it by 0.015 (which is 1.5 percent), which equals a theoretical loss of $105 per four hours. A theoretical loss is not an actual loss; you could win a session, lose a session, win a lot, or lose a lot more. Over time, your theoretical loss will be close to your actual loss, but for the casino this is neither here nor there. With the millions of decisions the casinos have each day, they have usually banked the theoretical loss for *all* the players, as if all the players are one monstrous entity—a player gestalt, if you will.

Most casinos will give back between 30 percent (the really cheap ones) and 50 percent—known as the "Jackie Gleasons," because these are the "great ones" for comping—of your theoretical loss. Let's speculate that your casino gives back 40 percent of $105 in comps, which is $42. What does that $42 mean? They certainly don't hand you $42 in cash, although sometimes they do send you cash back in the mail or, more likely, match play.

As a $25 average bettor at blackjack, you can reasonably expect to get a free room at locals and low-end Vegas casinos, plus some meals, especially during off-peak times, like Sunday through Thursday. At midrange casinos you can get a decent discount on the rooms (called "casino rates") and the buffet, again especially during off-peak times. At high-end places, you'll get the buffet. In the Midwest, a $25 bettor is treated the way a $100 bettor is treated in Vegas, and a $100 bettor is treated like a god. Of course, in Atlantic City, a $25 bettor is treated like everyone is treated out East:

$25 Player: Sir? Sir, may my wife and I have a comp?

Pit Boss: "Youse talkin' ta me?"

(Okay, okay, I'm just having a little fun with my fellow East Coasters.)

By the way, the casino puts a price tag on all the freebies. So a room at Hairy Harry's Outhouse Casino might have a price tag of $15 per night, which will be subtracted from your $42; and the gourmet room at "Harry's" might come in at $25 (how much can they charge for predigested franks and beans, anyway?); and the breakfast buffet will come in at $2. Voila! You have used your $42 in comps for that day.

At Venetian you won't get a discount for the room (except in really slow, snowball-in-hell seasons) because the Venetian will put a price tag of about $250 or more on the room, and you won't get more than $42 as a comp for their café.

You can plug any game into the formula and come up with what the casino will give you back for those games. Some games, such as roulette, have fixed house edges (5.26 percent), which means it doesn't matter how long you play because the edge is always the same. Other games, such as craps, have house edges that vary from bet to bet, and the casino rater will "estimate" what your average bet is based on the totality of the bets he sees you make over the time you are at the table. Usually, however, casinos will rate craps players as playing against a 3 percent house edge, give or take. And all games have different speeds—roulette has fewer decisions per hour than blackjack, baccarat has far fewer decisions per hour than craps, etc.

If you *really* want to be a savvy comp commander, I'm going to tell you a secret way that only I know about to discover what *exact* formula the casinos you play in use to rate you. Here goes: ask them! Yes, no one knows this secret, but you can actually ask to see your rating. When you go to your host (by all means get a host, even if you are a low roller), just ask to see "the screen." He or she will show you exactly how they are rating you—what house edge they are using, how much your average bet is, what your theoretical loss is, and what they are willing to give you back in terms of comps. And you'll get what you deserve.

Let's start moving into the fun territory of the *undeserving*, shall we?

How to Stretch Your Comps

True-story time. I played three days at a very nice Las Vegas casino, just a notch below an A+, where I was RFB, which means I was a big shot and got everything "free"—gourmet restaurants; room service; shows; limos; and a big big-shot suite with two bathrooms, a Jacuzzi, a living room, a dining room, four televisions, a huge bedroom, and a stable for my polo ponies.

When it was time to leave, I checked out my "screen" and asked my host if the casino would pick up the airfare for me and my wife, the beautiful A.P., and he said, "That would put you way over the return we can give you based on your theoretical." I looked at the screen, and next to my "room" was $1,500! Yep, that's what they "charged" me for the suite—per night! Thus, $4,500 of my comp return based on my "theoretical loss" was eaten up by the big-shot suite, in which I basically slept, showered, and did a couple of unmentionable things with my wife. So I asked him how much a regular room would have been "charged" to me. It turned out to be $250. And he then volunteered the information that I would have gotten the airfare "no problem" had I taken a regular room.

So right there, I learned a very valuable lesson. Did I really have to stay in a suite if not doing so would have allowed me to have our airfare covered? In good Vegas hotels all the rooms are good, by definition, and I really don't do much in a big-shot suite that I wouldn't do in a regular room.

Here's another little trick. When you ask for a comp for the café for two, don't let the floor person or pit boss write it out for the "normal amount"—say, $50 for two—because often they take that whole $50 off your comp allowance even if your meal came to $30. If you know what you're going to eat, or if you know approximately what you're going to spend in the café, when you ask for a comp, say, "Make the comp for two for $37." This way you only use up the actual money you spend.

Again, feel free to ask your host how they handle a meal price that comes in under the comp value. Many casinos return the unused portion to you.

Secrets of the Undeserving Only I Know

Now I'm going to share with you the secrets of getting much more than you deserve in comps. Most of these secrets are only known by me and everyone I've ever talked to about comps. But some of the following secrets are actually being revealed here for the first time because that's the kind of guy I am—a blabbermouth!

If you are a tipper—and you should be, because if you don't tip the dealers, they will hate you—then always tip *on top* of your bet, not next to it or in front of it or wherever the casino wants the bet placed (like directly in the dealer's bank account). Let's say you are still that $25 blackjack player, still solvent, alive and kicking, and you want to give the dealers a $5 tip. If you put it in front of your bet, two things happen: the dealer is happy that you made a bet for him, and if it wins, the dealer takes the winnings and the bet.

Here's what doesn't happen: the bet is *not* counted as a part of *your* bet. But if you put the bet on top of your $25 and say to the dealer, "You're riding on top," then three things happen: the dealer is happy that you made a bet for him; if it wins, it stays up and might win some more for the dealer with no extra risk for you; and, most important for your comps, that $5 will count as a part of your bet. The floor person will rate you as a $30 player. Hey, every little bit helps.

Craps players can try a classic ruse that I invented when I saw someone else do it. You can put your Place bets on the numbers during the Come-Out roll but keep them off! That's right. If you are a Place bettor, going right up on the numbers gets you noticed right away, rated right away, but with no risk. Even better, if you are, say, a $30 bettor on the 6 and 8, you might just go to $60 on each during the Come-Out roll—accompanied by much fanfare ("Give me a $60 6 and 8. Did you hear me? I said a sixty dollar—six-oh—6 and 8!" and in a whisper: "Off on the Come-Out"). But here's the sneaky part: when the shooter establishes his point, you reduce those two bets to $30 each. You can't do this too much, but a few times during the course of a session will help pump up your average bet rating at no extra risk.

Craps players should also look to play in casinos that count the total spread, which means that a $30 6 and 8 come in with a $60 rating. It's rare—I mean really, *really* rare—for the casinos to count the "odds" bet for comping purposes, because the house has no edge on this bet. (If you have no idea of what I am talking about, it will be more fully explained in the craps section of this book. Hang in there.)

Here's a nice ploy for those of you who are in the netherworld between RLFB (room limited food beverage)—which means you get a free room but limited food and beverage, with no gourmet fare—and RFB (room food and beverage), which means you are a big shot, where everything is free (based on paying for all this stuff based on your theoretical losses!). Often when you are RLFB/RFB borderline, you'll be told that you can charge your food to your room and at the end of the trip, "We'll take a look at it and see what you deserve." Do that, and you will get what the casino thinks you deserve. Fair enough. But maybe you can do better than this.

There is a way around this that sometimes works wonderfully (and sometimes fails miserably). I discovered this supersecret technique in the mid-1990s during my stays at the old Wynn properties, and when I was in the RLFB/RFB netherworld, I always employed it. When you want any nongourmet fare such as the café or buffet, ask a floor person for it. Some floor people will give you the comp no questions asked because of your average bet, rating, etc. Others will ask if you are staying in the hotel. They'll say to charge it to your room. Don't lie if they ask you that, just tell them that you prefer to get the comp up front. I once invented a story that I didn't want my wife to know I was having an extra meal because I was on a diet. The floor person, a portly fellow, sympathized and wrote out the comp.

So why "comp up front," as I call it? Because when your stay is over, there is a chance that none of your comps-as-you-went will show up on "the screen." Everything that you charged to your room will be there—all those gourmet dinners where you ate like a pig...uh...I mean, like a king or queen—but none of your "little" comps will register. Your host, who has allotted you X amount for food, will subtract that X from your gourmet fare. Had you put all the "little" food expenses on your room, that X would have probably covered them, but you'd be charged for the gourmet meals.

As I said, this doesn't always work. Sometimes some floor people are obstinate—thinking they are spending their own money—and you'll be given no choice but to charge it to your room or starve. Also, sometimes the "little" comps will show up on the "screen" when your host looks. So what? You'll at least get what you deserved and maybe a heck of a lot more than you deserved.

Given a choice between casinos where floor people rate you by hand on a piece of paper or those where they rate you by swiping your card through a computer, if all other things are equal (the games, amenities, stables for your polo ponies), then go with the pen and paper. Tradition counts! Also, those who have to rate you with pen and paper will, if they like you (tipping the dealers helps them like you), add some points to your rating at the end when they put it into the computer. This can't be done when they constantly enter your bets into the computer after every round.

I've played in places where I have been rated much higher than my actual betting would warrant, largely because I was related to the floor person doing the rating—just kidding. Rather, largely because of my tipping of the crew and the fact that I was a regular and an easy player who made no demands or intemperate remarks, win or lose.

The flipside of the pen and paper is also a possibility. I recently had the floor person from hell rate my average bet at a level that was two-thirds less than what every other floor person in that particular casino rated me. I wasn't betting any differently, mind you. I was just *perceived* differently. The guy probably took an instant dislike to me (those of you who know me must find that *impossible* to believe)—and my rating plummeted.

Getting the Edge

If you think the tricks above were, well, tricky, now we get into some serious comp-duggery, which will allow you to actually get what I call the "monetary edge" over the casino. Which means that between the comps you don't deserve and the ratings on the game that you don't deserve, you'll actually be getting more back from the casino then you're shelling out at the table game of your choice. (Sadly, none of these methods work on the slot machines.)

I'll give you two examples of how this works in the two most popular games, first in blackjack and then craps, but it can be applied to whatever your favorite game is.

In blackjack you are once again a $25 player. Your theoretical loss is $105, and your comp points come to $42. However, if you play basic strategy, you will not be facing a house edge of 1.5 percent but rather about 0.5 percent—as long as you avoid those games that pay black-jacks at 6-to-5, that is. Your real expectation at "normal" blackjack is to lose $35 per four hours of play, not $105. Wow! That means just by learning basic strategy, or bringing a basic strategy card to the table with you, you have a $7 edge over the casino as a $25 player in my example.

Want to add to that edge? Simply sit out 10 percent of the hands. Play 63 hands instead of 70 hands, and your expectation will be to lose a mere $31.50. Your monetary edge will be greater than $10, just for playing basic strategy and sitting out a hand every now and then ("I want to change the flow of the cards" is a good ploy when you've lost a couple of hands).

But here are some more little tricks to use. When the dealer is shuffling—and do make sure you play with real dealers shuffling and not those continuous-shuffle machines, which should all be destroyed—put out a bigger than normal bet. Let it sit there for all the world—and raters—to see. Then when the dealer finishes, take the bet down and go to the bathroom. Do this a couple of times every four hours, and you could increase your average bet with no risk to you. You'll also reduce the number of hands you play by heading for the john. You might also get some sympathy, as the raters will think you are having trouble with your bladder.

If you find that you must play the continuous-shuffle machines because aliens from space have put a phaser to your head and said, "Beep! Play shuffle machine or die. Beep!" then you must sit out at least 30 percent of all the hands. Here's a nifty trick to do even more than that. If the dealer puts the cards back into the infernal machine after every round, then you will sit out the next round of cards if you saw seven or more 10s come out on the last round. This is a "kind-of" card counting that can reduce the number of hands you play to make up for the fact that a continuous-shuffle machine will increase your play by approximately 20 percent.

In craps, follow my recommendations for Place betting above, but as soon as your Place bets are active and at risk, start to replace them with Come bets. Unless you know that a member of the Golden Touch dice-control crew is at your table, then assume everyone is just a random roller, and reduce the house edge by utilizing the Come with odds. To reduce your total action, all you have to do is follow the superstitions of the craps world. When the dice go off the table, call off your bets. Leave them off for a couple of rolls. You'll still be getting your comp credit, but you aren't at risk. If the shooter should seven out, then keep the bets up but off! Utilize the 5-Count (to be discussed later), which will eliminate 57 percent of all the random rolls, the ones that seven out in the blink of an eye. If the dice hit someone's hand, call off your next bet because "the dice have been disturbed."

Play craps this way, and you'll find that with the casino rating you at a 3 percent disadvantage for 60 decisions per hour, you will actually be playing about 25 to 30 decisions per hour with a house edge of between 0.5 to 1.5 percent. In this scenario, you will probably also have the monetary edge over the casino.

In short, follow my advice in this chapter, and you'll be the most undeserving player you can be. It's always fun to get what you don't deserve.

CHAPTER 6
Tips on Tips

I grew up in Brooklyn, where the size of a man's tip told you something important about him. All the big shots tipped like crazy. If you saw the hilarious movie *My Cousin Vinny*, you know that when in doubt, which was most times, Vinny tipped. He tipped waiters, waitresses, and even prison guards. So here's a tip from me: there's a certain amount of tipping expected in the casinos—that is, if you get good service. Good patrons tip good service.

Many casino workers are in the service business, and that means they rely on tips to make ends meet. For some reason, certain jobs in our society have been deemed jobs where the one served should tip the server. I'm not exactly sure why we tip a waiter who serves us our soup but we don't tip a nurse who serves us our medicine. I was once a waiter, and I can tell you, those tips were almost the be-all and end-all of my salary, which was, at the time, a mere 90¢ per hour. I've never been a nurse, but I have been a patient at and a visitor to the hospital, and I haven't once seen a nurse tipped for good service. Perhaps that's because the hospitals pay the nurses a living wage.

Be that as it may, tips are a part of life for many workers, and I am a firm believer in tipping those whose lives depend on tips. *I am a Vinny!* (In the casinos, good tippers are actually called "George.")

But how much should one tip those who provide various services?

The following is merely my opinion on how much and who to tip in the casino world. If I've left out anyone, that means that particular job hasn't really crossed my path often enough to be in my consciousness. So I'm sorry if I've forgotten you.

Valets should get a minimum of $3 when they retrieve your car. Remember, valeting it saves you time walking from the garage to the casino and is safer for your car (usually) and a wonderful way to avoid some of those bad guys who sometimes show up in self-parking garages looking to steal your car, your wallet, and maybe your life.

"I lug, therefore I am!" That's anyone who moves something for you from point *A* to point *B*. Bellhops should get a minimum of $2 per piece of luggage lugged to room or car. Once in a casino, if maintenance or housekeeping brings you something special—such as an extra bed, cot, or refrigerator—a minimum tip of $5 would be nice. Most of us wouldn't want to lug the things they are lugging.

Waiters and waitresses should get 20 to 25 percent of the pretax check if they are friendly and professional. If they are cold and professional, give them 15 percent. If they are disdainful, give them 10 percent. If they are disdainful, haughty, arrogant, verbally abusive, and aloof, just ask them how long they worked in the New York theater district before coming to this casino restaurant, and leave them nothing.

The cocktail waitress who serves your drinks should get a minimum of $1 to $2 per drink. If you are playing in the high-roller room, you might want to give $3 to $5 per drink.

Maitre d's in swanky restaurants who bring you to your table and place the napkin on your lap and give you the wine list are a tough sell to me. There's really no service there that I can see, yet for some reason this group seems to expect tips. I'll leave this up to you. I usually don't give anything unless I know that the person actually got me the preferred seating arrangement or held my reservation if I was a few minutes late. Then I give a few dollars.

Dealers should be tipped by putting up a bet for them. There are no rules of thumb that say what dealers' tips should be as there are guidelines with waiters and waitresses. A few bucks by a red-chip player, a few reds by a green-chip player, and a few more reds— maybe even a green—for a black- or purple-chip player every 20 to 40 minutes would be generous. Or you can use the method of tipping that I will recommend later when discussing each individual game. These methods will save you money but can also make the dealers quite a lot of money if you only have, as the song from *My Fair Lady* says, "a little bit of luck."

When you win an epic jackpot, a tip is generally expected by the person who pays it to you or, in our new credit-voucher world, the individual who certifies the win. In the good old days, it was usually the change person (I don't quite know why; after all, what did they actually do for you?). Follow your instincts here. Luckily I've never had to worry about this, because I've never won an epic jackpot. I've never won a non-epic jackpot either.

If you work out in the spa, it is customary to leave a tip if the attendants have been attending to you. Did they bring you water? Did they give you a towel? Ten to 20 percent of the spa fee is a generous tip. By the way, for masseuses and trainers, different clubs have different rules. Don't be afraid to ask, "Is it customary to tip the masseuse and trainer?" when you make your reservation. My wife, the beautiful A.P., enjoys a good massage, and she says, "Ten to 20 percent, depending on how long the massage is and how much it costs." When I massage her, my tip is a warm kiss, which is fine with me.

If you use the barbers and hairstylists at the casino, a tip of 20 percent seems right.

Maids should be tipped generously. To me, they have the roughest job in the hotel (my God, they clean strangers' bathrooms!), and yet folks tend to give them $1 or $2 per day. No, no, a thousand times no. I'd rather stiff one of those good fellows who leads you to your table at a Las Vegas show than be cheap with a maid. Give them five to 10 bucks per day! I prefer to give $20 if a maid is really attentive.

> **Oh, Please:** *I know a person who says, "I don't want to hurt my bottom line by tipping when I am in a casino. It just costs me money." Hey, if you can't afford to tip a few bucks here and there, what are you doing in a casino? Go home and watch television!*

The problem for the poor maids is the fact that you tip them at the end of your stay in a casino-hotel, after you've (probably) lost all your money and when you're suddenly trying to economize. So to avoid that, to assure really, really prompt service, I tip the maid immediately upon my arrival. I find out who my maid will be, I introduce myself to her, tell her I'm staying in such-and-such room, and that this (the money) is for her. I also make it known that I will tip at the end of the trip as well. An important caveat here: sometimes the maid who slaved in your room is off on the day you leave to go home. You leave a tip, and her substitute gets it. Make a point of finding out who your maid is and leave the tip with her directly or with her supervisor. And remember, *she cleans your toilet!*

For economical gamblers, you should figure in advance whom and for what you will most likely tip, and bring along a special "tip sheet" and envelope. This way your tips don't come out of your gambling stake. You don't want to get to a point where you ever have to decide, *Do I tip this nice person or stiff him in order to gamble a little more?*

If you use limos or if the casino comps your limo ride, a tip of $10 to $20 would be a decent one. Often you tip based on how far the limo driver drives you. Also find out if the tip has already been added to the cost of the fare, as some limo companies automatically charge you a tip to use their service. If your service does this, then no extra tip is necessary—unless you have the driver lug your baggage.

What about taxi drivers? If you know they are taking the correct route to your destination and not screwing you by going the long way, a 20 percent tip would be appropriate.

I know that some people don't like to tip certain other people, but let's face it—when in Rome, you do like the Romans; when in a tipping world, you should tip as well.

Being a George is a good thing. If you should hear the word "flea" applied to someone, that is a bad thing. Fleas are not liked by puppy dogs or dealers or anyone who needs tips to survive.

CHAPTER 7

Gambling Is a Numbers Game

ambling is a numbers game. For casinos, it has nothing to do with luck, although on any given table at any given time, it looks as if luck predominates. At least gamblers are convinced the casinos rely on luck too.

For casinos, luck isn't an operant condition, because they have enough tables and machines to be in the long run in a very, very short time. The long run favors the math, and a very "short" long run means the casinos can confidently go to the bank, oh, like tomorrow or the day after.

Casino gamblers fervently believe in luck—short-term luck, long-term luck, luck today, luck tomorrow, luck for a week, a month, a lifetime—and these casino gamblers firmly believe that such luck will dominate over time, either for good or bad. The sad truth is that it's almost always for the bad. Casinos know how in love gamblers are with luck, so they play up the concept that you will have good luck all the time by using deceptive advertising: pictures and billboards showing happy winners, radio and television advertisements depicting people smiling and applauding at table games and slot machines, etc.

In casinos' pitches to players, you won't see commercials where a player is cursing and foaming at the mouth or kicking the slot machine in a mad rage. Besides the true-life pictures of dazzled winners, the commercials show the beautiful people, usually drinking out of martini glasses with the whitest of white teeth gleaming in the glow of the slot machines. You won't see one of these beautiful people being dragged out of the casino by security guards for improper conduct.

Smart players know that luck is almost always bad over time for casino gamblers who are not playing with an edge and who have to go up against the house edge on the games they play.

Gamblers are almost all losers over almost any prolonged series of decisions. Casinos, on the other hand, are almost always winners over any such prolonged period of time. Indeed, casinos—with all their tables, all their machines, and all their decisions per hour—are almost always winners *right now*.

When referring to a casino's edge, it means a mathematical edge, not an edge in luck. On the Pass Line in craps, for example, the casino's edge is about 1.41 percent. That means the casino will win $1.41 for every $100 wagered. It translates easily: the casino wins 251 bets on the Pass Line, while the player wins 244 bets. That seven-bet difference gives the casino a mathematical edge on the bet.

If a casino player plays the Pass Line day in and day out for years and years, that player is most probably cursed to be a loser, and the casino is blessed to be a winner. That seven-number edge is all the casino needs to make a nice chunk of change from a craps player. And that's a *good* craps player, not the ploppies who make foolish bets.

So what about the bad craps players, who are legion in the casinos? It isn't pretty.

The bottom line is that the longer a player plays, the worse his or her prospects will be. That's a fact, because that is the math of the game. Those sad ploppy players think they can overcome randomness by discovering patterns in such randomness—patterns that are predictable and therefore bettable, making the game beatable. They can't; they are merely deluded in this regard, although they are quite strong in their declarations that their losing trend-betting systems are actually the way to play. I think it was Einstein who said, "Insanity is doing the same thing over and over again and expecting different results." That's the typical casino gambler.

The casino obviously wants as many decisions as it can get, to allow the mathematical probabilities to work themselves out. If a player were to make one single bet in all his or her life, then the player could come out ahead for his rather short gambling career. If the player won a stupid bet with a high house edge and never played again, the math of the game would not have time to work itself out to guarantee the casino a real monetary win.

But let's take one million players across the country all making just one bet on a proposition: red coming up in roulette. What happens then? Even if the number of the reds comes up exactly as probability indicates, even if the number of players winning comes up exactly as probability indicates, the players—as a group—will lose 5.26 percent of all the money wagered on this proposition.

That's the math inexorably working itself out. You can't escape the math even if you are deluded enough to think you can.

So the more decisions a casino gets, the better chance it will be ahead. In craps, casinos look to get in 120 decisions per hour per table. Do they? Easily. At a full table, there are players betting three, four, five, or more bets each round of play, so 120 decisions is actually a rather modest goal.

Even a single shooter at a craps table getting the dice back every 30 seconds can roll the dice 120 times. The more bets, the more decisions, the better the chance the casino will be ahead in a relatively short time.

Yes, when a monster roll at craps is going on, the number of rolls will decrease, but the number of decisions will rise and rise as the players bet more and more types of wagers. Keep this in mind: it doesn't matter if the casino wins or loses a given decision, the total number of decisions will allow probability to work itself out to the casino's benefit.

That's the be-all and end-all of the house's mathematical edge over the player still adamantly relying on luck to win. The casino has the right idea; the player has the wrong one. The casino lives in the real world of fact; the casino gambler lives in the fantasy world of hope.

And what about players who have an edge at the games they play? They now reverse places with the casinos. The math becomes on the advantage player's side over time. The only problem is that a single advantage player has to play a lot of hours (make that years' worth) to get in enough time for his or her edge to assert itself enough to be a long-term winner.

For advantage players, the road is up and down, down and up, but over time, the advantage player should be ahead. It's the reverse for a nonadvantage player—it's up and down, down and up, but the thrust is a steady down over time.

It's a numbers game, pure and simple. Whoever has the edge wins over time; whoever faces that edge is ultimately knocked out.

CHAPTER 8

Money Management at Slots and Table Games

There are many casino gamblers who believe that, through various money-management methods, they can overcome the house edges on the bets they make and come out ahead in the long run. They are under the impression that they can beat the casino by managing their money properly. They are wrong.

Money management only works positively when players play games in which they have the edge over the house, such as using dice control at craps and card counting at blackjack, among others. However, because the casino has the edge over the player in almost all games at almost all times, there is no amount of money management that can turn such a negative situation into a positive one. That would be called a "miracle" if it could happen.

So what is money management when it comes to slot machines and table games? Are they the same, or will different types of games provide different formulas for managing one's money? The answer is a little of "they are the same" and a little of "they are all different." As you can plainly see, I'm not a man who straddles a fence.

In slots, where the casino has edges ranging from a decent 2 percent to an outrageous 17 percent, money management is a lifeline to prevent players from losing their shirts, blouses, pants, skirts, wallets, pocketbooks, arms, and perhaps legs. Realistically put, managing your money properly at slots prevents you from losing your discipline and subsequently losing more money than you wanted—or worse, losing more money than you can afford to lose.

Remember what house edges actually mean in terms of money. Quoting percentages in gambling articles or books often goes flying over gamblers' heads in terms of what these numbers mean. The gambler thinks, *Yeah, okay, this percentage; yeah, that percentage. Who cares? I don't even know what these things really mean.* Translated into monetary terms, the impact of the house edge is dramatic. If the slot machine you play has an edge of 17 percent, your expected loss is $17 for every $100 you wager. Ouch!

And think of how fast you can play those slot machines! Combining lightning-fast speeds with high house edges is a prescription for you to lose big bucks and for the casino to treat you to a buffet for doing so. The exchange rate between losses and a buffet is quite high.

> **Anticipation:** *One of the main elements of fun in gambling is the anticipation of the next decision, the excitement that such antici- pation brings. Playing slowly does not decrease your anticipatory excitement; rather, it increases it. If you play fast, your anticipation is diluted, and the predecision excitement is far less.*

Think of money management in terms of the reins on a horse: done properly it can rein you in, especially if you're the type who has a ten- dency to go gallop in your play. Sticking to a solid money-management plan can make playing fun and *safe*. That is the maximum role of proper money-management techniques at the machines. For some people, money management saves them from themselves.

The Slots

Because there are now more types of slot machines in the casinos than ever before, my advice about money management has to be sifted through your own logic and risk tolerance. As a general principle, I will state the following unequivocally: when in doubt, don't spend new money trying to make up for money you previously lost. Conservative is by far the best way to play casino games. In fact, in my opinion, it is the *only* way to play casino games. Your money is important and is not to be risked because you have become too emotionally involved in your play. Lose your mind, lose your money—a simple but totally true statement.

Figure out how much you play on a machine in a spin. Let's say you put in $3 per spin. Take that spin and multiply it by six, which will be the number of spins you will make in a minute (no more)—which comes to $18 played per minute. Multiply that by 60 minutes, and you play $1,080 through the machine every hour.

That's a lot of money for just betting $3 per spin. In baccarat, betting $25 per hand, you stand to put out about $1,000 per hour—but with a house edge close to 1 percent! So you can see how those fast machines can clobber you even if you think you are a low roller.

Unless you hit a losing streak of galactic proportions, the chance of losing all $1,080 is remote—that is, if your bankroll for that one hour is $1,080. So that is what you bring to the machine for a one-hour session of play—the full amount of a possible galactic loss of $1,080. You play this money, called a "session stake," through the machine once—*only once*—and whatever you win, you keep. So whatever comes out of the machine is yours to keep.

It is possible (and quite desirable) that what comes out of the machine will be more than what you put in—more than likely, over time it won't be. Still, you will never go back to your room totally broke. You'll always have some money that you take away from the machine. That beats ambling back to your room, head down and busted.

What happens if, after one hour of play and maybe a few drinks along the way, you are substantially ahead and you want to keep playing? Take the original $1,080 and put it aside, and take half of your win and play with that.

Let's say you won $800. Take $400 as your playing money and put $400 aside as your win. Doing so guarantees that you will leave the session a winner—one of the few guarantees you'll ever get in a casino, that's for sure.

Let's get really positive and say you just won another $800 during your second run-through. Well, do the same thing if you want to continue playing. Take $400 and put it in the bank, and play with the other

$400. As long as you keep winning when putting your money through the machine—*one time*, I remind you—then you can keep playing if you so desire.

If you wind up with less than $1,080 after putting your money through the machine, your session is over. Do not play any more of that session stake. It is time for a break.

Once your session is over, you do not play with any money you won. That money is put away for keeps. You take a second $1,080 and use that for your next session. Using this type of money-management system will prevent you from experiencing disasters at the machines. It will allow you to come home with some money after each and every trip. You might not come home with a win, but you won't come home with empty pockets.

In the above example I was using $3 as the amount of a single bet, but you can make the amount whatever your bet is on the machines you enjoy playing. If you bet 75¢ per spin, then multiply by six, which is $4.50, then by 60, which is $270 per hour. Use these as your figures, but play exactly as I explained above.

The Table Games

In this book, we are covering quite a few table games. The basic premise of money management for table games where you can't get an edge is quite similar to the money-management techniques for slot machines. You want to have enough money to allow you to last at the game, and you want to make sure you do not lose your mind and start betting like a ploppy maniac.

Money management can't save you from the house edge at a table game, but it can save you from allowing that edge to destroy you. Unlike slot machines, edges at table games are usually smaller—at least, the better bets at those games are smaller—and the speeds of the game are quite slower. *Smaller edges, slower games*...those are magical words. Yes, there are some table games where the house edges are just as high as a slot machine's, but these are never (I repeat, *never!*) to be wagered on.

The outside bets at roulette (the red/black, high/low, odd/even); the Bank and Player bets at baccarat; blackjack; and the best bets at craps, such as Pass, Don't Pass, Come, Don't Come, and the Placing of certain numbers have sometimes been called "50/50" wagers by some writers. Naturally, as I already showed, these games are not actually 50/50 games either, because the casino either wins more decisions—for example, the craps Pass Line bet where the casino wins 251 decisions to the player's 244 decisions—or the casino takes a cut from the winning bet, as in roulette's short payouts of 35-to-1 on a number when the true ("fair") payout would be 37-to-1 or the casino's payout of 1-to-1 on the propositions mentioned above when the bets lose 10 times but only win 9 times. The casino is sharing in the player's win by paying too little!

So get the concept of 50/50 out of your mind; there are no fair games. The casinos do not want, nor will they ever want, to offer fair games. They want games where they are assured of winning, and thus they have to manipulate the games to make that happen. For players, that is the "cost of business."

However, because the best bets at the above games are relatively close contests, the likelihood of going on a galactic horror ride is really, really, really remote. Therefore, unlike the slot player who can be devastated in a single hour if he or she doesn't hit some decent payouts, that is not really a common occurrence at the table games; that is, if those games are played properly, using the correct bets with the correct strategies. You can probably do just fine with more or less half of what the slot player should bring to the table.

I'll give one example here and—later, with each game—will go into more specifics.

So let's take baccarat. If you do not bet the awful Tie bet, which comes in with a slot-like edge of higher than 14 percent, then the game fluctuates between two bets, Player and Bank. The Player bet will win about 49 percent of the time; the Bank bet will win a little more than 51 percent of the time (a commission is charged on a Bank win).

I have seen streaks of 10 to 12 of either of these propositions coming up in a row. So let me just take a loss of 10 in a row as a baseline for this money-management example. Given 40 actual decisions per hour, with 10 winning Bank bets in a row, the other 30 decisions (in theory) should come out 15-to-15 (give or take). So the Bank will win 25 decisions, and the Player will win 15 decisions. Let's say you only bet on the Player in this session; at $25 per decision, you lost $625.

To be safe then, let's say the largest expected loss you will likely (but not definitely) encounter will be about $700. If you bring $1,000 to a $25 game, you will probably be in good shape to play for a single hour without having to worry about going back to your spouse in your room to hear, "I told you not to play baccarat. You ain't James Bond, kiddo!"

Safe, mindful money-management methods can therefore keep you both safe and sane. And that's saying something.

The 401(g)

If you want to be a serious player, my strong recommendation is to start a 401(g). The 401(g) is a money-market checking account that you use for your gambling dollars. You should never be using "real" money when you play in the casinos; you should only be using money that you have set aside specifically for playing. This 401(g) (the G stands for *gambling*) can go a long way toward strengthening your emotional bankroll too. Knowing you have the proper amount of money in a single account to play at the level you feel comfortable will make you feel even more comfortable.

As you win money, you put it in your 401(g); when you lose money, you lose it from your 401(g). What should you do if you lose, say, 20 percent of your total bankroll in a horrendous series of defeats? A smart move would be to reduce your total betting by 20 percent so that your risk of ruin (ROR) stays at 5 percent or whatever level you feel comfortable with. If you win and increase your 401(g) by 20 percent, you can increase your betting by this percentage as well. Keep in mind, though, that in a negative-expectation game, the movement will ultimately be down.

You can also consider putting money into your 401(g) from your paychecks or business. You do not have to put in a lot, just a little on a regular basis. In a relatively short time, that 401(g) could be big enough to withstand a tough losing streak.

CHAPTER 9

Legal Stealing or Real Theft?

I asked members of my private website, www.goldentouchcraps.com, to comment on the various moral scenarios in which one can be during casino play. I'll give you the basic types of incidents, the law, and what board members had to say. (The laws might not apply to every state. These are based on Nevada.)

The Situation: The dealer overpays you or hold a major blunder in a game. Are you legally allowed to keep the chips?
The Law: Yes, you are. The law does not hold you responsible for a dealer error in a game. If the error isn't caught, you have no legal responsibility to hand back the money.

The Situation: You find a chip on the floor. Can you keep it?
The Law: No, it belongs to the casino.

The Situation: There is money in the slot tray or the slot machine still has credits to be played. Can you take the money? Can you play the credits?
The Law: No, the money and the credits belong to the casino.

What would you do in such cases? Here are some responses from my Golden Touch website members:

Dr. Crapology: "The [blackjack] dealer looked at her hole card every time she had an ace up. It took me about three times to realize that if she had a face card down she asked for insurance. If she did not have a face card down, she immediately began to ask anyone if they wanted to hit. So every time she asked for insurance, I took it and was successful. The other players thought I was a genius. She was a new dealer and not properly supervised, and I did not feel it my job to police the casino employees."

Section 8: "I've had Come bets [in craps] with full odds out on the table. I made my point, and the next Come-Out roll was a winning 7, except for my [losing] Come bets. The dealers ignored taking down my losing Come bets. They left all three Come bets up and working."

The Retired Ballplayer: "I notice many mistakes by dealers—in payoffs, change, or paying the wrong player. If a dealer makes a mistake in my favor, silence is a beautiful thing. If the dealer shorts me, I jump their ass in a heartbeat!"

The Goddess explained a situation she experienced. "In Pai Gow poker, the dealer's hand beat the player's hand, but the dealer called the hand a push and left it." She didn't have to do a thing. The dealer did it for her.

Skinny: "I took out a marker at a craps table in Las Vegas. I had done that before on the trip, so they cut out the chips right away. About roughly five to ten minutes later, they brought the marker over for me to sign. It was filled out for a lesser amount than what I had requested and already received in chips. I told them of their error, and they were extremely grateful. I expect it was the correct thing to do morally and legally."

Rodrigo: "I tend to be honest, but when a dealer makes a mistake, I tend not to be honest. What if a dealer deliberately leaves up a bet of yours that lost as a thank-you for tipping? Do you tell on him?"

And here's one that's becoming increasingly relevant in this computer age:

The Situation: What if there are malfunctions in casino software?
The Law: Malfunctions void the payouts.

Section 8: "One particular player's card issued me an extra 0 in my total Tier points. Instead of having 8,500 tier points, I suddenly had

85,000, which was well above their highest and most prized status level. I often wonder when this actually occurred, but I only noticed it a few summers back while playing video poker.

"Yes, the moral thing would have been to advise someone. How about doing nothing? I neither took advantage of it during several trips, nor did I tell anyone. However, when I returned home, I would just monitor the thing and see if the mistake would be caught. Nothing.

"After about a year of watching this and receiving all sorts of free monthly show tickets, free golf offers, and discounts for weddings and the like, I finally asked someone at the casino player's [club] about it. They said I had had the points for more than a year and that I had been receiving offers and all the benefits for having the points on the card. I was basically told that these are my points and had been such for a while.

"I'm still leery about it, though, and the points are still on the card."

Steven C.: "First time we visited Lake Tahoe we took a van from Reno to the Cal Neva resort. I was watching the bags while the ex-wife went in search of a phone to call her parents at their condo to let them know we were there, so they could pick us up.

"As it happened, there were several banks of slots right there, and I thought, *Why not?* Unfortunately, I only had a couple quarters in my pocket, and this was before you could stuff paper in the slots.

"I remember putting the first quarter in a machine, pulling, and nothing. Then on the second pull, with no fanfare, bells, or whistles, the machine emptied its little bowels right into the tray.

"Naturally, I was excited about the win. My ex, who had returned and was playing a machine opposite me, asked what I had won. Scanning the tumblers, the answer was...*nothing.* There were no winning combinations showing, and I had *won nothing.*

"Nobody from the casino responded, and my ex was asking what we should do. Well, I did some quick 'constipating' [sic] and came up with my Jimmy the Greek theory. I grabbed several buckets and started filling them. It wasn't until they were full and I started putting the remainder in her purse that the ex thought to ask what I was doing.

"I then educated her on my theory. 'They're getting off easy,' I told her. She gave me one of those *you've got to be kidding me* looks that only ex-wives can do so well. I could tell she didn't understand, so I gave her the rest of the theory. 'What odds,' I asked, 'would Jimmy give me if I told him I was going to walk into this very casino with only two quarters, play them one quarter at a time on a randomly selected machine, and hit a jackpot with no winning combination showing?' She looked at me strangely and said, 'I don't know.' 'Astronomical, bazillions-to-1,' I declared. 'They're getting off easy.'

"I beat a hasty but happy retreat from the scene of the crime."

PART 2:

The Games

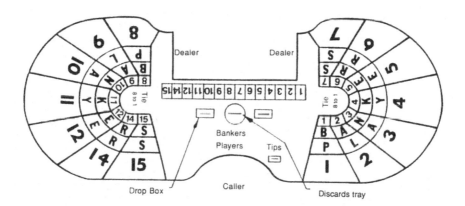

CHAPTER 10

Size Does Matter: Baccarat and Mini-Baccarat

"My name is Bond...James Bond." No, no, sorry, not anymore, Mr. Bond. The old baccarat Bond is dead; long live the new baccarat players—a baccarat legion strongly composed of Asians and Russians, as well as Americans and Europeans of every stripe. The game of baccarat is no longer solely the province of just the European elite; it is now an international game, played north, south, east, and west.

Go to any Las Vegas casino that has the full-blown high-roller-room game of baccarat, and there will be a large contingent of Asians playing. Indeed, some casinos have eliminated some seat numbers from their baccarat tables because Asian players consider particular numbers unlucky. For example, the number four is missing, because that number sounds like death in Chinese, and who wants to sit in the seat reserved for death?

The baccarat tables are the United Nations of gambling, with many tongues spoken and even more superstitions adhered to by the players... and for the players' emotional well-being by the superfriendly casino personnel. And superstitions from all geographic regions dominate the thinking of most baccarat players. It's not just the "unlucky" numbers; it's all sorts of things—some of them completely wild, as I'll show you later in this chapter.

Baccarat presents you with an *almost* 50/50 game against the casino—indeed, one of the two best bets at the game, the Bank, will actually win more than 50 percent of the time. That's how tight a contest it can be. Players have a good chance on any given night to "take home the money" because the game is *this close.*

Helpful Hint: *Baccarat is not pronounced* back-a-rat *but* bahh-kaa-rah. *That end* T *is silent. You definitely do not want to say, "Let's play back-a-rat," because you'll tip the dealers off to your novice status and lack of James Bond–like smoothness!*

As with any casino game, the first question is this: can baccarat be beaten? Unless you have the amazingly unusual and completely rare skill (say "rare" many times over) to follow cards in a shuffle, there is no way to actually get an edge at this game. (I have only known one person who could follow cards in a shuffle, and he has long since passed away.) Yes, card-counting systems have been developed for the game, but none of these can really reduce the house edge by more than one-tenth of a percent. Indeed, every card-counting system at baccarat is truly laborious and usually winds up with this statement, "Bet the Bank hand!" Yes, 90 percent of the time, baccarat card-counting systems tell us that the best hand to bet on is Bank.

However, even with that said, *how* you bet the hands at baccarat, how you actually structure your attack at the game, will go a long way to the possibility of winning money at any given session, and it will go an even longer way toward getting what I call a "monetary edge" over the casino.

Baccarat is perhaps the most accessible of all the table games because it is, when you play it correctly, betting on the equivalent of a coin flip. Despite this simplicity, baccarat also has a charm, an old-world ambience, a "this is the way casinos should be" atmosphere about it. It is a game of elegance, played in high-roller rooms with several dealers and pit people catering to your needs. This is James Bond time for real, no matter what country the players come from. There are quite a few truly enjoyable eccentrics who love playing the game too.

How Baccarat Is Played
The full-blown high-roller-room games, where the players get to deal the cards and the game moves along at a snail's pace, will usually be

$100- minimum games. Don't panic; that minimum does not translate into big expected losses. In fact, you will lose more in the long run at a 25¢ slot machine than at a $100-minimum baccarat game because the game is so slow that you play maybe 40 decisions per hour—which means you put into play about $4,000 against a house edge of a little more than 1 percent if you bet either of the two best bets. A player stands to lose on average about $50 per hour, or the equivalent of half a bet. You only need to win one more hand than you lose to be ahead. Again, it's that close a game.

Baccarat is usually dealt from an eight-deck shoe. All 10s, jacks, queens, and kings equal zero. The ace equals one. All the other cards equal their face value. The highest possible hand is nine.

The objective of baccarat is for the players to correctly guess which of three possible propositions will win on the next round: Bank, Player, or Tie. After the casino dealer shuffles, discards cards, and places the yellow card in the decks, two cards are dealt to the Bank hand and two cards are dealt to the Player hand. Sometimes a third card is dealt to either or both hands. Whichever hand is closest to nine is the winner. A two-card hand of nine and a two-card hand of eight are considered naturals and do not take any hits. However, a two-card hand of nine beats a two-card hand of eight.

In baccarat the deal goes counterclockwise around the table from player to player. The player who is dealing continues to deal as long as the Bank hand keeps winning—even though the player dealing does not have to bet the Bank hand. As soon as a Player hand wins, the next player gets to deal. Thus the shoe makes its way around the table. Players can pass up their turn at dealing if they so wish. If you want to play baccarat and you want to deal, but you're timid, don't worry. The casino personnel assigned to the baccarat tables are always willing to take you through the deals step by step. In fact, the slower you deal, the better it is for you, because you will be playing fewer hands.

As Bank (or bank dealer), you send the first card to the casino's dealer. This is the Player's first card. Then you put a card under the lip of the shoe. That's the Bank's first card. Next the Player's hand gets a second card, then the Bank hand gets a second card. All these cards are dealt facedown. Remember, even though you are dealing, you can actually place your bets on the Player hand if you wish.

The individual who has bet the most on the Player then receives the two Player cards. Here's where the game becomes fun for me. Most baccarat players don't just look at the cards and flip them over to reveal what the fates have in store for the Player hand. Oh no, most baccarat players have extremely elaborate ways of checking to see what hand they have. Some squeeze the cards together and then slowly move them apart—I'm talking nano-inches at a time—in order to see what hand they have. Other players bend the sides of the cards to look at the pips. They do this slowly. If you are the type of gambler who likes speed, then these players will drive you crazy. But I love them! Playing slow in games where the house has the edge over the player is the only way to play.

Once the Player hand is put into the center of the table, you get to look at the two Bank cards. After the Bank and Player hands have received two cards, it is possible that either or both might need to draw an extra card. The rules for drawing cards are predetermined. They are also essentially irrelevant, because the players do not get to make any decisions concerning hitting or standing. The casino's dealer will tell you which hands need more cards. You just have to follow orders. (See tables for the rules; you don't have to memorize them!)

Rules for Player Hands:

If first two cards total:	Action
1, 2, 3, 4, 5, 0	Player draws a card
6, 7	Player stands
8, 9	Player and Bank must stand

Rules for Bank Hands:

If Bank's first two cards total:	Draw when Player's third card is:	Do not draw when Player's third card is:
3	1, 2, 3, 4, 5, 6, 7, 9, 10	8
4	2, 3, 4, 5, 6, 7	1, 8, 9, 10
5	4, 5, 6, 7	1, 2, 3, 8, 9, 10
6	6, 7	1, 2, 3, 4, 5, 8, 9, 10

If Bank's first two cards total:	Draw when Player's third card is:	Do not draw when Player's third card is:
7	stands	stands
8	Natural stands	Natural stands
9	Natural stands	Natural stands

A winning Player hand is paid off at 1-to-1. Thus, if you bet $100, you win $100. A winning Bank hand is paid off at even money with a commission, usually 5 percent, extracted on each win. This means that if you bet $100, you win $95. This commission is collected after the shoe is finished, but you can request to "pay as you go." The Tie hand is paid at 8-to-1. Thus, a winning tie wager of $10 will return $80. If you bet on either Bank or Player and the Tie wins, you do not lose your bet. It is a push.

The Tie bet is one of the worst bets in the casino—with higher than a 14 percent edge, which means your expectation is to lose $14 for every $100 you wager on the Tie, so let's not even consider making it. Because the Tie bet does not affect the other two bets, Player and Bank, we'll concentrate on how we arrive at the house edge for these bets.

The Player bet wins 49.32 percent of the time.

The Player bet loses 50.68 percent of the time.

Translate that into money, and for every $100 wagered on the Player bet, you will lose $1.36. ($50.68 minus $49.32 equals $1.36.) The casino edge is therefore 1.36 percent.

The Bank bet wins 50.68 percent of the time.

The Bank bet loses 49.32 percent of the time.

Without any interference, the Bank bet would have a 1.36 percent edge in its favor. If the casinos allowed this to stand, no one would bet Player, and everyone would bet Bank until the casinos went bankrupt. To avoid this, the casinos charge that 5 percent commission on all winning Bank bets. In actuality, you only win 95¢ on the dollar on a winning Bank wager, as stated. This reverses the situation and gives the casino a smallish 1.17 percent edge.

How does a 5 percent commission reduce the edge to 1.17 percent? When you lose the Bank bet, you lose $49.32 for every $100 wagered.

But when you win the bet, you win $50.68 x 95¢, which comes out to $48.15. Therefore, $49.32 minus $48.15 equals $1.17 lost per $100 dollars wagered—in short, a 1.17 percent edge for the casinos.

Purists would dispute the above figures, because they want to count the Tie bet in the equations. I prefer not to, because making the Tie bet does not—I repeat, *does not*—exist in my baccarat world. When Tie bets appear, I just think of it as more time between hands and not as a part of the game. The bet does not exist. The Tie bet appears approximately 10 percent of the time and pays off at 8-to-1. Still, to be comprehensive, here are the house edges if we count the Tie bet.

Player = 1.24 percent

Bank = 1.06 percent

Tie = 14.36 percent (ugh!)

> **So What?:** *Some casinos will pay the Tie bet off at 9-to-1, and this cuts the house edge to about 5 percent, still not a good bet. Bottom line is, never bet the Tie bet even if you see someone hooting and hollering when he hits it. Over time, the Tie bet sinks all players; it is the Tie-tanic of baccarat!*

New Wrinkles on the Old Game

Today you will also find baccarat games where the casinos have changed how they handle the Bank bet. Instead of charging a commission on the bet, the casino will pay only one-half of a winning Bank hand totaling six. Therefore, if the Bank beats the Player by a score of 6–5 or less, then the casino only pays the Bank bets at half value. So a $100 wager is paid $50.

On the other winning Bank hands no commission is charged. Now this new rule helps casinos in a straightforward way—it makes the game faster because no commissions have to be figured out at the end of a round of play, and it increases the house edge by 0.3 percent. Over time that 0.3 percent coupled with the speedier payouts will win the casinos more money—more of *your* money.

Another Bank and Player change concerns the new "push" rule. If the number three is the winner, the winner does not get paid. This simple change nudges up the house edge and also increases the number of hands being played.

Some Wrinkles Are Good

There are some casinos that have occasionally reduced the commission on the Bank bet to 4 percent; some casinos have even gone down to 3 percent. Obviously, these commissions are terrific for those players betting on Bank, as a 4 percent commission reduces the house edge to 0.6 percent, and the 3 percent commission reduces the edge further still, to 0.14 percent. These are far better bets than even the original Bank percentage—which is darn good in its own right.

Mini-Baccarat Means Maxi-Losses

There are three major differences between mini-baccarat and full-blown baccarat aside from the fact that mini-baccarat is played on a blackjack-style table or a lower midsize table:

1. Players do not deal the cards; the casino dealer is in charge of that.
2. The size of the minimum bets can be as low as $10 but tend to be $25.
3. The speed of mini-baccarat is fast, faster, and fastest.

Casino dealers are trained to swiftly move the games along. The faster a game is played, the better for the casinos, as more decisions bring the real results of the game into the realm of math. Probability works itself out more precisely over extended periods of time. In short, the more decisions in baccarat, the better it is for the casino.

And mini-baccarat does not disappoint! The number of hands that can be played in an hour often range from 120 to almost 200! You'll never find anything close to that number of decisions in the full-blown game. If no player crimps, bends, spins, taps, moans, yells, or throws the cards into the air, the speed is about 70 hands per hour. In fact, the actual speed is closer to 40 to 50 hands per hour—a much smaller average number than 120 to 200. (I am basing all of my figures on my own scouting of the games.)

If we postulate that a full-blown baccarat player betting $100 per decision on the Bank or Player, with no bets on Ties, plays 40 hands per hour, his expectation is as follows: He actually plays only 36 hands, because 10 percent of the hands will be Ties, on which no money is won or lost on the Bank or Player bets. If he does make a combination of these two bets, we can postulate that he is playing against an approximately 1.25 percent house edge.

- He bets a total of $3,600.
- Betting a combination of both Bank and Player, he has an expected loss of $45 per hour.
- If he only bets Player, his expected loss is about $49 per hour.
- If he only bets Bank, his expected loss is $42 per hour.

Now look at a mini-baccarat player. If we say he plays 160 hands per hour, never betting on Ties, he will face 144 decisions.

- If our player bets $25 per decision, he will place $3,600 into action.
- Betting the combination of Bank and Player, his expected loss is $45 per hour.
- If the mini-baccarat player only bets Player, his expected loss is about $49 per hour.
- If he only bets Bank, his expected loss is about $42 per hour.

Imagine thinking of yourself as a $25 bettor and being frightened of the $100 minimums in the high-roller-room version of baccarat when, over time, your expected results will be the same or similar.

What you will discover—as some casinos attempt to strain the money out of the wallets of baccarat players—is the complete or partial elimination of the big baccarat tables or the reducing of their action to weekends only. Instead you'll discover that the lower, midsize tables will be opened for business, composed of one dealer dealing as fast as he or she can. Those $100+ players take a shellacking at those games!

Variance

In the short run, a $100 player will have a bigger variance in his wins and losses. If you are a $25 player who decides to jump to $100 in the full-blown baccarat game, you will find that the swings in your bankroll will be greater in the short run. If a $25 mini-baccarat player plays a dozen hands per minute, he gets into the long run four times faster than a $100 baccarat player playing only seven hands per minute. The more decisions, the more the game starts to resemble its mathematical underpinnings, so mini-baccarat will reach the long run in a shorter period of time. Still, if you have the bankroll to withstand the short-term ups and downs, playing the big baccarat game is the way to go. Why? Comps! Betting $100 brings in more comp value for a $100 player, despite the fact that the averages come out the same. Most casino raters don't know what I just explained to you.

What Is Scoblete Talking About?

Wait a minute; I just said that playing a $100 game is better than playing a $25 game, when it is clear that the $100 player clearly loses more per hour. Is something wrong with me?

No, you see, if you use my slow-down-the-game strategies, you will play fewer than 40 decisions per hour. You'll spin the cards, tap the cards, bend them, and talk to them when you are the dealer, and if you're the individual with the highest bet on the Player hand, you'll do all of that too. You'll take oodles of time to decide which bet to make. Your goal will be to cut down the number of decisions by 10 to 25 percent. This is easier to do in full-blown baccarat than in mini-baccarat, because you get to play around as the dealer.

So, let's look at some of the best strategies you can use to play baccarat the most intelligent way. I want you to become a fast learner in slowing down the game!

Try to Play at Crowded Tables

The more players at the table, the slower the game goes. This is true of every casino game in which the player faces a house edge he can't overcome with skill. More players are good for you because it automatically cuts down the number of decisions you face and the average hourly hit on your money. Because baccarat players are a supremely superstitious lot, the more of them, the merrier. Almost all of them will have strange habits that tend to slow down the game. Also, the dealers will have to take all those losing bets and pay off all those winning bets.

The Scorecard Is Your Friend

Baccarat is the scorecard game of all scorecard games. Every baccarat and mini-baccarat table will usually have scores of scorecards so the players can keep track of the past streaks in the game. Naturally, most baccarat players fall into the category of gamblers who know nothing about why trend betting can't be winning betting. The past trends tell you nothing about the future hands coming out.

No matter; those scorecards are a godsend to the smart baccarat player—meaning you. Keep score...slowly. Analyze the trends that have appeared; debate with yourself, maybe even out loud ("Hmm, the Bank has appeared four times in a row. Is it hot? Will it continue? Or is it going to cool off right now? I wish I could make up my mind."). Most baccarat players will fully (foolishly) understand the dilemma you face: how do you bet those darn trends? Most of the other players are in the same boat, killing themselves trying to predict the future; the difference is, your boat is moving really slow!

By the way, enjoy the posturing. Have fun with your new superstitious persona. Be a part of the crowd, even if some of them seem crazed to you. You can enjoy a game by playing it in such a way, even if you actually don't believe that such a way has any bearing on the outcome.

Bet Bank Every Hand or Every Other Hand

Distance runners pride themselves on their slow heart rates; it shows they are in shape. Well, my bet-Bank-only strategy will clearly show the slow heartbeat of the smart baccarat player.

Obviously the Bank bet is the premier bet at the game. (Don't get trapped into playing one of the baccarat anti-Bank wrinkles.) It will win more than 50 percent of the time. You could, if you wish, just bet it each and every hand. The casino's hit on your money doing this, as clearly shown above, will be noticeably less than if you bet only the Player hand.

As a $100 player, your expected loss is $42 per hour as opposed to an expected loss of $49 betting only on the Player wager. But you can stomp that hourly loss on the Bank bet down even more. Yes, you will still only bet Bank, but you will only bet it once it has already shown. I call this "intermittent betting." Here is how it works:

You buy in and get your chips.

Then you put down your first Bank bet. If the Bank wins, you bet it again. If it loses, you sit out the next hand. If Player wins the next hand, you keep sitting out. As soon as another Bank hand wins, you bet on the Bank again. If the Bank wins, you bet it again. You keep betting Bank until it loses; then you sit out. You wait for the Bank to hit again, and then you bet it again. If the dealers should say anything to you, just respond, "I use the streak method. Yesterday I did Player streaks; now I'm using Bank streaks. I like playing those streaks." Then laugh, "I'm a streaker!"

This technique is excellent for mini-baccarat as well. It dramatically reduces the number of hands on which you bet. I would also recommend that at the mini version of the game to just sit out some hands for the heck of it. If you are trying to reduce the mini-baccarat hit on your bankroll, you have to get the number of decisions down to about 80—not an easy thing to do.

You could, if you have patience, wait for two Banks to hit in a row and then bet Bank. The more you incorporate intermittent betting into your methods, the less the house's edge has the ability to grind away at your money.

What About Adding Player Bets?

It is not a crime against nature to bet the Player as it is a crime against all that is holy to bet the Tie. Do the same method as above—wait for a Player win and then bet Player. Continue to bet Player until it loses, sit out, and if Bank hits a second time or Player hits once again, bet whichever one just hit. You'll still reduce the number of decisions betting this way.

Bet the Hot Player

If there is a player at the table who is winning or even just won a single hand, then bet with that player. Let everyone know you are doing this: "Hey, guy, I'm betting with you. You look lucky tonight!"

No, he doesn't have an edge; he just has had some current luck, and that luck translates into good fortune for you because, to determine who is winning, you have to wait to see who wins or who loses one or (even better!) a few hands. So you are sitting out a few hands in the meantime, looking for that hot player.

If the "lucky" player loses a hand, sit out a couple more to find the next lucky player. Many Asian baccarat players love this style of play—although they will bet with or against certain players for other reasons also (I am not always sure how they decide in such cases on whom to bet with or against), and they bet each and every hand. You don't want to do this.

The Bathroom Break

When ya gotta go, ya gotta go...but never go while the decks are being shuffled. This is dead time, but it is time where your comps are still adding up. Go to the bathroom as the game begins—your comps will still be adding up, but your money will not be at risk.

And take your time in there. If you are playing in the high-roller room, you will have your own bathroom. Lock the door, and the bathroom is yours. Make sure you wash your hands, comb your hair, and check your face in the mirror. Then slowly count to 100. If you are going to the public bathroom, amble, don't walk; enjoy the sights of the casino.

Oh, Dealer, My Dealer

I am not the garrulous type. I usually prefer to play silently. But trying to slow down the game often comes down to getting the dealers involved with you. This works at the high-roller-room game where the dealers are pros at talking to the customers; but it works even better to slow down the game at the mini-baccarat tables.

The more the dealer talks, the fewer hands the dealer deals. Just ask a few questions and give your opinions, or tell the dealer about your life, your wife, your husband, your kids, your best buddies, or your abduction by space aliens—whatever you want. Wait to put your bet out while you talk, and never put a bet out when the dealer is talking, as that could stop the dealer, who now thinks she has to deal those cards because you've put your bet onto the layout.

Many people believe that small talk is a waste of time; it isn't when you are playing baccarat. In such cases, small talk is a big help.

Commission Now, Not Later

The typical baccarat game will collect the commissions of the winning Bank bets at the end of the shoe. This is a tradition, not a law of nature. Always pay your commission while the game is in progress, preferably after every Bank win. The dealers might not like it; the other players might not like it, but your bankroll will thank you for it.

Tippy Top

This bears repeating: I am not one of those gambling writers who think tipping is a waste of time and money. Casino dealers don't make much more than minimum wage, and they need those tips to make a decent living. However, if you keep tipping in front of your bet, with each win, the casino will take the win and the original bet. To tip again, you'll have to put more money out, which can get expensive.

My recommendation—as I mentioned before—is to always tip on top of your bet. Doing this will accomplish three important things:

1. Your tip will continue to stay active if you should win two or more hands in a row, making the dealer more money but not costing you any more money.
2. The tip will count as a part of your wager, adding to its comp value.
3. Dealers will appreciate such tips because, as you will see, many, if not most, players do not tip at all.

When placing the tip on top of your bet, let the dealers know that it is a bet for them, and make it obvious that you really, *really* want to win one for them.

Money Management at Baccarat

For a $25 player, a bankroll of $700 would be more than sufficient to play one hour without much worry of losing every penny at the big baccarat game in the high-roller room—if you can find one that has a $25 minimum bet, that is. Indeed with a bankroll per hour of $1,000 you would have to lose 40 out of 40 hands each hour, something I have never seen happen in my playing career. So if you wish to play four hours in a day, $4,000 is a guarantee that you will probably never be busted.

With the normally slow big baccarat game in the high-roller room—made even slower by your wise incorporation of eccentric dealing, spinning, tapping, bending, and peeking slooooowwwly at the cards—you will probably only play 40 decisions per hour. So if you are playing $100 per decision, you can confidently figure a bankroll of $2,800 per hour would be enough. If you wish to totally guarantee you will leave the table with money, then jack up your one-hour betting bankroll to $4,000.

Yikes! A bankroll for one hour of $4,000—that's crazy! It is and it isn't; that depends on your ability to handle risk.

> **Risk:** *Many people think they can tolerate more risk than they actually can. When asked by their investment broker if they have a strong stomach for risk, these people will answer, "Yes!" But if their investments tank, they get all shook up because, in truth, they couldn't handle as much risk as they thought they could. That is a valuable lesson for a gambler.*

You do not need $16,000 per four-hour play day. Let's say that after the first hour you are down $800, which means you lost eight more bets than you won, and now your bankroll has been reduced to $2,000. You have a choice; you can take a break before your second session, or you can decide to play another hour or until you lose another $800 to $1,200, and then you can call it a session. Chances are, you will make it through that second hour.

Nonetheless, with a big loss at the end of one or two hours, it is always best to take a break.

For the sessions after your break, you take what was left over from your former playing session(s), add to it enough money to bring you to $700 in a $25 game or $2,800 in a $100 game, and play another session.

Okay, the above shows the negative possibility of losing money. But baccarat, especially big baccarat, is a very close contest between the player and the house, owing to the low house edges on the Bank and Player bets and the slow speed—you will therefore find, with proper betting, you will have many winning sessions.

Let's say that you win $800 in that first hour-long session; what then? Put that $800 aside, never to be touched. When you play your second session, just play against your first $2,800. No session wins are ever to be played at subsequent games. For the $25 player, a $200 win would be put aside—never to be played.

Keep in mind that I am giving you a very conservative money-management system for baccarat, one that I think will stand you in good stead and make the possibility of being devastated remote. But all baccarat games are not either $25 or $100 minimum bets; some are $10, $15, $50, and $200. Some higher-than-high rollers (or high rollers who are actually high) will want tables with $500, $1,000, or higher minimums to keep...well...to keep you and me away!

My first discussion had to do with one-hour sessions; but what if you intend to actually play four hours per day, and you are going to be at the casino for three days? How much should you bring to reasonably prevent a wipeout? The following chart will give you a decent idea of what to do:

Baccarat Stakes

(40 Decisions Per Session)

Minimum Bet	Session Stake	Daily Stake (Four Hours)
$10	$280	$1,120
$15	$420	$1,680
$25	$700	$2,800
$50	$1,400	$5,600
$100	$2,800	$11,200
$200	$5,600	$22,400
$500	$14,000	$56,000

If your tolerance for risk is far greater than mine, you can reduce the above figures. For me, I want to know that I have enough money to thwart any possibility of going home empty-pocketed. Oh, keep this in mind too: I talk about sessions being an hour long, but that is only a rule of thumb for discussion purposes. Sessions can be whatever length you determine—longer or shorter than one hour, although I wouldn't make them more than two hours at a clip.

Mini-Baccarat Money Management

The chart concerning minimum bets, session stakes, and daily stakes for big baccarat are based on 40 decisions per hour. Mini-baccarat will have 80 decisions per hour—if you use my slow-down-the-darn-game strategies. You can't—I repeat *can't*—have a game where you are betting 100 to 200 decisions per hour. The speed of that type of game will make those low house edges on the Bank and Player bets become razor-sharp swords looking to slice your bankroll to shreds.

Mini-Baccarat Stakes

(80 Decisions Per Session)

Minimum Bet	Session Stake	Daily Stake (4 hours)
$10	$560	$2,240
$15	$840	$3,360
$25	$1,400	$5,600
$50	$2,800	$11,120
$100	$5,600	$22,400
$200	$11,200	$44,800
$500	$28,000	$112,000

CHAPTER 11

The Wild Men and Women of Baccarat

Baccarat is not just its rules or even its edges; no, sir, the players define this wonderful game. They create the excitement and the madness. But if you think baccarat as played in the high-roller rooms of America is a sweet and demure game, you are mistaken. It is more akin to war—war against fate, war against the casino and, more important, war against the players who are winning while you are losing or who are losing when you are winning. It's a wonderful study of human nature too.

The juice in a baccarat game comes from the adrenaline flowing in abundance from myriad players who often come from all over the world and whose competitive, though highly superstitious, natures make them create explanations for why they win and why the lose. Many of these reasons are quite wild, to say the least.

There is no randomness in a baccarat game, according to the over-whelming majority of players. You are playing against the gods, the fates, the furies, and your destiny. Remember this when you sit down at the game.

Many of the players will be playing against y-o-u. That's right; there are players who think other players change the fate of the table, and if they think you are one of *those*, they will let you know it with sneers, shakes of the head, glares, growls, and loud cries of anguish. Be prepared...and enjoy the show even if you become an object of it.

A baccarat table is like the U.N.—plenty of accents, plenty of disputes, and plenty of money being spent.

If you were to just peer into the high-roller room and look casually at a baccarat game, you might think that everything is peaceful and sedate. You would be mistaken.

At the magnificent Taj Mahal in Atlantic City, my friend Dominator and I were playing baccarat, and the two men on my side of the table were from Russia. I know this because Fingernail, a man with an incredibly long nail on his left pinky (I wonder what he used *that* for and also why he had all that white stuff under his nostrils), said in a heavy accent, "Guess where we are from," indicating himself and the weaselly man next to him. But before I could say anything, he gave away the secret, "Okay, we are from Russia, and we love America!" Patriotism for your new country is a good thing. This man was high...on...ah...patriotism.

The weaselly guy with him did not have a long fingernail, nor could I tell how he felt about America. He just kind of looked—to be unkind—really dopey. Also his nails looked as if they had been bitten down to almost nothing by his large overbite. He never spoke, but he grimaced a lot. Across the long table from these two patriots were three Chinese players, two men and a really, *really* diminutive, decidedly ugly woman who scowled when she lost and frowned when she won. These Chinese players each bet anywhere from $500 to $2,000 per hand, but they *always* bet in opposition to the Russians, who would each bet the same way.

They would wait for the Russians to bet—and the Russians took their time as they pored over their scorecards trying to determine the Lord's patterns—and when they had placed their bets, the Chinese contingent would then place theirs. If the Russians bet Player, the Chinese bet Bank. If the Russians changed their bets quickly, so did the Chinese.

Both Russians were getting really annoyed by the three Chinese players.

"You don't bet against me," said Fingernail across the table to the Chinese, who ignored him or didn't understand him—or both. "I *never* lose!" he shouted. Then he mumbled something in Russian, and the weaselly Russian showed a slight smile.

It was Fingernail's deal. He always said "I never lose" when he turned over his Bank hand. He won five hands in a row for Bank. Incredible!

He'd squeeze the cards and bend them to look at the pips. He had a routine, and he was intense about his routine. But even more incredible, Fingernail was betting on Player, so he lost all five hands he dealt in a row. The Chinese won five hands in a row because they were betting Bank in opposition to him. Fingernail won a continued deal and lost money at the same time. Fingernail's head was visibly throbbing.

The Russians were both martingaling it—doubling their bets when they lost. They went from $100 to $200 to $400 to $800 to $1,600. Getting crushed on five hands in a row was deflating. They had taken a pounding.

The weaselly Russian quit first. He just sat there, glum, busted, his lips making a circuit around his large teeth, which were engaged in biting his nubby nails. Then a young man with Elvis hair and an aging girlfriend who supplied him with his $5,000 buy-in sat down. "You mind if I sit here?" he asked shyly.

"Sure, sure," said Dominator. "Sit down, relax."

Fingernail quit right then and there. He looked at Elvis and harrumphed. The diminutive Chinese woman had a sneery smile on her ferociously fierce face, and she just looked right back at Fingernail. You could plainly see she delighted in destroying the Russians, and I guessed she was taking full credit in her beastly brain for their utter, exasperating termination.

A half hour later, Elvis, so shy and quiet, had turned angry and agitated—and loud. Losing hurts, and he was a big loser because he also increased his bets tremendously when he won a couple of hands in a row. He rarely kept one of his wins. He also had about five *big* glasses of Merlot—so he was kind of tanked as well.

"You people there," he shouted at the Chinese group. "Why are you betting against me? You gonna learn a lesson now. My deal. Now I destroy you."

The diminutive Chinese woman glared at him derisively, her lips tight, but the men with her ignored him. When he put his bet down, they bet the opposite. "You gonna learn a lesson now, you bitch!" shouted Elvis. He could have been Fingernail's twin, emotionally speaking, as he had begun to look upon the Chinese contingent as his bitterest enemies.

Elvis lost.

He ordered another drink as the shoe was passed to Dominator. Elvis was cursing under his breath. This Elvis was not about to leave the building; his anger was about to explode its roof and walls.

Dominator has a particular style of play. As dealer, before he looks at the Bank hand, he spins the cards on the table—many times: *spin, spin, spin*. "This changes the cards to make me win," smiles Dominator, and everyone looks at him as if he is nuts. Let me change that—the dealers look at him as if he is nuts; many of the players are right in there with him, thinking that what he is doing is actually having the desired effect upon the results. The spin takes up time and fits right into the superstitious natures of the other players.

The Chinese players must have liked him, because they bet with him and not against him. I bet with him too—as the two of us always bet the same way—Bank.

"Spin those cards, Dom, spin 'em!" I'll shout. "The cards will change, and we will win!" Yes, sometimes I do feel like an idiot shouting such things, but most of the time I am into the act and actually enjoy the nonsense. We are actually playing two games at baccarat—the game against the house and the game against time.

Dom spins the cards for a minute, more or less, looking intense, with his eyes blazing, an insane man just let loose. Why does he do this? Obviously, it reduces the number of hands per hour, and it also entertains us. "Spin, baby, spin!"

There have been times when the whole table, betting as one, will yell, "Spin! Spin! Spin!"

We've even played alone in Vegas casinos, and as we shouted "Spin! Spin! Spin!" so did the dealers. Dom and I both like to tip when we deal, so everybody would shout, "Spin! Spin! Spin!" The dealers knew why we enjoyed the spinning, and we knew why they enjoyed us playing at their table.

By the way, at one of our favorite baccarat places, when you order a drink, they will bring the drink and a small table on which to place the drink. This way you don't have your drink on the baccarat table. In all the baccarat rooms we've played, they serve your drinks in the best of cups and glasses. If you wish to eat, they will also bring your food and a table for you. You are treated like royalty. Not bad for an anticipated average loss of $50 per hour.

Some baccarat players are too intense, however. One harsh, young, overly made-up woman at the Rio casino in Vegas, her body strategically bulging with both of her awesomely enlarged fake breasts falling out of her skintight dress, outdid the Taj's Elvis in the drinks department... really outdid him. I mean, she left the building without even having to leave her chair! She was completely, utterly blitzed. I thought of her as Skintight.

I was dealing, and the Bank had won eight hands in a row. Dom and I were betting Bank. Skintight had been encouraging her older, gray-haired sugar daddy to bet Player against us. Dom was yelling "Bank, bank, bank!" as I tapped the cards. That's my thing. I play the piano on top of the cards—to get them to change their numbers so we win—*tap! tap! tap!* I prefer long piano solos!

On the ninth Bank win, with Sugar Daddy betting a stack of orange chips, Skintight went ballistic. She started slurringly cursing Dom, slurringly cursing me, and slurringly cursing the dealers for allowing us to win. She cursed anything that could be cursed, including Sugar Daddy. Her elephantine glands bounced up and down, up and down, as she shouted and gesticulated and frothed. The dealers at the Rio were real pros. They were calm and handled Skintight's outburst with true professionalism. She and Sugar Daddy left the table at his urging—Sugar Daddy having lost most of his chips.

"She gave me a lap dance at a club. That's how I met her," said Sugar Daddy, sneaking back to give the dealers a tip. "She's very excitable."

Oh, yes, baccarat is a war indeed. If you can afford that $100 minimum bet, then give the game a try. Keep the number of hands you play low, and enjoy the antics of your fellow players. And *spin, spin, spin!*

CHAPTER 12

Blackjack: A Beatable Game

Blackjack is the most popular casino table game, with about 10 percent of all casino gamblers making it their preferred game. Blackjack makes a fortune for the casinos for several reasons. It's a relatively fast game that requires players to know the correct strategy for the play of their hands against the dealer's up-card, a card that can be seen by the players.

Sadly, the majority of the players do not play perfect basic strategy or anything close to it—which is a shame, because they can bring a basic-strategy card to the table and use it to play their hands. Players give up a situation when they can play an extremely strong game against the house and instead choose a far weaker method of play.

Many blackjack players think they can hop onto streaks, basing their raising and lowering of bets on what has happened in terms of wins and losses of previous hands. As we know, this is a foolish way to play, especially when the casino wins far more hands than the players at this game.

Although there is a truly simple and effective card-counting system known as Speed Count (see my book *Beat Blackjack Now!*), most players eschew any attempt at actually achieving an edge at the game—even if that edge is relatively simple to get.

What does it all add up to? More losses than are necessary and the giving up of the potential to actually have a real, mathematical edge over the casino.

How Blackjack Is Played

The best hand in blackjack is a two-card 21. This is a natural, also called a blackjack, and beats every other hand, although the player and the dealer can tie (push) if both have blackjacks. However, the player does not have to get a 21 to win. A player can have a lousy hand and still win because the purpose of the game is to beat the dealer's hand. The player can do that in two ways: have a higher hand than the dealer that does not go over 21 or have the dealer bust his hand by going over 21 and the player does not.

There is a strong element of skill in blackjack. A player who knows the computer-derived basic strategy can keep the house edge around 0.5 percent—a loss of 50¢ per $100 wagered. That is quite good.

Card Values

- Jack, queen, and king count as 10
- Aces count as 1 or 11
- All other cards are face value
- Card suits are irrelevant (except in bonus games, which are usually rip-offs for the player)

For example, a hand containing a 5-4-8 totals 17. Another containing a jack-4 totals 14. The ace always counts as an 11 initially, but if a player draws one (or more) cards, and the hand totals more than 21, then the ace can be counted as 1. For example 4-ace-8 counts as 13, because counting the ace as 11 would bust the player.

Soft Hands and Hard Hands

Any hand that counts the ace as 11 is known as a soft hand; ace-6 is a soft 17, and ace-3-3 is also a soft 17. A hard hand is any hand that either does *not* contain an ace or, if it does, the ace counts as 1; 10-8 and 5-ace-10-2 are hard-18 hands. Soft hands are played differently than hard hands.

Number of Players

Blackjack tables can accommodate five, six, or seven players. The cards are always dealt by the casino dealer. Players compete against the dealer and not against each other.

Many casinos do not allow players to enter midgame. If this is the case, wait until the dealer finishes the deck(s) or shoe and begins to reshuffle before you place your cash on the table for chips or your chips in the betting circle in front of you. This rule is called "no midshoe entry."

No midshoe entry is done for two reasons. Some players get annoyed when a new player enters in the middle of a game because they think the order of the cards will change for the worse. The other reason has to do with the casinos' fear of card counters, many of whom wait for the game to become player-favorable before jumping in and taking advantage of a game when the player has an edge.

Number of Decks

Blackjack games go from one to eight decks. Single-deck and double-deck games are usually dealt by hand. On four-deck, six-deck, and eight-deck games casinos almost always use a box-like device called a "shoe."

The Deal

Once all players have made a bet by placing chips in their individual betting spots, each player and the dealer receive two cards. One of the dealer's cards is dealt face up so players can see its value. The other dealer's card, the hole card, is unseen.

The two player cards can be dealt either face up, facedown, or sometimes one up and one down. In general, in games that are dealt from shoes, the players' cards are dealt face up. In this case you should not touch the cards. In games in which the dealer deals from his hand by pitching the cards to the players, the players' cards are usually dealt facedown. However, in some casinos that use a double deck, both cards are dealt face up. When the cards are dealt facedown, it is permissible for the player to handle the cards with *one hand only,* and the cards must always be held above the table.

Blackjacks

When a player is dealt an ace and a 10-value card (10, jack, queen, or king) as his first two cards, it is called a "blackjack" or "natural" and generally is paid one and a half times the original bet, meaning a 3-to-2 payoff. It is this payout that keeps the game close between player and dealer, as blackjacks will occur about 5 percent of the time.

> **Double Yuck:** *Some casinos pay 6-to-5 on player blackjacks, which gives the casino a much higher edge over players. A normal blackjack game will pay $15 for $10 on a blackjack; an "abnormal" 6-to-5 game will pay $12 for $10 on a blackjack. The casino just kept three dollars of what used to be your money! These games should be avoided. In blackjack we all want to be normal.*

Push

When your hand totals the same as the dealer, this is known as a "push" or "tie," and you get to keep your bet. If you have a blackjack and the dealer has a blackjack, that is also a push, so a player blackjack does not automatically win every time.

Player Options

If the dealer doesn't have a blackjack, players have to make a decision on how they want to proceed. Players' options include the following:

Hit: If you want to be dealt another card, you call for a "hit." In a game where the initial two player cards are dealt face up, if you want a hit, make a beckoning motion with your finger or tap the table behind your cards with your finger. In a game where the cards are dealt facedown (i.e., usually a single- or double-deck game), you signify to the dealer that you want a hit by scratching the edges of the cards lightly on the felt.

Stand: If you are satisfied with the total of your hand, you can stand with the cards you have. In face-up games, indicate that you want to stand by waving your hand over the cards. In facedown games, tuck your cards under the chips that you wagered in your betting spot.

Double Down: You are allowed to double your bet on your first two cards and receive one additional card. You cannot ask for any cards once you have doubled down. To double down, just place your chip(s) next to the original chip(s) you bet. In facedown games, you must toss your cards on the table face up and then make the secondary double-down wager.

In face-up games, simply make the secondary double-down bet as above. Most casinos allow players to double-for-less, which means you can wager less than the original bet.

Splitting Pairs: If you are dealt two cards of the same rank (say, a pair of 8s or aces), you may split them, making two hands. When you split, you must make another bet equal to your original bet. By pair-splitting you play each card as a separate hand, and you can draw as many cards as you like to each hand with one exception: a pair of aces. Most casinos will only allow one card to each ace, because it is such a powerful card.

> **Oh, Pairs:** *If you are dealt a pair of 8s (16) and you split them, you now have two separate hands, each containing an 8. You would be required to play out one of the split hands first before taking any action on the second hand.*

In face-up games, you place another bet of equal size next to the original bet. For facedown games, flip over your cards on the table and then make the secondary wager. Most casinos will allow players to split all 10-value cards, such as a jack-ten or queen-king, although this is an awful thing to do when sitting at 20. Some casinos will also allow a player to resplit up to four hands. Many casinos will also allow players to double down after pair-splitting, a player-favorable rule. Keep in mind that if you split aces and receive a 10 to an ace, you have a 21 and *not* a blackjack.

Surrender: A rare option nowadays. Surrender allows a player to forfeit his initial hand with an automatic loss of half the original bet. Surrender cannot be used if the dealer has a blackjack. Surrender can only be made based on the first two cards. A player surrenders by simply saying to the dealer, "Surrender." Some casinos have implemented a hand signal for surrender, so if you are lucky enough to find a game with this option, ask beforehand if you need to use a hand signal and, if so, what it is. The dealer will remove the player's cards from the table, taking one-half of the player's wager.

Early Surrender: *If you find this option, give my publisher a call, because it is as rare as seeing Bigfoot! It is a great rule for the player. With early surrender, a player can surrender his hand before the dealer checks to see if she has blackjack, and he will not lose his entire bet if she has one. The playing strategy for early surrender is much different than late surrender, but you'll have more luck trapping Bigfoot than finding this option.*

Insurance: When the dealer has an ace up-card, he will ask players if they want to make the insurance wager. Insurance is a side bet on whether the dealer's hole card is a 10-value card. The insurance bet is one-half of the initial bet made on the hand, although you can insure for less. To wager on insurance, just put your chips on the insurance line of the layout. You win your insurance bet at 2-to-1 odds if the dealer has a 10-value card in the hole.

Even Money: If the player has a blackjack and the dealer has an ace showing, the dealer will ask if the player wants "even money," which means a payoff of 1-to-1 (even money) on the bet before he checks his down-card for a potential blackjack. Taking even money is the same as making an insurance bet on a player's blackjack.

Busting: If a player's hand exceeds a total of 21, he has busted and loses the hand, even if the dealer busts also. When a player busts, his cards and bet are immediately whisked off the table. This is why the casino has the mathematical edge over players; if a player busts, he loses even if the dealer subsequently busts in the same round.

Dealer's Playing Strategy: Unlike players, the dealer has no playing options. Casino rules specify that a dealer must draw when the dealer's hand totals less than 17 and stand when the total is 17 to 21. In some casinos, dealers stand on soft 17 (ace-6), but in other casinos they hit soft 17. The dealer standing on a soft 17 is better for the player.

Shuffle Machines: Many casinos use automatic shufflers to shuffle the cards in multiple-deck games. Automatic shufflers eliminate the down-time that occurs when the dealer manually shuffles the cards. Another type of automatic shuffler is known as a "continuous-shuffle machine" (CSM). With this device, the discards from one round are placed back into the shuffler to be mixed with the undealt decks of cards. With a CSM there is never a pause in action, and more hands are dealt per hour than with an automatic shuffler, resulting in a higher theoretical hourly loss.

> **I Repeat Myself:** *The more hands you play, the more the house edge will eat away at your bankroll. It is better to play where the dealers shuffle by hand; next-best is where dealers use an automatic shuffler; but never play where they use a CSM, which increases by about 20 percent the number of hands a player receives in an hour.*

What's Good for the Casino Is *Not* Good for You!

Given a choice, always play games that have the best rules. If you are not playing with an edge, you want to play games where fewer cards are dealt from the shoe. The dealer will have to shuffle more often, which slows down the game; and the slower the game, the better for the blackjack player.

The card counter is in a different situation. He wants deep cuts in the cards so he can see more cards played from the shoe. The more cards, the better his edge becomes.

Guess What? *The fewer the decks, the better the game—as long as the rules are the same. So a one-deck game is better that an eight-deck game! But keep in mind, the rules should be the same...or just about the same.*

Good Rules:
Blackjack pays 3-to-2
Suited blackjacks pay 2-to-1
Early surrender allowed
Surrender allowed
Player may resplit aces
Dealer stands on soft 17
Player may split any pair
Resplitting allowed
Player may double down after splits
Player may double down on any first two cards

Bad Rules
Dealer hits on soft 17
Continuous-shuffle machine is used
Blackjack pays 6-to-5
Limited double downs or no doubling down
No splitting
No splitting aces
Player loses pushes

Money Management at Blackjack
Even though blackjack is a close game with the house, unless you count cards, you are going to find that, over time, you will lose. If you select the games with the best rules as shown above, the house edge can go below 0.5 percent. If you choose games where the rules are antiplayer,

then the house edge will start to inch up toward 1 percent. If you choose a 6-to-5 game, the house edge will go well beyond 1 percent.

In general, the casino wins about 48 percent of the time, the player wins about 44 percent of the time, and the other 8 percent of the decisions are pushes. The reason blackjack is a close game concerns the fact that players have options on certain hands that will bring in more money to them, including doubling down, splitting, doubling after splits, and payments of 3-to-2 on naturals.

In the past I used to recommend a 40-unit session bankroll for blackjack, so if your bet was $10, you'd need $400 for the session. However, on a hand where you split and double down on those splits, you can have 10 percent or more of your session stake at risk during that round. Now I lean toward 50 units as a session bankroll. I also know from bitter experience that long losing streaks, 10 or more hands in a row, are not all that rare. You want the money behind you to weather those awfully long streaks.

Blackjack is a fast game; many gambling writers use 100 hands per hour as the number of hands a player faces. As a basic-strategy player, you do not want to play 100 hands per hour. So look for tables that are almost full, and sit down to play at those. The more players, the fewer hands you'll play; the fewer the hands, the better for you. Also look for games where the casino cuts a lot of cards out of play, because the dealer will have to shuffle more often. Take your time making decisions, so you slow down the game still more. You want to play no more than 80 hands per hour—and it is preferable if you can cut that down to 60 hands per hour. Small house edges become deadly when the number of decisions skyrocket.

Money-Management Ideas That Don't Work

There is a belief that if you lose three or four hands in a row, the table is cold and you should leave and go to another table, where your luck will change. Doing this might indeed find you at another table, where suddenly you start to win. Doing this might also find you at a table where the dealer is even hotter than the dealer you just left. Or you could go to the next table and find that you win some, lose some, and get a little ahead there or a little behind there.

Winning and losing streaks at blackjack are common for all tables. Switching tables will not help you to win more or lose less.

Now for my big *but* (I get the innuendo!): Changing tables usually means you will be playing fewer hands. Playing fewer hands means you will lose less. Walking to another table is a good thing *only* for this reason.

Another silly idea that costs you money is to take "even money" when you have a blackjack and the dealer is showing an ace. You win more money over time simply allowing what is going to happen to actually happen. Your blackjack wins 3-to-2, and that overcomes all those even-money bets. You lose more money if you take the bird in the hand because that bird in the bush is worth a lot more to you. So don't insure or even-money any of your blackjacks.

When to Call an End to a Session

I think a two-hour session should be the maximum length of time. You're probably better simply quitting after an hour or so. You can also play based on the money you have won or lost.

If you are ahead by X amount at the end of an hour but are still eager to continue, you might want to take half of that X (if it is large enough) and play until you double it or lose it all. You'd still be able to leave the session ahead.

If you are behind at the end of the hour, then maybe taking a break to do something else would be the best thing for you.

The fact is, when you are playing against a house edge, anything you do in the money-management department is not going to change the fact that, in time, you will lose. Still, taking breaks and splitting up your wins to play a little longer but never playing all that you have won are good ways to extend your ability to play without losing too much of your stake at any one session or trip.

The *key* ingredient in playing a powerful game of blackjack is the use of basic strategy. Check out the next chapter, which contains the basic strategies for just about all blackjack games. Don't panic because they look intimidating—you can photocopy the strategy you wish to use and take it to the table with you.

CHAPTER 13

Basic Strategies for Blackjack

Even if you do not wish to become an advantage player, if you use basic strategy, blackjack is a really close contest. You can photocopy these on a piece of paper, laminate it, and you're ready to go. There are subtle changes in the basic strategies for different types of games and rules. If you think these are too many, just take the first one and use it for *all* games. Most casinos will allow players to refer to basic strategy charts. You can buy smaller plastic cards from www.smartgaming.com.

Above the top of the chart you'll see the number of decks, whether the dealer stands or hits on soft 17, and whether you can split your pairs. Under that there is a letter for the recommended action, with *S* meaning *stand*, *H* meaning *hit*, *D* meaning *double down*, *P* meaning *split*, and *U* meaning *surrender*.

On the chart, the columns represent the dealer's up-card, and the rows represent the player's hand. Follow the playing strategies on the chart, and you will be playing the strongest possible game against the house, other than card counting.

There are eight fundamental moves players should make in all games *regardless* of the rules of the game:

1. Always split aces
2. Always split 8s
3. Never split 5s
4. Never split 10-value cards
5. Never double down on a hand you can bust—12 or higher
6. Never insure a hand
7. Never take even money on your blackjacks
8. Never give anyone at the table advice on how to play

4-6-8 decks; dealer STANDS on 17; no double after splits. *For boxes with a slash, use play on the left if permitted; if not, use play on the right.*

S=Stand; H=Hit; D=Double Down; P=Split; U=Surrender

Hand	2	3	4	5	6	7	8	9	10	Ace
8	H	H	H	H	H	H	H	H	H	H
9	H	D/H	D/H	D/H	D/H	H	H	H	H	H
10	D/H	D/H	D/H	D/H	D/H	D/H	D/H	D/H	H	H
11	D/H	D/H	D/H	D/H	D/H	D/H	D/H	D/H	D/H	H
12	H	H	S	S	S	H	H	H	H	H
13	S	S	S	S	S	H	H	H	H	H
14	S	S	S	S	S	H	H	H	H	H
15	S	S	S	S	S	H	H	H	U/H	H
16	S	S	S	S	S	H	H	U/H	U/H	U/H
17	S	S	S	S	S	S	S	S	S	S
A-2	H	H	H	D/H	D/H	H	H	H	H	H
A-3	H	H	H	D/H	D/H	H	H	H	H	H
A-4	H	H	D/H	D/H	D/H	H	H	H	H	H
A-5	H	H	D/H	D/H	D/H	H	H	H	H	H
A-6	H	D/H	D/H	D/H	D/H	H	H	H	H	H
A-7	H	D/S	D/S	D/S	D/S	S	S	H	H	H
A-8	S	S	S	S	S	S	S	S	S	S
A-9	S	S	S	S	S	S	S	S	S	S
A-A	P	P	P	P	P	P	P	P	P	P
2-2	P	P	P	P	P	P	H	H	H	H
3-3	P	P	P	P	P	P	H	H	H	H
4-4	H	H	H	P	P	H	H	H	H	H
5-5	D/H	D/H	D/H	D/H	D/H	D/H	D/H	D/H	H	H
6-6	P	P	P	P	P	H	H	H	H	H
7-7	P	P	P	P	P	P	H	H	H	H
8-8	P	P	P	P	P	P	P	P	P	P
9-9	P	P	P	P	P	S	P	P	S	S
10-10	S	S	S	S	S	S	S	S	S	S

4-6-8 decks; dealer STANDS on 17; no double after splits. *For boxes with a slash, use play on the left if permitted; if not, use play on the right.*

S=Stand; H=Hit; D=Double Down; P=Split; U=Surrender

Hand	2	3	4	5	6	7	8	9	10	Ace
8	H	H	H	H	H	H	H	H	H	H
9	H	D/H	D/H	D/H	D/H	H	H	H	H	H
10	D/H	D/H	D/H	D/H	D/H	D/H	D/H	D/H	H	H
11	D/H	D/H	D/H	D/H	D/H	D/H	D/H	D/H	D/H	H
12	H	H	S	S	S	H	H	H	H	H
13	S	S	S	S	S	H	H	H	H	H
14	S	S	S	S	S	H	H	H	H	H
15	S	S	S	S	S	H	H	H	U/H	H
16	S	S	S	S	S	H	H	U/H	U/H	U/H
17	S	S	S	S	S	S	S	S	S	S
A-2	H	H	H	D/H	D/H	H	H	H	H	H
A-3	H	H	H	D/H	D/H	H	H	H	H	H
A-4	H	H	D/H	D/H	D/H	H	H	H	H	H
A-5	H	H	D/H	D/H	D/H	H	H	H	H	H
A-6	H	D/H	D/H	D/H	D/H	H	H	H	H	H
A-7	S	D/S	D/S	D/S	D/S	S	S	H	H	H
A-8	S	S	S	S	S	S	S	S	S	S
A-9	S	S	S	S	S	S	S	S	S	S
A-A	P	P	P	P	P	P	P	P	P	P
2-2	H	H	P	P	P	P	H	H	H	H
3-3	H	H	P	P	P	P	H	H	H	H
4-4	H	H	H	P	P	H	H	H	H	H
5-5	D/H	D/H	D/H	D/H	D/H	D/H	D/H	D/H	H	H
6-6	H	P	P	P	P	H	H	H	H	H
7-7	P	P	P	P	P	P	H	H	H	H
8-8	P	P	P	P	P	P	P	P	P	P
9-9	P	P	P	P	P	S	P	P	S	S
10-10	S	S	S	S	S	S	S	S	S	S

4-6-8 decks; dealer HITS soft 17 (Ace-6); double after splits. *For boxes with a slash, use play on the left if permitted; if not, use play on the right.*

S=Stand; H=Hit; D=Double Down; P=Split; U=Surrender

Hand	2	3	4	5	6	7	8	9	10	Ace
8	H	H	H	H	H	H	H	H	H	H
9	H	D/H	D/H	D/H	D/H	H	H	H	H	H
10	D/H	D/H	D/H	D/H	D/H	D/H	D/H	D/H	H	H
11	D/H	D/H	D/H	D/H	D/H	D/H	D/H	D/H	D/H	D/H
12	H	H	S	S	S	H	H	H	H	H
13	S	S	S	S	S	H	H	H	H	H
14	S	S	S	S	S	H	H	H	H	H
15	S	S	S	S	S	H	H	H	U/H	H
16	S	S	S	S	S	H	H	U/H	U/H	U/H
17	S	S	S	S	S	S	S	S	S	U/S
A-2	H	H	H	D/H	D/H	H	H	H	H	H
A-3	H	H	H	D/H	D/H	H	H	H	H	H
A-4	H	H	D/H	D/H	D/H	H	H	H	H	H
A-5	H	H	D/H	D/H	D/H	H	H	H	H	H
A-6	H	D/H	D/H	D/H	D/H	H	H	H	H	H
A-7	D/S	D/S	D/S	D/S	D/S	S	S	H	H	H
A-8	S	S	S	S	D/S	S	S	S	S	S
A-9	S	S	S	S	S	S	S	S	S	S
A-A	P	P	P	P	P	P	P	P	P	P
2-2	P	P	P	P	P	P	H	H	H	H
3-3	P	P	P	P	P	P	H	H	H	H
4-4	H	H	H	P	P	H	H	H	H	H
5-5	D/H	D/H	D/H	D/H	D/H	D/H	D/H	D/H	H	H
6-6	P	P	P	P	P	H	H	H	H	H
7-7	P	P	P	P	P	P	H	H	H	H
8-8	P	P	P	P	P	P	P	P	P	P
9-9	P	P	P	P	P	S	P	P	S	S
10-10	S	S	S	S	S	S	S	S	S	S

4-6-8 decks; dealer HITS soft 17 (Ace-6); no double after splits. *For boxes with a slash, use play on the left if permitted; if not, use play on the right.*

S=Stand; H=Hit; D=Double Down; P=Split; U=Surrender

Hand	2	3	4	5	6	7	8	9	10	Ace
8	H	H	H	H	H	H	H	H	H	H
9	H	D/H	D/H	D/H	D/H	H	H	H	H	H
10	D/H	D/H	D/H	D/H	D/H	D/H	D/H	D/H	H	H
11	D/H	D/H	D/H	D/H	D/H	D/H	D/H	D/H	D/H	D/H
12	H	H	S	S	S	H	H	H	H	H
13	S	S	S	S	S	H	H	H	H	H
14	S	S	S	S	S	H	H	H	H	H
15	S	S	S	S	S	H	H	H	U/H	H
16	S	S	S	S	S	H	H	U/H	U/H	U/H
17	S	S	S	S	S	S	S	S	S	U/S
A-2	H	H	H	D/H	D/H	H	H	H	H	H
A-3	H	H	H	D/H	D/H	H	H	H	H	H
A-4	H	H	D/H	D/H	D/H	H	H	H	H	H
A-5	H	H	D/H	D/H	D/H	H	H	H	H	H
A-6	H	D/H	D/H	D/H	D/H	H	H	H	H	H
A-7	D/S	D/S	D/S	D/S	D/S	S	S	H	H	H
A-8	S	S	S	S	D/S	S	S	S	S	S
A-9	S	S	S	S	S	S	S	S	S	S
A-A	P	P	P	P	P	P	P	P	P	P
2-2	H	H	P	P	P	P	H	H	H	H
3-3	H	H	P	P	P	P	H	H	H	H
4-4	H	H	H	H	H	H	H	H	H	H
5-5	D/H	D/H	D/H	D/H	D/H	D/H	D/H	D/H	H	H
6-6	H	P	P	P	P	H	H	H	H	H
7-7	P	P	P	P	P	P	H	H	H	H
8-8	P	P	P	P	P	P	P	P	P	P
9-9	P	P	P	P	P	S	P	P	S	S
10-10	S	S	S	S	S	S	S	S	S	S

TWO decks; dealer STANDS on 17; double after splits. For boxes with a slash, use play on the left if permitted; if not, use play on the right.

S=Stand; H=Hit; D=Double Down; P=Split; U=Surrender

Hand	2	3	4	5	6	7	8	9	10	Ace
8	H	H	H	H	H	H	H	H	H	H
9	D/H	D/H	D/H	D/H	D/H	H	H	H	H	H
10	D/H	D/H	D/H	D/H	D/H	D/H	D/H	D/H	H	H
11	D/H	D/H	D/H	D/H	D/H	D/H	D/H	D/H	D/H	D/H
12	H	H	S	S	S	H	H	H	H	H
13	S	S	S	S	S	H	H	H	H	H
14	S	S	S	S	S	H	H	H	H	H
15	S	S	S	S	S	H	H	H	U/H	H
16	S	S	S	S	S	H	H	H	U/H	U/H
17	S	S	S	S	S	S	S	S	S	S
A-2	H	H	H	D/H	D/H	H	H	H	H	H
A-3	H	H	H	D/H	D/H	H	H	H	H	H
A-4	H	H	D/H	D/H	D/H	H	H	H	H	H
A-5	H	H	D/H	D/H	D/H	H	H	H	H	H
A-6	H	D/H	D/H	D/H	D/H	H	H	H	H	H
A-7	H	D/S	D/S	D/S	D/S	S	S	H	H	H
A-8	S	S	S	S	S	S	S	S	S	S
A-9	S	S	S	S	S	S	S	S	S	S
A-A	P	P	P	P	P	P	P	P	P	P
2-2	P	P	P	P	P	P	H	H	H	H
3-3	P	P	P	P	P	P	H	H	H	H
4-4	H	H	H	P	P	H	H	H	H	H
5-5	D/H	D/H	D/H	D/H	D/H	D/H	D/H	D/H	H	H
6-6	P	P	P	P	P	P	H	H	H	H
7-7	P	P	P	P	P	P	P/H	H	H	H
8-8	P	P	P	P	P	P	P	P	P	P
9-9	P	P	P	P	P	S	P	P	S	S
10-10	S	S	S	S	S	S	S	S	S	S

TWO decks; dealer STANDS on 17; no double after splits. *For boxes with a slash, use play on the left if permitted; if not, use play on the right.*

S=Stand; H=Hit; D=Double Down; P=Split; U=Surrender

Hand	2	3	4	5	6	7	8	9	10	Ace
8	H	H	H	H	H	H	H	H	H	H
9	D/H	D/H	D/H	D/H	D/H	H	H	H	H	H
10	D/H	D/H	D/H	D/H	D/H	D/H	D/H	D/H	H	H
11	D/H	D/H	D/H	D/H	D/H	D/H	D/H	D/H	D/H	D/H
12	H	H	S	S	S	H	H	H	H	H
13	S	S	S	S	S	H	H	H	H	H
14	S	S	S	S	S	H	H	H	H	H
15	S	S	S	S	S	H	H	H	U/H	H
16	S	S	S	S	S	H	H	H	U/H	U/H
17	S	S	S	S	S	S	S	S	S	S
A-2	H	H	H	D/H	D/H	H	H	H	H	H
A-3	H	H	H	D/H	D/H	H	H	H	H	H
A-4	H	H	D/H	D/H	D/H	H	H	H	H	H
A-5	H	H	D/H	D/H	D/H	H	H	H	H	H
A-6	H	D/H	D/H	D/H	D/H	H	H	H	H	H
A-7	S	D/S	D/S	D/S	D/S	S	S	H	H	H
A-8	S	S	S	S	S	S	S	S	S	S
A-9	S	S	S	S	S	S	S	S	S	S
A-A	P	P	P	P	P	P	P	P	P	P
2-2	H	H	P	P	P	P	H	H	H	H
3-3	H	H	P	P	P	P	H	H	H	H
4-4	H	H	H	H	H	H	H	H	H	H
5-5	D/H	D/H	D/H	D/H	D/H	D/H	D/H	D/H	H	H
6-6	P	P	P	P	P	H	H	H	H	H
7-7	P	P	P	P	P	P	H	H	H	H
8-8	P	P	P	P	P	P	P	P	P	P
9-9	P	P	P	P	P	S	P	P	S	S
10-10	S	S	S	S	S	S	S	S	S	S

TWO decks; dealer HITS soft 17 (Ace-6); double after splits. *For boxes with a slash, use play on the left if permitted; if not, use play on the right.*

S=Stand; H=Hit; D=Double Down; P=Split; U=Surrender

Hand	2	3	4	5	6	7	8	9	10	Ace
8	H	H	H	H	H	H	H	H	H	H
9	D/H	D/H	D/H	D/H	D/H	H	H	H	H	H
10	D/H	D/H	D/H	D/H	D/H	D/H	D/H	D/H	H	H
11	D/H	D/H	D/H	D/H	D/H	D/H	D/H	D/H	D/H	D/H
12	H	H	S	S	S	H	H	H	H	H
13	S	S	S	S	S	H	H	H	H	H
14	S	S	S	S	S	H	H	H	H	H
15	S	S	S	S	S	H	H	H	U/H	U/H
16	S	S	S	S	S	H	H	H	U/H	U/H
17	S	S	S	S	S	S	S	S	S	U/S
A-2	H	H	H	D/H	D/H	H	H	H	H	H
A-3	H	H	D/H	D/H	D/H	H	H	H	H	H
A-4	H	H	D/H	D/H	D/H	H	H	H	H	H
A-5	H	H	D/H	D/H	D/H	H	H	H	H	H
A-6	H	D/H	D/H	D/H	D/H	H	H	H	H	H
A-7	D/S	D/S	D/S	D/S	D/S	S	S	H	H	H
A-8	S	S	S	S	D/S	S	S	S	S	S
A-9	S	S	S	S	S	S	S	S	S	S
A-A	P	P	P	P	P	P	P	P	P	P
2-2	P	P	P	P	P	P	H	H	H	H
3-3	P	P	P	P	P	P	H	H	H	H
4-4	H	H	H	P	P	H	H	H	H	H
5-5	D/H	D/H	D/H	D/H	D/H	D/H	D/H	D/H	H	H
6-6	P	P	P	P	P	P	H	H	H	H
7-7	P	P	P	P	P	P	P	H	H	H
8-8	P	P	P	P	P	P	P	P	P	P
9-9	P	P	P	P	P	S	P	P	S	S
10-10	S	S	S	S	S	S	S	S	S	S

TWO decks; dealer HITS soft 17 (Ace-6); no double after splits. *For boxes with a slash, use play on the left if permitted; if not, use play on the right.*

S=Stand; H=Hit; D=Double Down; P=Split; U=Surrender

Hand	2	3	4	5	6	7	8	9	10	Ace
8	H	H	H	H	H	H	H	H	H	H
9	D/H	D/H	D/H	D/H	D/H	H	H	H	H	H
10	D/H	D/H	D/H	D/H	D/H	D/H	D/H	D/H	H	H
11	D/H	D/H	D/H	D/H	D/H	D/H	D/H	D/H	D/H	D/H
12	H	H	S	S	S	H	H	H	H	H
13	S	S	S	S	S	H	H	H	H	H
14	S	S	S	S	S	H	H	H	H	H
15	S	S	S	S	S	H	H	H	U/H	U/H
16	S	S	S	S	S	H	H	H	U/H	U/H
17	S	S	S	S	S	S	S	S	S	U/S
A-2	H	H	H	D/H	D/H	H	H	H	H	H
A-3	H	H	D/H	D/H	D/H	H	H	H	H	H
A-4	H	H	D/H	D/H	D/H	H	H	H	H	H
A-5	H	H	D/H	D/H	D/H	H	H	H	H	H
A-6	H	D/H	D/H	D/H	D/H	H	H	H	H	H
A-7	D/S	D/S	D/S	D/S	D/S	S	S	H	H	H
A-8	S	S	S	S	D/S	S	S	S	S	S
A-9	S	S	S	S	S	S	S	S	S	S
A-A	P	P	P	P	P	P	P	P	P	P
2-2	H	H	P	P	P	P	H	H	H	H
3-3	H	H	P	P	P	P	H	H	H	H
4-4	H	H	H	H	H	H	H	H	H	H
5-5	D/H	D/H	D/H	D/H	D/H	D/H	D/H	D/H	H	H
6-6	P	P	P	P	P	H	H	H	H	H
7-7	P	P	P	P	P	P	H	H	H	H
8-8	P	P	P	P	P	P	P	P	P	P
9-9	P	P	P	P	P	S	P	P	S	S
10-10	S	S	S	S	S	S	S	S	S	S

SINGLE deck; dealer STANDS on 17; double after splits. *For boxes with a slash, use play on the left if permitted; if not, use play on the right.*

S=Stand; H=Hit; D=Double Down; P=Split; U=Surrender

Hand	2	3	4	5	6	7	8	9	10	Ace
8	H	H	H	D/H	D/H	H	H	H	H	H
9	D/H	D/H	D/H	D/H	D/H	H	H	H	H	H
10	D/H	D/H	D/H	D/H	D/H	D/H	D/H	D/H	H	H
11	D/H	D/H	D/H	D/H	D/H	D/H	D/H	D/H	D/H	D/H
12	H	H	S	S	S	H	H	H	H	H
13	S	S	S	S	S	H	H	H	H	H
14	S	S	S	S	S	H	H	H	H	H
15	S	S	S	S	S	H	H	H	H	H
16	S	S	S	S	S	H	H	H	U/H	U/H
17	S	S	S	S	S	S	S	S	S	S
A-2	H	H	D/H	D/H	D/H	H	H	H	H	H
A-3	H	H	D/H	D/H	D/H	H	H	H	H	H
A-4	H	H	D/H	D/H	D/H	H	H	H	H	H
A-5	H	H	D/H	D/H	D/H	H	H	H	H	H
A-6	D/H	D/H	D/H	D/H	D/H	H	H	H	H	H
A-7	S	D/S	D/S	D/S	D/S	S	S	H	H	S
A-8	S	S	S	S	D/S	S	S	S	S	S
A-9	S	S	S	S	S	S	S	S	S	S
A-A	P	P	P	P	P	P	P	P	P	P
2-2	P	P	P	P	P	P	H	H	H	H
3-3	P	P	P	P	P	P	P	H	H	H
4-4	H	H	P	P	P	H	H	H	H	H
5-5	D/H	D/H	D/H	D/H	D/H	D/H	D/H	D/H	H	H
6-6	P	P	P	P	P	P	H	H	H	H
7-7	P	P	P	P	P	P	P	H	U/S	H
8-8	P	P	P	P	P	P	P	P	P	P
9-9	P	P	P	P	P	S	P	P	S	S
10-10	S	S	S	S	S	S	S	S	S	S

SINGLE deck; HIT soft 17 (Ace-6); no double after splits. *For boxes with a slash, use play on the left if permitted; if not, use play on the right.*

S=Stand; H=Hit; D=Double Down; P=Split; U=Surrender

Hand	2	3	4	5	6	7	8	9	10	Ace
8	H	H	H	D/H	D/H	H	H	H	H	H
9	D/H	D/H	D/H	D/H	D/H	H	H	H	H	H
10	D/H	D/H	D/H	D/H	D/H	D/H	D/H	D/H	H	H
11	D/H	D/H	D/H	D/H	D/H	D/H	D/H	D/H	D/H	D/H
12	H	H	S	S	S	H	H	H	H	H
13	S	S	S	S	S	H	H	H	H	H
14	S	S	S	S	S	H	H	H	H	H
15	S	S	S	S	S	H	H	H	U/H	H
16	S	S	S	S	S	H	H	H	U/H	U/H
17	S	S	S	S	S	S	S	S	S	U/S
A-2	H	H	D/H	D/H	D/H	H	H	H	H	H
A-3	H	H	D/H	D/H	D/H	H	H	H	H	H
A-4	H	H	D/H	D/H	D/H	H	H	H	H	H
A-5	H	H	D/H	D/H	D/H	H	H	H	H	H
A-6	D/H	D/H	D/H	D/H	D/H	H	H	H	H	H
A-7	S	D/S	D/S	D/S	D/S	S	S	H	H	S
A-8	S	S	S	S	D/S	S	S	S	S	S
A-9	S	S	S	S	S	S	S	S	S	S
A-A	P	P	P	P	P	P	P	P	P	P
2-2	H	P	P	P	P	P	H	H	H	H
3-3	H	H	P	P	P	P	H	H	H	H
4-4	H	H	H	D/H	D/H	H	H	H	H	H
5-5	D/H	D/H	D/H	D/H	D/H	D/H	D/H	D/H	H	H
6-6	P	P	P	P	P	H	H	H	H	H
7-7	P	P	P	P	P	P	H	H	U/S	U/H
8-8	P	P	P	P	P	P	P	P	P	P
9-9	P	P	P	P	P	S	P	P	S	S
10-10	S	S	S	S	S	S	S	S	S	S

SINGLE deck; STAND on 17; no double after splits. *For boxes with a slash, use play on the left if permitted; if not, use play on the right.*

S=Stand; H=Hit; D=Double Down; P=Split; U=Surrender

Hand	2	3	4	5	6	7	8	9	10	Ace
8	H	H	H	D/H	D/H	H	H	H	H	H
9	D/H	D/H	D/H	D/H	D/H	H	H	H	H	H
10	D/H	D/H	D/H	D/H	D/H	D/H	D/H	D/H	H	H
11	D/H	D/H	D/H	D/H	D/H	D/H	D/H	D/H	D/H	D/H
12	H	H	S	S	S	H	H	H	H	H
13	S	S	S	S	S	H	H	H	H	H
14	S	S	S	S	S	H	H	H	H	H
15	S	S	S	S	S	H	H	H	H	H
16	S	S	S	S	S	H	H	H	U/H	U/S
17	S	S	S	S	S	S	S	S	S	S
A-2	H	H	D/H	D/H	D/H	H	H	H	H	H
A-3	H	H	D/H	D/H	D/H	H	H	H	H	H
A-4	H	H	D/H	D/H	D/H	H	H	H	H	H
A-5	H	H	D/H	D/H	D/H	H	H	H	H	H
A-6	D/H	D/H	D/H	D/H	D/H	H	H	H	H	H
A-7	S	D/S	D/S	D/S	D/S	S	S	H	H	S
A-8	S	S	S	S	D/S	S	S	S	S	S
A-9	S	S	S	S	S	S	S	S	S	S
A-A	P	P	P	P	P	P	P	P	P	P
2-2	H	P	P	P	P	P	H	H	H	H
3-3	H	H	P	P	P	P	H	H	H	H
4-4	H	H	H	D/H	D/H	H	H	H	H	H
5-5	D/H	D/H	D/H	D/H	D/H	D/H	D/H	D/H	H	H
6-6	P	P	P	P	P	H	H	H	H	H
7-7	P	P	P	P	P	P	H	H	U/S	H
8-8	P	P	P	P	P	P	P	P	P	P
9-9	P	P	P	P	P	S	P	P	S	S
10-10	S	S	S	S	S	S	S	S	S	S

CHAPTER 14
Card Counting at Blackjack

Blackjack can be beaten. That is a simple, unassailable fact. Given a decent amount of penetration, just about every game can give the player the edge if the player does four things:

1. Knows the basic strategy for the game
2. Knows a legitimate card-counting system
3. Raises the bet when the remaining cards favor the player
4. Lowers the bet when the remaining cards favor the house

> **Penetration:** *When the dealer finishes the shuffle, she will put a plastic card, called the "cut card," into the deck or shoe, cutting some cards behind it out of play. This card is usually yellow. How many cards she cuts off decides whether there is good, average, or poor penetration.*

There are many card counting systems, ranging from the extremely difficult to learn and the overly complex to the traditional one-level systems that can still be a chore for most players to learn and play, going right up to the best and easiest system ever developed, known as Speed Count. If you are a basic-strategy player (which you better be after reading the last chapter), I recommend you try Speed Count if you wish to take the next step upward. Or if you are a traditional card counter who makes too many mistakes that cost you what little edge you have, then Speed Count is for you too.

Speed Count was developed by blackjack mathematician and computer expert Dan Pronovost over a three-year period. Countless millions of computer simulations were run and my Golden Touch teams played the method in casinos all over America and in Canada.

So my bottom line when it comes to blackjack is simple: Why not play with an edge? If a game can be beaten, then why not beat it?

Introduction to Card Counting

There have been many misunderstood and downright wrong card-counting concepts floated out to the general public by casinos and popular literature and film, the foremost of which is that card counting is against the law. Not so. It is perfectly legal. There are no laws that state you must stop using your brain once you enter a casino.

Now, yes, while it does seem that many people do stop using their brains in the castles of Lady Luck, doing so is a matter of choice and not some mandate of the gods, nature, or the state legislatures, whose members are voted in by people who likewise seem to have forsaken their brains when voting.

The fact that card counting is legal does not mean that the casinos must like it or lump it. As private enterprises, casinos can tell a card counter he cannot play blackjack; they don't even have to give the card counter a reason. However, they usually will give a reason, such as, "You are too good for us. We don't want you playing blackjack here." It's the equivalent of a restaurant offering an "all you can eat" buffet and then kicking out the world's eating champion because he is "too good for us." Indeed, restaurants offering "all-you-can-eat" buffets actually hope only anorexics show up.

Strangely, I have been at tables where the pit boss has said to me, "You're too good; you can't play here anymore," and I always glance at the other players to see if they realize by telling me that I am "too good," the casinos are also telling these other players that they are bad enough to be welcomed at the blackjack tables. Putting their brains into deep freeze before entering the casino obviously makes them oblivious to what is actually taking place around them. Only twice in more than two decades has another player questioned the casino in these situations.

Some movies, such as *Rain Man*, make it sound as if a card counter has to have a mind like Albert Einstein's in order to keep track of every card in the deck or shoe. This is nonsense. Traditional card counting is simply adding, subtracting, and dividing small numbers—and remembering the total results from round to round. And Speed Count is far easier than that!

There will be counts where the casino has the edge, and there will be counts where the player has the edge. Anyone with normal intelligence can do this; no genius-level IQ is required.

There is also the myth that card counting only works in single-deck or double-deck games and that four-, six-, and eight-deck games are immune to it. Again *Rain Man* pushed this false idea when a scene showed two security personnel in the control room saying (and I paraphrase), "He can't be counting because no one can count into six decks!" Maybe the movie producers had to add that line to the script in order to be allowed to film in the casino. No matter; the movie is fiction, as is that false statement made by those actors playing security agents.

There are many card-counting systems, and I will take a look at two, the traditional Hi-Lo system and the amazingly simple Speed Count.

The Traditional Hi-Lo Card-Counting System

The Hi-Lo system tracks the 2s, 3s, 4s, 5s, and 6s, along with the 10-value cards and aces, giving them plus or minus points as they come out of the deck or shoe.

Plus Cards	*Neutral Cards*	*Minus Cards*
2 = +1	7 = 0	10 = -1
3 = +1	8 = 0	Jack = -1
4 = +1	9 = 0	Queen = -1
5 = +1		King = -1
6 = +1		Ace = -1

There are 20 plus cards and 20 minus cards. The count is at zero when the game begins. When more plus cards come out of the deck or shoe, the count will become favorable to the player. When more minus cards come out of the deck or shoe, the count will be unfavorable for the player. Naturally, having a deck that favors the player does not mean the player must automatically win the next hand. It simply means that the player is statistically more likely to make money over time when the deck or shoe contains more high cards.

When the count is at a certain plus level, then the player will start to make bigger bets to take advantage of his edge. When the count is in a neutral or minus level, the player will make smaller bets.

Because the casino starts off with an edge at the beginning of the game, even though the count is zero, the game will still favor the house in small plus counts. The plus count has to get to different levels, depending on the game, for the player to have a real mathematical advantage over the house.

Language: *We call a player-favorable deck or shoe a "high count" or "positive count"; we call an unfavorable deck or shoe a "low count" or "negative count."*

So why do the large cards remaining in a deck or shoe favor the player and the small cards favor the casino? Large cards make a blackjack more likely, and although players and dealers will get the same percentage of blackjacks, the players are paid 3-to-2. The reverse is also true. With more small cards remaining, the likelihood of a blackjack is less—and that favors the house.

Even though in positive counts the dealer will stand more often, he is also more apt to bust his 16-and-lower hands because there are more high cards in the shoe waiting to come out, and the dealer must hit any hand that is 16 or less. Conversely, with more small cards remaining, when he hits those 16-or-lower hands, he has a better chance of not busting.

Executing the Hi-Lo Count

Card counting using the traditional Hi-Lo system has you add the positive cards (2, 3, 4, 5, and 6) when they come out of the deck or shoe and subtract the negative cards (10, jack, queen, king, and ace) when they are dealt. The 7, 8, and 9 are neutral cards and are ignored.

When the deck or shoe is at zero, what is the count when the following cards come out?

Player One: ace-10

Player Two: 5-6-7

Player Three: 7-4-6
Dealer: 8-2-5-3

Player One brings the count down to minus two (-2), as both the ace and 10 are negative ones. Player Two brings the count up to zero again, because 5 and 6 are each a plus one (+1), while 7 is neutral. Player Three brings the count to plus two (+2), because the 7 is neutral, but the 4 and 6 are plus ones (+1s). With the dealer's 8 (neutral), 2 (+1), 5 (+1), and 3 (+1), the count is now +5. It is a positive.

Is this positive count of +5 enough to give the player the edge over the casino, or is it just not enough? Let's see.

The Running Count and the True Count in Shoes and Single-Deck Games

The +5 count above is called the "running count" and indicates the number of plus and minus cards that have come out of the deck. However, to understand whether you have an edge or not, the player must bring into play his skills at division in order to arrive at the "true count." It is the true count that tells a player whether he has an edge, how large that edge is, and what he should bet into that edge.

Let's take a look at multiple-deck shoe games first.

The true count is arrived at by dividing the number of remaining decks to be played into the running count. So if five decks remain to be played in the shoe, with a running count of +5, the true count is +1. What if the true count results in a fraction, such as +2.6? In that case you always drop the fraction and use +2 as the true count; if it is a -2.6, you round the fraction and make the true count -3. These are safety measures and should be followed.

Because many shoes cover the cards so the players cannot see them, arriving at the true count requires the player to look at the discard pile to determine as best he can how many decks have already been played. You subtract the decks played from the number of decks in the game to arrive at your figure. So if you are playing a six-deck game and two decks have come out, four decks remain. You divide these four decks into your running count to get your true count.

Although the math is relatively simple in Hi-Lo, probably the simplest of the traditional counts, it can still be difficult doing this in a casino because of all the constant distractions. It takes time to master, and you shouldn't expect to become proficient without a lot of practice in and out of the casinos. Patience will pay off, however, and after a while, doing the count in the casino will be second nature...well, for some players, that is.

Single-deck games (with a 3-to-2 payout for blackjacks) are a different story.

Arriving at the true count for single-deck games will always require you to deal with fractions. That can be a tortuous, head-spinning procedure. Instead, you can use just the running count for single-deck games without too much worry about not being accurate. In single-deck games, the true count conversion of the running count is just not that important, especially for a relatively new player.

So what would that running count of +5 be in a single-deck game? It would be a *monster* plus count, because the impact of a single card in a single-deck game is far stronger than the impact of a single card in a multiple-deck game.

Betting Your Edge

In single-deck games with decent rules, you can use the following betting scheme:

Bets for a Single-Deck Game

Count	Units	$10 Player	$25 Player	$100 Player
0 or lower	1	$10	$25	$100
+1	2	$20	$50	$200
+2	3	$30	$75	$300
+3	4	$40	$100	$400
+4	4 or 5	$40 or $50	$100 or $125	$400 or $500
+5	4 or 5	$40 or $50	$100 or $125	$400 or $500
+6 or higher	4 or 5	$40 or $50	$100 or $125	$400 or $500

The single-deck chart goes as high as five units, but the more you increase your bet in jumps, the better the chance the casino floor person or pit boss will wonder why you are doing so. Increasing your bet does not have to be done in whole numbers as shown above. You could go to two units on +1, and when the count jumps to +4 just go to three units, and if you win the hand—even if the count goes down to +2—you can then increase your hand to four units or 3.5 units, etc. Playing around with your bets in high counts can at times reduce your edge somewhat, but it can also allow you to stay at the tables for longer periods of time.

> **Caution:** *I do not recommend that you count cards at the same table at the same casino for more than 45 minutes at single-deck or for more than one hour at multiple-deck games. Shorter sessions in a single casino are always the best sessions for staying under the radar.*

Bets for a Double-Deck Game

True Count	*Units*	*$10 Player*	*$25 Player*	*$100 Player*
0 or lower	1	$10	$25	$100
+1	1	$10	$25	$100
+2	2	$20	$50	$200
+3	4	$40	$100	$400
+4	6	$60	$150	$600
+5	8	$80	$200	$800
+6 or higher	8 to 10	$80 to $100	$200 to $250	$800 to $1000

Bets for a Four-Deck Game

True Count	Units	$10 Player	$25 Player	$100 Player
0 or lower	1	$10	$25	$100
+1	1	$10	$25	$100
+2	2	$20	$50	$200
+3	4	$40	$100	$400
+4	8	$80	$200	$800
+5	8	$80	$200	$800
+6 or higher	8 to 10	$80 to $100	$200 to $250	$800 to $1000

Bets for a Six-Deck Game

True Count	Units	$10 Player	$25 Player	$100 Player
0 or lower	1	$10	$25	$100
+1	1	$10	$25	$100
+2	2	$20	$50	$200
+3	4	$40	$100	$400
+4	6	$60	$150	$600
+5	12	$120	$300	$1200
+6 or higher	12 to 14	$120 to $140	$300 to $350	$1200 to $1400

Bets for an Eight-Deck Game

True Count	Units	$10 Player	$25 Player	$100 Player
0 or lower	1	$10	$25	$100
+1	1	$10	$25	$100
+2	2	$20	$50	$200
+3	4	$40	$100	$400
+4	6	$60	$150	$600
+5	12	$120	$300	$1200
+6 or higher	12 to 14	$120 to $140	$300 to $350	$1200 to $1400

As I stated, you do not have to increase your bets by whole numbers. You can change your betting scheme each and every time you decide to increase your bet. These charts are really for reference—albeit a strong reference—but you do not have to be a slave to them.

The Insurance Paradox: *Basic-strategy players never take insurance, as it is a long-term losing bet. However, card counters will find that at certain high counts, insurance becomes a player-favorable bet. A Hi-Lo card counter should take insurance in single-deck games when the count is +2 or higher and in all multiple-deck games when the true count is +3 or higher. I have eliminated using fractions in assigning the numbers to insurance bets, and the above are ultra-safe levels.*

CHAPTER 15
Welcome to Speed Count

On average the player and the dealer will receive 2.7 cards per hand, one being a small card. In speed count, you simply add up the small cards that have come out (2, 3, 4, 5, and 6), and you subtract the number of completed hands (including the dealer's hand) from the total.

You *do not* add or subtract while the cards are being dealt. You are not interested in the cards; you are interested in *the hands,* and hands only matter when the player *stops playing his cards.*

And what is the total from which you subtract these numbers, because you aren't adding and subtracting +1 or -1 from each other as you do in the traditional Hi-Lo count?

Okay, let's take a typical two-deck game first.

My resident genius and creator of Speed Count, Dan Pronovost, has determined through computer simulations that the count for a double-deck game starts at 30. Oh, and forget everything you just read about Hi-Lo, because you have now entered the wonderful and brave new world of Speed Count.

Let's say there are two players and the dealer. That's *three hands* being played. So you will subtract three from the total after a round.

Splits: *If there is a split, you will subtract four hands. If there are two splits, you will subtract five hands. Splits count as separate hands. Are splits a big deal? Not really; they occur about 2 percent of the time.*

When the dealer deals out the cards, you get a 10 and a 2, the other player gets a 6 and 4, and the dealer shows a 6 as the up-card. So do you start counting right then?

No, no, no. Why not? *Because no hand has been played.*

Traditional card counters are busily counting high cards and low cards and adding and dividing right then, but you are doing nothing. You do not count a small card until *a hand has been played,* even hands swept off the board by a dealer's blackjack.

What makes Speed Count unique is the fact that you are adding and subtracting small cards based on *the number of hands,* and if a hand is not finished, there is no counting.

Okay, let's do a round:

You stand on your 10 and 2 against the dealer's 6. Your hand is finished. The count is 31—you started with 30 on the two-deck game, added one for your small card of 2, which equals a 31 count.

Next it's the other player's turn. He doubles on his 6 and 4 and gets a 5. His hand is finished. You add three small cards to your 31 (6, 4, and 5), and the Speed Count is at 34.

The dealer turns over the hole card, a 10, and she has 16. She hits and busts with a 10. You add her small card (the 6) to the total of 34, and you have 35.

Three hands were played, so you subtract 3 from 35 and get 32. That is your count, 32, which means a real mathematical edge over the house. Counts of 31 and higher show a positive expectation for the player in *every* blackjack game!

You started the two-deck game at the count of 30. When a hand was completed, you added all the small cards to your starting number of 30. You went to 35 at the end of the round. You then subtracted the number of hands from the total to arrive at your new count. You subtracted three hands from 35 to arrive at 32.

And that is Speed Count. Easy as can be!

There are none of the mathematical gymnastics you have to do with Hi-Lo or any of the other traditional card-counting systems. You just add the small cards when a hand is finished, then you subtract the number of hands from the initial count. Voila! As I said, when the count is 31 and higher, you have the edge; when it is 30 or lower, the casino has the edge.

Number of Decks

Of course, not all games are two-deck games. While the player will have the edge every time the count is at 31 in *every* game, the *starting* number for Speed Count will change based on the number of decks. Here's how to begin your Speed Count with various decks:

Number of Decks	Speed Count Begins at:	Edge Begins at:
1	30	31
2	30	31
4	29	31
6	27	31
8	26	31

The rules of the game and the penetration of the game will determine how strong your edge is at 31—but 31 will always mean an edge at *all* games. If the casino allows DAS, S17, resplits, and surrender, your 31 will be stronger than a 31 in a game where the dealer hits soft 17 (H17), where you can't double after splits, and where you can't resplit or surrender. As the count goes up to 32, 33, 34, 35, and higher, your edge over the casino gets stronger.

At 30, the casino has an edge in all games. As the count goes down to 29, 28, 27, 26, 25, etc., the house's edge over you becomes stronger.

Speed Count Betting Ranges
Single Deck: Count Starts at 30

Speed Count	Units	$10 Player	$25 Player	$100 Player
27 or lower	Exit game	Exit game	Exit game	Exit game
28 to 30	1	$10	$25	$100
31	2	$20	$50	$200
32	3	$30	$75	$300
33	4	$40	$100	$400
34 or higher	5	$50	$125	$500
33 or higher	Insure hand	Insure hand	Insure hand	Insure hand

Double Deck: Count Starts at 30

Speed Count	Units	$10 Player	$25 Player	$100 Player
26 or lower	Exit game	Exit game	Exit game	Exit game
27 to 30	1	$10	$25	$100
31	2	$20	$50	$200
32	4	$40	$100	$400
33	5	$50	$125	$500
34 or higher	6	$60	$150	$600
34 or higher	Insure hand	Insure hand	Insure hand	Insure hand

Four Decks: Count Starts at 29

Speed Count	Units	$10 Player	$25 Player	$100 Player
23 or lower	Exit game	Exit game	Exit game	Exit game
24 to 30	1	$10	$25	$100
31	2	$20	$50	$200
32	3	$30	$75	$300
33	4	$40	$100	$400
34	5	$50	$125	$500
35	6	$60	$150	$600
36 or higher	7	$70	$175	$700
37 or higher	Insure hand	Insure hand	Insure hand	Insure hand

Six Decks: Counts Starts at 27

Speed Count	Units	$10 Player	$25 Player	$100 Player
21 or lower	Exit game	Exit game	Exit game	Exit game
22 to 30	1	$10	$25	$100
31	2	$20	$50	$200
32	4	$40	$100	$400
33 or higher	8	$80	$200	$800
38 or higher	Insure hand	Insure hand	Insure hand	Insure hand

Eight Decks: Count Starts at 26

Speed Count	Units	$10 Player	$25 Player	$100 Player
20 or lower	Exit game	Exit game	Exit game	Exit game
21 to 30	1	$10	$25	$100
31	2	$20	$50	$200
32	4	$40	$100	$400
33	6	$60	$150	$600
34	8	$80	$200	$800
35 or higher	10	$100	$250	$1000
40 or higher	Insure hand	Insure hand	Insure hand	Insure hand

There you have it: the simplest card-counting system ever developed that can give the player a decent edge. Is Speed Count as powerful as the Hi-Lo count? No, it isn't. But again, a player will tend to make more mistakes at Hi-Lo than at Speed Count, so it can often be a wash between the two. Obviously, if you are a successful Hi-Lo counter, there would be no reason to switch to Speed Count. However, basic-strategy players should seriously consider an upgrade in their game when it comes to Speed Count.

> **Bankrolls for Blackjack:** *As a basic-strategy player, over time your bankroll will go down—that is inevitable. A competent card counter's bankroll will go up over time, although there will be wild swings of fortune because a card counter's edge is small, between 0.5 to 1 percent or so. So the more money you have behind you, the less your losing sessions will throw you off kilter. I would recommend $8,000 for a $10 player and higher as your minimum bet increases over time.*

More Info on Blackjack

There is far more information on Speed Count and other areas of blackjack in my book *Beat Blackjack Now!*

The book lays out methods for increasing one's edge—even as a basic-strategy player. It gives you a new "optimum" basic strategy that can only be used with Speed Count, to increase its power. There are detailed bankroll recommendations as well, based on a concept called "risk of ruin" (ROR). You'll also find excellent information about tournament blackjack.

If you are looking to really hammer the casinos at blackjack, this is the book to read.

Dan Pronovost has also created excellent software programs that I highly recommend:

For Basic Strategy: Blackjack Mentor
http://www.deepnettech.com/blackjack.html#mentor

For Hi-Lo: Professional Bundle
http://www.deepnettech.com/bjbundles.html#professional

For Speed Count: Speed Count Bundle
http://www.deepnettech.com/bjbundles.html#speedcount

All Bundles:
http://www.deepnettech.com/bjbundles.html#bundles

Another excellent resource for blackjack players is Henry Tamburin's monthly newsletter *Blackjack Insider*, which features the top blackjack writers in the country: www.bjinsider.com/main.shtml#page_start.

CHAPTER 16
Casino Dementia: Blackjack Is Not Slots

lackjack has been the most popular casino table game since the early 1960s, when it became known that card counting could beat the game. Edward O. Thorp's publication *Beat the Dealer* first posed a difficult but successful card-counting system, and from that point, the blackjack explosion commenced. The game soon eclipsed craps as the No. 1 table game in the casino, a position it still holds today.

Of the tens of millions of blackjack players since that publication, only a small percentage ever got good enough to beat the casinos at the game using traditional count systems such as Hi-Lo—but that didn't stop the casinos from panicking in the first blush of the card-counting revolution.

The first step the casinos took was to change the game drastically. Not only were more games implemented that used more than one deck, but the rules were changed to make the game far less attractive.

So what happened? Players started to reduce their time at the tables, and many gave up the game completely. The casinos soon realized that a game that made them a lot of money was about to go down the drain. So they brought back the good rules and even continued offering excellent single- and double-deck games. The crowds returned, and blackjack sailed off into the sunset with tons of the players' gold.

Blackjack players with long memories can recall the wealth of excellent blackjack games offered in the 1980s in Las Vegas. Just about every casino had them. On my first trip to Vegas, after years of playing in Atlantic City, my jaw dropped when I saw all those great single- and double-deck games.

True, some excellent blackjack players did win money over the years, and a small fraction of those excellent players won a lot of money, but no one player and no one team won even a tiny nanopercentage of the heaping mountains of money the casinos were harvesting daily from the game. Blackjack profits soared, year after year after year...and then something happened.

Somewhere, on some desolate shore, a casino executive stumbled over a bottle, rubbed it, and released an evil genie. This genie told him in strictest confidence, "Change the nature of the game. Give players only a 6-to-5 payment on their blackjacks, hit all soft 17s, create continuous-shuffle machines that make the players play 20 percent more hands, limit doubling and splitting options, and don't penetrate too deeply into the decks. The casinos will win much more money if you do all these things. You will start to make the kind of money you make at the slot machines."

Logically this sounded right. Today's casinos need to always make more and more money each and every year. To do so, they either have to get people to play more or get more people to play or reduce the returns of their games so they take ever more money from the same people for the same amount of play. The hat trick would be to do all three. That's the way to be crowned Casino Executive of the Year.

Unfortunately, logic and profit don't always work out in the real world. Instead of increasing the profits from blackjack, even the dumbest blackjack players could see they were losing more money, and as they did in the late 1960s, they decreased their play, and some of them even quit. Blackjack has flattened out as a moneymaker—you can look it up.

Sadly, the casinos have not yet figured out that blackjack has been losing its stranglehold on the table-game world as the games have gotten far, far worse. Atlantic City, in the face of Las Vegas' blackjack blues, decided to do what Vegas did: offer inferior games where the casino hits a soft 17. The casino motto seems to be, "If it doesn't work, just do more of it, and then it will work!" Remember Einstein's dictum that it is the sign of insanity to do the same thing over and over and expect different results.

Blackjack is still the most popular table game—it will be some time before it is replaced—but it is not the mega-monster it once was. Making the game hold more for the casino might have seemed like a noble and brilliant idea when discussed in the boardrooms by various MBAs, but in truth the new rules and new games are disasters...for the players and for the casinos.

The true irony of this situation is that the casinos have as many misconceptions about blackjack as the players do. The players think they can win more money at blackjack by becoming either positive- or negative-progression players or clumping proponents or trend seekers. The casinos think they can make good money by offering bad games.

Perhaps what has blinded the casinos' thinking is slot machines. There doesn't seem to be any end to the numbers of players willing to spend their money on the one-armed bandits. Slot players face very large house edges ranging from 2 percent to a monstrous 17 percent on some mega-moola progressives.

Slot players have been trained to accept the fact that they will lose time and time again and once in a while will get a "big one" to keep the juices flowing. This big one rarely brings them into the black, and the losing just continues again into the future.

Blackjack players are not like slot players. They expect to have a close contest with the house—win some, lose slightly more. Yes, the typical *traditional* blackjack player is a loser, but the pattern of his losses is radically different from the pattern of the slot players' losses. To try to make blackjack win the kind of money the slot machines do—in the way the slot machines do it—is to change the nature of the game and make it the type of game that will put off a lot of players.

Slot machines and blackjack are indeed moneymaking animals for the casinos, but they are animals from different species. Trying to force one to become like the other will ultimately kill the one.

Blackjack facts are tough to digest. They are tough for the players, who wish to use idiosyncratic methods that don't actually work to beat the game, and they are tough for the casinos, who wish to see blackjack win the kind of money the slots win.

Blackjack players love the game, and many play it exclusively. They wish to get the type of game that gives them that "blackjack feel," and they don't want to play a game that is closer to slots in its house edges. That's the nature of blackjack and blackjack players.

Casinos should learn from the lines of that old Chiffon Margarine commercial: "It's not nice to fool Mother Nature!"

Come on, casinos. Go back to the best blackjack games.

CHAPTER 17

Spanish 21

(This chapter is excerpted from my book *Beat Blackjack Now!*)

A popular new variation of blackjack called Spanish 21 has entered the casino fray, although it has actually been around since the late 1990s. With the proper Spanish 21 basic strategy, the house edge can hover between 0.40 percent and 0.76 percent. That translates into long-term losses between 40¢ and 76¢ per $100 wagered.

In short, played properly, Spanish 21 is a good game.

The following strategies were created by Michael Shackleford, also known as "the Wizard of Odds." Michael is a professional actuary, an expert in the math of casino games, and he consults for many of the top casino websites. His consulting services are also highly valued by casino games developers and casino gaming writers, such as me. He is currently an adjunct professor of Casino Math at the University of Nevada. He is the author of the book *Gambling 102* (Huntington Press). Michael's websites are www.wizardofodds.com and www.gamingmath.com.

The Rules

Spanish 21 uses six or eight Spanish decks, each deck consisting of 48 cards—the regular 52 cards minus the four 10s. Any card counter can tell you that removing any 10-point card from the cards moves the odds in favor of the dealer. To make up for this, Spanish 21 gives to the player a host of bonuses and favorable rules. The rules are based on liberal six-to-eight-deck blackjack rules, including double after split, late surrender, and resplitting aces. In addition, Spanish 21 offers the following rule enhancements:

- A player 21 always wins.
- Player's blackjack beats dealer's blackjack.
- Player may double down on any number of cards.
- At some casinos, a player may usually hit and double down after splitting aces.
- Players may surrender after doubling, known as "double-down rescue," and forfeit an amount equal to their original bet.
- A five-card 21 pays 3-to-2, a six-card 21 pays 2-to-1, a seven-or-more-card 21 pays 3-to-1. However, the bonuses are not paid if the player doubled.
- A 6-7-8 or 7-7-7 of mixed suits pays 3-to-2, of the same suit pays 2-to-1, and of spades pays 3-to-1. These bonuses do not pay after doubling.
- Suited 7-7-7 when the dealer has a 7 face up pays $1,000 for bets of $5–$24 and $5,000 for bets of $25 or greater. In addition, all other players receive a $50 "envy bonus." This bonus does not pay after doubling or splitting.

Variable Rules
- Dealer may hit or stand on a soft 17.
- Usually six or eight Spanish decks are used.
- Some casinos allow redoubling, up to three times.
- Some casinos allow late surrender on the initial two cards.

Basic Strategy for Spanish 21

Dealer Hits Soft 17

S = Stand; H = Hit; P = Split

S4 = Stand except hit with four or more cards

D = Double; PS = Split except hit with suited 7s

S5 = Stand except hit with five or more cards

D3 = Double except hit three or more cards; @ = Hit if suited or spaded 6-7-8 is possible

S6 = Stand except hit with six or more cards

D4 = Double except hit with four or more cards; *Hit if any 6-7-8 is possible; R = Surrender

D5 = Double except hit with five or more cards

** Hit if spaded 6-7-8 is possible; R/H = Surrender if allowed

Hand	2	3	4	5	6	7	8	9	10	Ace
4–8	H	H	H	H	H	H	H	H	H	H
9	H	H	H	H	D	H	H	H	H	H
10	D5	D5	D	D	D	D4	D3	H	H	H
11	D4	D5	D5	D5	D5	D4	D4	D4	D3	D3
12	H	H	H	H	H	H	H	H	H	H
13	H	H	H	H	S4*	H	H	H	H	H
14	H	H	S4*	S5@	S6**	H	H	H	H	H
15	S4*	S5@	S6	S6	S	H	H	H	H	H
16	S6	S6	S6	S	S	H	H	H	H	R/H
17	S	S	S	S	S	S	S6	S6	S6	R/H
18–21	S	S	S	S	S	S	S	S	S	S
Soft 12	H	H	H	H	H	H	H	H	H	H
Soft 13	H	H	H	H	H	H	H	H	H	H
Soft 14	H	H	H	H	H	H	H	H	H	H
Soft 15	H	H	H	H	D4	H	H	H	H	H
Soft 16	H	H	H	D3	D4	H	H	H	H	H
Soft 17	H	H	D3	D4	D5	H	H	H	H	H
Soft 18	S4	S4	D4	D5	D6	S6	S4	H	H	H
Soft 19	S	S	S	S	S	S	S	S	S6	S6
2-2	P	P	P	P	P	P	P	H	H	H
3-3	P	P	P	P	P	P	P	H	H	H
4-4	H	H	H	H	H	H	H	H	H	H
5-5	D5	D5	D	D	D	D4	D3	H	H	H
6-6	H	H	P	P	P	H	H	H	H	H

Hand	2	3	4	5	6	7	8	9	10	Ace
7-7	P	P	P	P	P	PS	H	H	H	H
8-8	P	P	P	P	P	P	P	P	P	R
9-9	S	P	P	P	P	S	P	P	S	S
10-10	S	S	S	S	S	S	S	S	S	S
A-A	P	P	P	P	P	P	P	P	P	P

Basic Strategy for Spanish 21

Dealer Stands on Soft 17
S = Stand; H = Hit; P = Split

S4 = Stand except hit with four or more cards
D = Double; PS = Split except hit with suited 7s

S5 = Stand except hit with five or more cards
D3 = Double except hit three or more cards; @ = Hit if suited or spaded 6-7-8 is possible

S6 = Stand except hit with six or more cards
D4 = Double except hit with four or more cards; *Hit if any 6-7-8 is possible; R = Surrender
D5 = Double except hit with five or more cards
** Hit if spaded 6-7-8 is possible; R/H = Surrender if allowed

Hand	2	3	4	5	6	7	8	9	10	Ace
4–8	H	H	H	H	H	H	H	H	H	H
9	H	H	H	H	D4	H	H	H	H	H
10	D5	D5	D	D	D	D4	D3	H	H	H
11	D4	D5	D5	D5	D5	D4	D4	D4	D3	D3
12	H	H	H	H	H	H	H	H	H	H
13	H	H	H	H	H	H	H	H	H	H
14	H	H	S4*	S5*	S4*	H	H	H	H	H
15	S4*	S5*	S5**	S6	S6	H	H	H	H	H
16	S5	S6	S6	S	S	H	H	H	H	H
17	S	S	S	S	S	S	S6	S6	S6	R/H
18–21	S	S	S	S	S	S	S	S	S	S
Soft 12–15	H	H	H	H	H	H	H	H	H	H
Soft 16	H	H	H	H	D4	H	H	H	H	H
Soft 17	H	H	D3	D4	D5	H	H	H	H	H
Soft 18	S4	S4	D4	D5	D5	S6	S4	H	H	H

Hand	2	3	4	5	6	7	8	9	10	Ace
Soft 19–21	S	S	S	S	S	S	S	S	S6	S
2-2	P	P	P	P	P	P	P	H	H	H
3-3	P	P	P	P	P	P	P	H	H	H
4-4	H	H	H	H	H	H	H	H	H	H
5-5	D5	D5	D	D	D	D4	D3	H	H	H
6-6	H	H	P	P	P	H	H	H	H	H
7-7	P	P	P	P	P	PS	H	H	H	H
8-8	P	P	P	P	P	P	P	P	P	P
9-9	S	P	P	P	P	S	P	P	S	S
10-10	S	S	S	S	S	S	S	S	S	S
A-A	P	P	P	P	P	P	P	P	P	P

Please Note: *If drawing to split aces is not allowed, and the dealer stands on soft 17, then hit A-A against an ace.*

Basic Strategy for Spanish 21

Double Double Down / Dealer Hits Soft 17

Player Has Not Already Doubled

S = Stand; H = Hit; P = Split

S4 = Stand except hit with four or more cards
D = Double; PS = Split except hit with suited 7s

S5 = Stand except hit with five or more cards
D3 = Double except hit three or more cards; @ = Hit if suited or spaded 6 7 8 is possible

S6 = Stand except hit with six or more cards
D4 = Double except hit with four or more cards; *Hit if any 6-7-8 is possible; R = Surrender
D5 = Double except hit with five or more cards
** Hit if spaded 6-7-8 is possible; R/H = Surrender if allowed; $ Hit with Super Bonus

Hand	2	3	4	5	6	7	8	9	10	Ace
5	H	H	H	H	D	H	H	H	H	H
6	H	H	H	H	D	H	H	H	H	H
7	H	H	H	H	D	H	H	H	H	H
8	H	H	H	D	D	H	H	H	H	H
9	H	D4	D	D	D	H	H	H	H	H

Hand	2	3	4	5	6	7	8	9	10	Ace
10	D5	D5	D	D	D	D	D5	H	H	H
11	D4	D5	D5	D5	D5	D5	D5	D4	D3	D3
12	H	H	H	H	H	H	H	H	H	H
13	H	H	H	H	S4*	H	H	H	H	H
14	H	H	S4*	S5@	S6**	H	H	H	H	H
15	S4*	S5@	S6	S6	S	H	H	H	H	H
16	S6	S6	S6	S	S	H	H	H	H	R/H
17	S	S	S	S	S	S	S6	S6	S6	R/H
18–21	S	S	S	S	S	S	S	S	S	S
A2	H	D3	D	D	D	H	H	H	H	H
A3	H	D3	D4	D	D	H	H	H	H	H
A4	H	H	D4	D4	D5	H	H	H	H	H
A5	H	H	D3	D4	D5	H	H	H	H	H
A6	H	H	D3	D4	D5	H	H	H	H	H
A7	S4	S4	D4	D5	D6	S6	S4	H	H	H
A8	S	S	S	S	S	S	S	S	S6	S6
2-2	P	P	P	P	P	P	P	H	H	H
3-3	P	P	P	P	P	P	P	H	H	H
4-4	H	H	H	H	H	H	H	H	H	H
5-5	D5	D5	D	D	D	D4	D3	H	H	H
6-6	H	H	P	P	P	H	H	H	H	H
7-7	P	P	P	P	P	PS	H	H	H	H
8-8	P	P	P	P	P	P	P	P	P	R
9-9	S	P	P	P	P	S	P	P	S	S
10-10	S	S	S	S	S	S	S	S	S	S
A-A	P	P	P	P	P	P	P	P	P	P

Double Down Surrender: *12–16 against 8–Ace; 17 against an Ace. Never split 4s, 5s, or 10s.*

Basic Strategy for Spanish 21
Double Double Down, Dealer Hits Soft 17
Player Has Already Doubled

S = Stand; D = Double; R = Surrender

Hand	2	3	4	5	6	7	8	9	10	Ace
6	S	D	D	D	D	D	R	R	R	R
7	D	D	D	D	D	D	R	R	R	R
8	D	D	D	D	D	D	D	D	R	R
9	D	D	D	D	D	D	D	D	D	D
10	D	D	D	D	D	D	D	D	D	D
11	D	D	D	D	D	D	D	D	D	D
12	S	S	S	S	S	D	D	R	R	R
13	S	S	S	S	S	S	R	R	R	R
14	S	S	S	S	S	S	R	R	R	R
15	S	S	S	S	S	S	R	R	R	R
16	S	S	S	S	S	S	R	R	R	R
17	S	S	S	S	S	S	S	S	S	R
18–21	S	S	S	S	S	S	S	S	S	S
Soft 13	D	D	D	D	D	D	D	D	D	D
Soft 14	D	D	D	D	D	D	D	D	D	D
Soft 15	D	D	D	D	D	D	D	D	D	D
Soft 16	D	D	D	D	D	D	D	D	D	D
Soft 17	D	D	D	D	D	D	D	D	D	D
Soft 18	S	S	D	D	D	S	S	S	S	S
Soft 19	S	S	S	S	S	S	S	S	S	S
Soft 20	S	S	S	S	S	S	S	S	S	S
Soft 21	S	S	S	S	S	S	S	S	S	S

Please Note: *Some players have expressed doubt about Shackleford's advice to hit 17 against an ace with three or more cards. The player will save about 2.8 percent of the initial wager by hitting as opposed to standing. The dealers will advise against this play, as might other players, but the odds favor hitting.*

House Edges

Following are the house edges under various common rules, before considering the Super Bonus.

- Dealer stands on soft 17 = 0.4 percent
- Dealer hits on soft 17 and redoubling allowed = 0.42 percent
- Dealer hits on soft 17 and redoubling *not* allowed = 0.76 percent

Super Bonus

The probability of hitting the Super Bonus is 1 in 668,382 with six decks and 1 in 549,188 with eight decks. The reduction in the house edge depends on the bet amount and, to a lesser extent, the number of players. With no other players and bets of exactly $5 or $25, the Super Bonus lowers the house edge by 0.03 percent in a six-deck game and 0.036 percent in an eight-deck game.

At a bet of exactly $5, the Envy Bonus lowers the house edge by an additional 0.0015 percent in a six-deck game and 0.0018 percent in an eight-deck game, per additional player.

For bet amounts other than those indicated above, the benefit of the Super Bonus will go down as the bet amount goes up.

Rule Variations

- **No Draw to split aces:** This rule increases the house edge by 0.29 percent (29¢ per $100 wagered). Therefore hit A-A against an ace if drawing to split aces is not allowed and the dealer stands on soft 17.
- **Ace and 10 after splitting aces pays 3-to-2:** This lowers the house edge by 0.16 percent (16¢ per $100 wagered).
- **Doubling only allowed on first two cards:** This increases the house edge by 0.16 percent.
- **Match the dealer:** In some locations there is a side bet available if either or both of the player's first two cards match the dealer's up-card. In a six-deck game a nonsuited match pays 4-to-1 and a suited match pays 9-to-1. In an eight-deck game a nonsuited match pays 3-to-1 and a suited match pays 12-to-1. The side bet has a house edge of 3.06 percent in a six-deck game and 2.99 in an eight-deck game—edges that are way too high to bother with.

CHAPTER 18
Craps: The Exciting Game!

C raps is the most exciting yet the most intimidating game in the casino and is witnessing a surge of popularity because some shooters can change the odds of the game to favor the players by reason of their "rhythmic rolling," "dice control," or "precision shooting"—three phrases that mean the same thing.

Still, the majority of craps players play the game so poorly that no amount of dice control can overcome the huge house edges that they give the casinos with their awful betting choices. And that doesn't have to be, because at its purist, craps is a very simple game with a very small house edge on its better bets.

DEALER   BOXMAN   DEALER

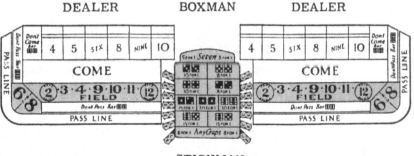

STICKMAN

The Dice

A die has six sides, with 36 possible combinations of two dice: 6 x 6 = 36 combinations. Each side (or face) of a die will have "pips": 1-pip, 2-pips, 3-pips, 4-pips, 5-pips, and 6-pips. The lowest number that can be rolled is a 2 (1-pip + 1-pip); the highest number is a 12 (6-pips + 6-pips). Therefore there is only one way to make a 2 and one way to roll a 12. The following graph shows you the possible combination of pips that can be made with two dice.

Number	Ways to Make It	Combinations of Pips
2	one	1:1
3	two	2:1, 1:2
4	three	3:1, 1:3, 2:2
5	four	4:1, 1:4, 3:2, 2:3
6	five	5:1, 1:5, 4:2, 2:4, 3:3
7	six	6:1, 1:6, 5:2, 2:5, 4:3, 3:4
8	five	6:2, 2:6, 5:3, 3:5, 4:4
9	four	6:3, 3:6, 5:4, 4:5
10	three	6:4, 4:6, 5:5
11	two	6:5, 5:6
12	one	6:6

The 7 is the number that comes up the most, and it is the key number in playing craps. If you look at a set of casino dice, you will find that the front side and back side of each add up to 7: opposite the 1-pip is the 6-pips, opposite the 2-pips is the 5-pips, and opposite the 3-pips is the 4-pips.

Casino dice can come in various sizes, colors, and opacity. The usual sizes are 5/8" and 3/4"; and while some dice are clear, some are frosted.

The Personnel

Craps tables usually have three dealers and a box person. In the diagram at the beginning of the chapter, note that one dealer, called the "stickman," stands on the players' side of the table. He has a long stick that he uses to beat sense into the ploppy players' thick skulls...sorry, just fantasizing. The stickman moves the dice to the shooter or brings the dice to the middle of the table between rolls, and he also announces the payoffs of the winning proposition bets in the middle of the table.

Two dealers stand on the opposite side of the table from the stickman—one on the left side of the table and one on the right side of the table. (It doesn't matter how you are looking at the table—one is always left and one is always right.) The dealers pay off winning bets and take the losing bets on their side of the table. Dealers do not stay in their positions throughout the game but will move from one position to another, generally in 20-minute intervals.

At the center of the table, across from the stickman, is the box person, who supervises the game. The box person also resolves most of the disputes at the table.

The Table

There are different types of craps tables with some minor changes in their layouts and sometimes in the payoffs of their bets.

The left and right sides of the layout offer the same bets. You have the Pass Line (a good bet), which goes in front of all players, and above that bet is the Don't Pass (also a good bet). Note the word *bar* at the 12; that means the 12 is a push or tie for those players betting the Don't Pass if it appears. These players are betting against the shooter—even if *they are* the shooter! On some tables you will note a 6/8 bet in the corners—a true ploppy bet.

Above the Don't Pass Line is the Field (a bad bet), which combines the numbers 2, 3, 4, 9, 10, 11, and 12. Above that is the Come bet, which is a good bet. At the top are the Point numbers, also called Box numbers—4, 5, 6, 8, 9, and 10. These Point/Box numbers can be good bets or bad bets depending on how the player is using them. In the upper corners of the layout are the Don't Come boxes.

In the center of the table sit the very worst ploppy bets at the game of craps, also known as Crazy Crapper or Proposition bets. Here are their names, which you should put out of your mind as soon as you read them: the Hardways (pips formed as 2:2, 3:3, 4:4, 5:5), the 2 (Snake Eyes), the 12 (Boxcars), the 11 (Yo), the 3 (Triad), and Any Craps. There are also other combinations of awful bets, such as the Whirl or the World, the Horn, a multitude of Hop bets, and the Any Seven, one of the worst bets in the whole casino! Some tables will add more Crazy Crapper bets, such as the Fire bet, an even worse bet than the Any Seven bet.

I'll fully explain the good, bad, and ugly of all the various bets later in this chapter.

How Craps Is Played

The game begins with the stickman pushing several dice to the player, who chooses two. The remaining dice are then put into a bowl on the stickman's side of the table. The shooter must have a bet on the Pass Line or the Don't Pass Line.

The Pass Line bettors make up more than 95 percent of the craps players. They are also called "rightside" players or "Do" players because they are betting *with* the shooter. Don't Pass players (or simply "Don't players") make up about 5 percent of the players and are called "wrong-side" players because they are betting *against* the shooter.

The shooter rolls the dice to the back wall, which is composed of foam-rubber pyramids. These pyramids are used to make the game of craps random, which it is, except for controlled shooters.

This roll is called the "Come-Out roll" and signifies the beginning of the game. If the shooter rolls a 7 or 11, the Pass Line bet wins; if he rolls a 2, 3, or 12, the Pass Line bet loses. He has six ways to win on the 7 and two ways to win on the 11, giving him a total of eight ways to win his Come-Out roll. But he has four ways to lose: one way on the 2, two ways on the 3, and one way on the 12. So on this Come-Out roll, the rightside players have a 2-to-1 edge over the casino. This edge reverses itself when the Come-Out is over and the Point Cycle begins.

On the Come-Out roll, the Don't players will lose on the 7 and 11, giving them eight ways to lose. But they will win on the 2 and 3, giving them three ways to win; they push on the 12.

There are 24 point or box-number combinations that can be rolled: the 4, 5, 6, 8, 9, and 10. If one of these numbers is rolled, it becomes the shooter's Point. The dealer then puts a puck on that number, white side facing up with the word *on* showing. The reverse side of this puck is black with *off* on it. When the Come-Out roll is taking place, the puck will be over on the side of the table on its black/off side.

The shooter has to roll the Point number before he rolls a 7 in order to win. If the 7 appears before the Point, all players who bet the Pass Line lose. The dice are passed to the next shooter. When that 7 appears, ending a roll, it is called "sevening out." The stickman will yell "Seven out!" in order to tell everyone the shooter's hand is finished.

Let's go over it again:

- The Come-Out roll: the 7 or 11 wins for the Pass Line player
- The 2, 3, or 12 loses for the Pass Line player
- The Don't player loses on 7 or 11
- The Don't player wins on 2 and 3 but pushes on 12
- The Point is established, which is one of these numbers: 4, 5, 6, 8, 9, or 10
- The Point must be hit again before the 7 to win for the Pass Line bettor and lose for the Don't Pass bettor
- If the 7 comes up before the Point, the Pass Line loses and the Don't Pass wins, and the dice are passed to the next shooter

The house edge on the Pass Line is 1.41 percent. That means for every $10 on the Pass Line, the expectation is a loss of 14¢. These dollar amounts are averages over time. The house wins 251 decisions; the player wins 244 decisions on the Pass Line. It's a very close contest. Those sad ploppies who insist on not using the Pass Line bet are fools. Avoid their advice.

The Don't Pass has a slightly lower house edge of 1.36 percent or 1.4 percent, depending on whether you count the 12 as an actual roll.

There, you just went through the essential game of craps. After I add some little tweaks to it, you'll be on your way to being an intelligent player at the most exciting game in the casino.

The Odds Bet:
Taking the Odds on the Pass Line

Once the shooter establishes his Point, the casino allows a second bet to be placed behind the Pass Line, called the "Odds." If the casino allows 2X or double Odds, a player making a $10 Pass Line bet can put $20 in Odds behind it. The house has no edge on the Odds bet, and the bet is paid off at the true odds.

Here are the payoffs for the Odds bets along with the total win, including Pass Line bet:

1. The 4 or 10 pay 2-to-1 (six ways to make the 7, three ways to make a 4 or 10). If you have $20 in Odds, you win $40. Coupled with the even-money payout on the $10 Pass Line bet, the player wins $50.

2. The 5 or 9 pay 3-to-2 (six ways to make the 7, four ways to make the 5 or 9). If you have $20 in odds, you win $30. Coupled with the even-money payout on the $10 Pass Line bet, the player wins $40.

3. The 6 or 8 pay 6-to-5 (six ways to make the 7, five ways to make the 6 or 8). If you have $20 in odds, you win $24. Coupled with the even-money payout on the $10 Pass Line bet, the player wins $34. (Some casinos will allow you to put $25 in Odds in a 2X game, making the payout $30, in which case the total Pass Line win would be $40.)

The Odds has the best return of any bet at the game. No house edge = good for the players. That is a hard and fast rule.

By the way, if you want to bet $30 on the Pass Line, take advantage of the Odds by putting $10 on the Line and $20 in Odds. Your losing expectation would be 14¢. If you were to put all $30 on the Pass Line, your losing expectation would be 42¢. That's a big difference.

Again, if some ploppy tells you not to take the Odds because it is a bad bet, just ignore him. Why would you want to join him in bankroll suicide?

> **Bad News:** *The Odds bet can only be made after the shooter has established a point. So the house always has an edge on you because that Pass Line bet comes in with a 1.41 house edge.*

You can just play the Pass Line without knowing anything else about craps, because it is the essential bet of the game for rightside/do players. I'll deal with the Don't Pass (and Don't Come) in a separate section.

The Come Bet

After the Point is established, you can place a Come bet on the layout. This bet is just like a Pass Line bet, so if the shooter rolls 7 or 11, the bet wins; if the shooter rolls a 2, 3, or 12, the bet loses. If the shooter rolls a Box number, the Come bet is placed on that number's box at the top of the layout. The shooter has to make that number before the 7 shows for the Come to win. If the 7 shows, the Come bet loses.

Odds can be taken on the Come bet. The dealer will place the Odds chips on top of the bet, a little skewed. The Come has the same house edge as the Pass Line—1.41 percent.

If you have both a Pass Line bet and a Come bet, if the shooter is on another Come-Out roll and rolls a 7, the Come bet will lose. The Come bet is a separate game between the Come bettor and the casino. The Odds are usually off for Come bets on the Pass Line's Come-Out roll, so those won't be lost on a Come-Out 7. However, you could keep those Odds working if you wish, although few players do that.

Once Pass Line or Come bets are on a number, they cannot be called off. They stay up until a decision. This rule protects the casino, because on the Come-Out roll the player has a 2-to-1 edge, but once the bet is on a number, the edge turns heavily in favor of the house. The Pass Line and Come bets are called "contract bets."

Reducing the House Edge

The Odds will reduce the house edge on the *total amount* wagered. But keep in mind, you will always lose 1.41 percent of your Pass Line and/or Come bets no matter how much you have in Odds. Again, if you intend to bet $30, as I showed above, you are always better putting the least on the Pass Line or Come and the most in Odds.

Odds	*House Edge*	*Losses & Added Information*
1X	0.85 percent	85¢ per $100 wagered
2X	0.61 percent	61¢ per $100 wagered
Full 2X Odds	0.57 percent	Allows 2.5X Odds on 6 and 8; 57¢ per $100 wagered
3X	0.47 percent	47¢ per $100 wagered
3X—4X—5X	0.37 percent	3X on 4/10; 4X on 5/9; 5X on 6/8; 37¢ per $100 wagered
5X	0.33 percent	33¢ per $100 wagered
10X	0.18 percent	18¢ per $100 wagered
20X	0.10 percent	10¢ per $100 wagered
100X	0.02 percent	2¢ per $100 wagered

The Don't Pass

Let's take a closer look at the Don't Pass bet. We already know that on the Come-Out roll this bet will lose on the 7 and 11, win on the 2 and 3, and push (bar) on the 12 (although some casinos use the 2 as the bar and allow a win on the 12). The Don't Pass player faces a horrible 8-to-3 house advantage on the Come-Out roll, but once the Point is established, the Don't Pass player has an edge over every number.

On the Don't Pass, the casino wins 976 decisions while the player wins 949 decisions, with 55 ties. The house edge, counting ties as bets, is 1.36 percent; not counting ties, it is 1.40 percent. Thus, for a $10 Don't Pass wager, your expectation is to lose 13.6¢ or 14¢. You decide how you want to figure it!

Laying the Odds on the Darkside

The Don't bettor can also take advantage of the Odds bet, only this time he *lays* the Odds because he has the better of the game during the Point Cycle. He puts up the long money to the casino's short money. Again, the Don't Odds can be made only once a Point is established.

Here are the Odds you can lay on the various Point numbers:

1. If you have a 4 or 10 with a $10 Don't Pass bet, you can lay $40 in odds to win $20. Total win would be $30.
2. If you have a 5 or 9 with a $10 Don't Pass bet, you can lay $30 to win $20. Total win would be $30.
3. If you have a 6 or 8 with a $10 Don't Pass bet, you can lay $24 to win $20. Total win would be $30.

The Don't Come

The Don't Come bet is made after the shooter's Point is established. It wins on the 2 and 3, loses on the 7 and 11, and pushes on the 12 (or 2 at some casinos). On a number, the 7 will win the bet; hitting the number loses the bet. You can lay Odds on the Don't Come. The house edge on the Don't Come bet is 1.36 percent (or 1.40 percent, depending on how you count ties), which means you will lose $1.36 or $1.40 for every $100 you bet.

Guess What?: *Once up on a number, Don't Pass and Don't Come bets can be taken down if you wish. Why? The house edge on the Don't Pass and Don't Come is derived on first placement of the bet, but during the Point Cycle, the edge shifts heavily in favor of the player. Taking a Don't bet down is a stupid strategy employed by dizzy-eyed ploppies. If you are up on the Don't Pass or Don't Come, don't take down your bets.*

How Odds Lowers the House Edge on the Don't

Odds	House Edge	Losses/Added Information
1X	0.68 percent	68¢ per $100 wagered
2X	0.46 percent	46¢ per $100 wagered
Full 2X Odds	0.43 percent	43¢ per $100 wagered
3X	0.34 percent	34¢ per $100 wagered
3X—4X—5X	0.27 percent	27¢ per $100 wagered
5X	0.23 percent	23¢ per $100 wagered
10X	0.12 percent	12¢ per $100 wagered
20X	0.07 percent	7¢ per $100 wagered
100X	0.01 percent	1¢ per $100 wagered

Using the Pass Line, Don't Pass, Come, and Don't Come bets, along with taking or laying Odds, you can now play the strongest game against the casinos. With such small house edges, your chances of winning are far greater than those of craps players who make foolish bets. The only way to play a stronger game is to learn how to control the dice.

Place Bets

Some players prefer to Place-bet the numbers, which the casino will allow. Just tell the dealer you want to Place the number(s), and he will put your chips on the number(s) you want. However to have such a Place-bet privilege, the numbers will not pay off at the correct odds. The casino will have a bigger edge on these bets than it does on the Pass Line, Come, Don't Pass, and Don't Come.

The following table will show you the difference between the true odds and the Place odds:

Numbers	True Odds	Place Odds	Payment	Casino Edge
4 and 10	2 to 1	9 to 5	$9 to $5	6.67 percent
5 and 9	3 to 2	7 to 5	$7 to $5	4.0 percent
6 and 8	6 to 5	7 to 6	$7 to $6	1.52 percent

The 6 and 8 are bet in increments of $6 to win $7. The placement of the 6 and/or 8 is a decent bet. Your expectation is to lose 9¢ for every $6 you bet or $1.52 for every $100. Place-betting the other numbers at the above payments is a waste. On a $10 bet on 4 or 10, the expectation is to lose 67¢ or $6.67 per $100 wagered. Your expectation on a $10 Place bet on the 5 or 9 is to lose 40¢ or $4 per $100 wagered.

Don't Place Bets and Lay Bets

These bets are the reverse of the rightside Place bets. You are placing them to win on a 7 and lose on the number. You can use a strict Don't Place bet or you can use a Lay bet. Not all casinos will allow Don't Place bets, though almost all allow Lay bets.

With the Don't Place Bet you put up the following wager to win the following amounts on the following numbers:

1. If you want to bet against the 6 or 8, you bet $5 to win $4. The house edge is 1.82 percent. That means for every $5 you bet, your expectation is to lose 9¢. For every $100 you bet, your expectation is to lose $1.82.

2. If you want to bet against the 5 or 9, you bet $8 to win $5. The house edge is 2.5 percent. Your expectation is to lose 20¢ for every $8 you bet. For every $100 you bet, your expectation is to lose $2.50.

3. If you want to bet against the 4 or 10, you bet $11 to win $5. The house edge is 3.03 percent. Your expectation is to lose 33¢ for

every $11 you bet. Your expectation for every $100 you bet is to lose $3.03

The second way to bet is to use a Lay bet. You pay a 5 percent commission on the bet, and the house will then pay you the true odds. Here is how it works:

1. If you want to Lay against the 4 or 10, you bet $40 to win $20. The 5 percent is taken out of $20. Your payment of the vig (commission) is $1. The house edge is 2.44 percent. Your expectation for every $100 you bet is to lose $2.44.
2. If you want to Lay against the 5 or 9, you bet $30 to win $20. Your payment of the vig is $1. The house edge is 3.23 percent. For every $100 you wager, your expectation is to lose $3.23.
3. If you want to Lay against the 6 or 8, you bet $24 to win $20. Your payment of the vig is $1. The house edge is 4 percent. For every $100 you wager, your expectation is to lose $4.

As on all bets, use the ones with the lowest house edges.

Put Bets

The Put bets are Pass Line or Come bets that are placed and do not go through the Come-Out or initial placement type of roll. These bets pay even money, but they can also have Odds placed on them. If the Point is 6 with double odds, you can bet $10 as the even-money portion and add $20 in Odds to the bet. The payoff will be $34 for your $30 wager. The house edge is 3.03 percent, an expected loss of $3.03 per $100 wagered.

The Odds that a casino lets you take will determine whether the Put bet is one worth making. Some casinos will not allow Put bets. But, yes, some Put bets come in with good edges—better than the Place house edges at times—but they are never as good as Pass Line or Come bets with Odds. Below, the bets in bold italics are decent Put wagers to make.

Odds Allowed	4 or 10 Put House Edge	5 or 9 Put House Edge	6 or 8 Put House Edge
No odds	33.33 percent	20 percent	9.09 percent
1X	16.67 percent	10 percent	4.55 percent
2X	11.11 percent	6.67 percent	3.03 percent
3X	8.33 percent	5 percent	2.27 percent
4X	6.67 percent	4 percent	*1.82 percent*
5X	5.56 percent	3.33 percent	*1.52 percent*
10X	3.03 percent	*1.82 percent*	*0.83 percent*
20X	*1.59 percent*	*0.95 percent*	*0.43 percent*
100X	*0.33 percent*	*0.20 percent*	*0.09 percent*

The Crazy Crapper/Proposition Bets

You know what? I don't even want to write this section, because the bets that follow stink to high heaven, which is the seventh heaven in mythology and is way, way up there. To get up that far is a stink of almost unimaginable scent-a-grades. These bets are beloved by ploppies who can't seem to sniff out putrid wagers. The Crazy Crapper bets come in with high house edges, every single one of them. So why do ploppies make them? The bets pay off big and hold the hope of giant wins *right now.* Of course, the poor ploppy does not realize that making these bets will guarantee monster losses over time.

There are two varieties of Crazy Crapper bets: one-roll bets decided on each roll of the dice and multiroll bets that don't have to be decided with each roll. The house edges on these bets come from being paid at much less (*much less*) than true odds. Take the Any Seven one-roll bet. The true odds are 5-to-1 or $5 to $1, but the casino pays $4 to $1. It literally takes that extra dollar from you to give it a 16.67 percent edge, meaning you lose $16.67 per $100 wagered on this ghoulish proposition.

Fancy, Fancy: *Don't let shifts of wording throw you. Casinos will sometimes use the word "for" as a substitute for "to" in an attempt to cloud a bet's true return. A bet that is 9-to-1 will be paid off as $9 on a $1 wager, or it might be paid off as $10 for $1. The different words actually mean the same thing. The 10-for-1 means the casino counts the initial bet as a part of the payoff. The real payoff is still actually $9-to-$1.*

Multiroll Crazy Crapper Bets

The Hardway 4 or Hardway 10 (also called Hard 4 or Hard 10): A Hard 4 is 2:2; a Hard 10 is 5:5. In order to win, the Hardway must be rolled before the 7 and before the number is made the soft way (that is, 3:1 or 1:3 for the 4; 6:4 or 4:6 for the 10). The Hard 4 or Hard 10 only occur once in 36 rolls, while the 7 and the soft ways can be made eight times. So the true odds are 8-to-1. The casino pays 7-to-1 (or 8-*for*-1), and the house edge is a large 11.11 percent, an expected loss of $11.11 for every $100 wagered.

The Hardway 6 or the Hardway 8 (also called Hard 6 or Hard 8): The player is looking to hit a 3:3 or a 4:4 before the 7 or a soft way appears. The true odds are 10-to-1; the casino pays off at 9-to-1 (or 10-*for*-1). House edge is 9.09 percent, which translates into an expected loss of $9.09 for every $100 wagered.

The Big 6 and the Big 8: This is the same as the Place bet of the 6 or 8 but paid even money as opposed to $7 to $6. The house edge is 9.09 percent. This bet is not found on most craps tables anymore.

Fire Bet: The devil's bet! This is a side bet that the shooter will hit each and every Point number during the Point Cycle of his roll. He must hit the 4, 5, 6, 8, 9, and 10 on the Pass Line before sevening out in order to win the big jackpot. If he hits four or five numbers, smaller jackpots are won. The *maximum* bet is usually $5. Here is the bad news: the house edge ranges from 20 percent to about 25 percent, depending on the payouts. Losses range between $20 and $25 for every $100 wagered. And you know what? Ploppies love this bet and make it whenever a layout allows. And that is a fiery hell of the first order.

The One-Roll Crazy Crapper Bets

The 2 or 12: These numbers hit once every 36 rolls, so the odds of hitting a 2 or 12 are 35-to-1. The casino does not pay you 35-to-1; instead it pays 30-to-1 (or 31-*for*-1), giving it a 13.89 percent house edge. The player's expectation is to lose $13.89 for every $100 wagered. Some casinos will change the payouts on these, but I have never heard of any casino making these bets worthwhile. Ploppies love these bets.

The 3 or 11: House edge is 11.11 percent. The payout is 15-to-1 (or 16-*for*-1), but the true odds are 17-to-1. The expectation is to lose $11.11 for every $100 you bet. Ploppies love these bets too.

Any Craps: The bettor wants one of these numbers to hit: 2, 3, or 12. The true odds are 8-to-1; the payoff is 7-to-1 (or 8-*for*-1), and the house edge is 11.11 percent. For every $100 wagered on this nutty proposition, the house will take $11.11. Ploppies flock to this bet.

Any Seven or Big Red: Comes in at 16.67 percent. Oh, yeah, you are betting that the next number thrown will be a 7. Ploppies are madly in love with this bet, even though their bankrolls will be in the "big red" if they habitually make it.

Craps/11 or C&E: The bet is that one of the following numbers will appear: 2, 3, 11, or 12. Half the bet goes on the craps numbers (2, 3, and 12); the other half goes on the 11. If a craps number appears, the payout is 7-to-1, but the 11 loses. If the 11 appears, the payoff is 15-to-1, and the craps numbers lose. The house edge is 11.11 percent or an expected loss of $11.11 for every $100 wagered. Ploppies eat up this bet.

Field Bet: The bet is that any one of these numbers will appear next: 2, 3, 4, 9, 10, 11, or 12. There are 16 ways to make these numbers and 20 ways to make all the other numbers. The 2 and 12 will pay 2-to-1. The house edge on this bet is 5.56 percent or an expected loss of $5.56 per $100 wagered. Some casinos will pay 3-to-1 on either the 2 or 12, and this will reduce the house edge to 2.78 percent, an expected loss of $2.78 per $100 wagered. You guessed it: ploppies love this bet.

Hardway Hop Bets: The odds are 35-to-1 to hit a particular Hardway, but the payoff is 30-to-1, a house edge of 13.89 percent, or an expected loss of $13.89 per $100 wagered. The Hardway hops are 1:1, 2:2, 3:3, 4:4, 5:5, and 6:6. Ploppies can't get enough of this bet.

Hop Bets: All combinations can be done as Hop bets. The payouts for all Hop bets of this type are 15-to-1; the true odds are 17-to-1. The house edge is 11.11 percent, an expected loss of $11.11 per $100 wagered.

Horn: The bet is that a 2, 3, 11, or 12 will be the next number. The bet is made in multiples of $4. You win on the number that shows (30-to-1 on the 2 and 12; 15-to-1 on the 3 and 11), but you lose the three other bets. The house edge on this bet is 12.5 percent, a loss of $12.50 per $100 wagered. There is an offshoot of this Horn bet, the Horn High variation. Here a ploppy throws out $5 and has the extra dollar put on any one of the four numbers. The house edge on this Horn High is 12.22 percent on the 3 or 11 and 12.78 percent on the 2 or 12. Ploppies love all versions of this bet.

Over 7 or Under 7: This started in churches at casino nights and is an ungodly horror. The house edge is 16.67 percent or a loss of $16.67 for every $100 wagered. Ploppies still love this bet, even though it should be considered a sin.

Whirl or World: The ploppy wants one of the following numbers: 2, 3, 7, 11, or 12. The house edge is 13.33 percent. Each number is paid off at house odds, but the other numbers are subtracted from it. A ploppy's dream.

As you can see, the Crazy Crapper bets are for crazy crappers only. My mentor, the late, legendary Captain, said, "You have to be crazy to make them." He was right.

I included side bets that are popular either in the casinos or in church games. Many casinos create new side bets to sucker the ploppies into losing more money. The rule of thumb is this: A casino is not going to put in a side bet that is a great deal for the player. Ignore all side bets.

Let's Go Over This Once More

1. Put a Pass Line or Don't Pass bet down. Come-Out roll will win even money for Pass Line bettors if a 7 or 11 is rolled. It will lose if a 2, 3, or 12 is rolled. The Pass Line bettor has a 2-to-1 edge on the Come-Out roll, as the 7 and 11 can be made eight ways, while the 2, 3, and 12 can be made four ways.

2. The other 24 dice combinations are no-decisions on the Come-Out but become the Point if rolled. Once the Point is established, the house gets a solid edge on each of the Point numbers.

3. If you are betting the Don't Pass, you win if a 2 or 3 is rolled (three ways), tie on a 12 (one way), and lose on a 7 or 11 (eight ways). The casino has an 8-to-3 edge on the Come-Out roll for Don't bettors. Again, the other numbers are no-decisions on the Come-Out roll but become the Point if hit. During the Point Cycle, the Don't bettor has a strong edge over the casino, which is the exact reverse of the rightside bettor.

4. Once a Point is established, you can take Odds or Lay Odds on your Pass Line or Don't Pass bets, respectively.

5. You can get on other numbers by betting Come or Don't Come. You may also take or lay Odds on these bets by putting the Odds down and telling the dealer, "Odds."

6. Rightside bettors can also Place the 6 and/or 8 after the Point is established.

7. The shooter continues until he sevens out. Rightsiders will not lose as long as the 7 doesn't show; Don't players will win if the 7 does show.

Strange: *Sometimes Don't players will shoot the dice, and if they make their Point or hit Box numbers they are betting against...they lose! If they seven out, they win! That's bizarro world for sure.*

The Placing of bets with house edges lower than 2 percent, such as the Placing of the 6 and 8, is okay but not as good as the Pass, Come, Don't Pass, and Don't Come with Odds. Smart players should not consider any other bets.

Something Else: *While the Placing of the 6 and 8 are good bets and the Placing of the 4 and 10, and 5 and 9 are bad bets, there is a wrinkle in this arrangement. Players can "buy" the 4 and 10 for $25 or $50—paying a $1 or $2 vig—and if the bet wins, they get paid based on the true odds. However, the commission must be taken out of wins only, as some venues and casinos will take the vig out of winning and losing bets—which then makes the bet nowhere near as good as just placing the 6 and/or 8. One last word of caution—only make the bets on $25 and $50 because the house edge drops all the way down to 1.3 percent by doing this; if the bet is made on any other amount, the house edge does not go down enough to make the bets worthwhile.*

CHAPTER 19

The Captain's 5-Count and Smart Betting Strategies

My craps mentor, and the man who taught me everything I know about gambling and advantage play, was the late Captain, the legendary Atlantic City player who has taken on mythic proportions over the decades I've been writing about him. His ideas and playing philosophies, his discovery of how to control the dice on a modern casino table, and his amazing 5-Count method are legacies that have stood craps players in good stead over the years, and these concepts should now become second nature to you, as they are to me.

In a random game of craps, even if the player makes the best of the low-house-edge bets, such a good player (and such players *are* good) is still doomed to lose over time. This is true for just about every player playing just about every game in the casino—the losses will outweigh the wins. Yes, advantage players can get an edge at blackjack by counting cards and, yes, there are certain slot machines that will become favorable at certain times, but until the Captain came along, no one thought that there was any way to beat the game of craps.

The Captain proposed three strict methods for playing the game and, for those who desired it, how to achieve an edge over the casino.

- Use the 5-Count on all random shooters.
- Make the lowest-house-edge bets.
- Learn how to control the dice—what he called "rhythmic rolling."

The 5-Count

When the Captain first analyzed the game of craps, he wanted to handle three things:

1. Reducing the number of random rolls a player bet on, to preserve the player's bankroll
2. Increasing the likelihood that the shooters a player bets on will win him money
3. Increasing the player's comps based on *body time* at the table as opposed to *risk time*

Through trial and error, through years of playing three to five days each week, the Captain discovered his 5-Count. He believed it would eliminate 50 percent of the random rolls and would position a player to make money if that player came across "rhythmic rollers" who were changing the nature of the game to give the players an advantage. He also knew that the 5-Count would simply look like the typical "qualifying event" that many craps players use to decide when to start betting on a shooter.

We now understand in no uncertain terms that the 5-Count accomplishes all three of the Captain's imperatives, based on mathematical studies. (Go to www.goldentouchcraps.com to read these.)

1. The 5-Count eliminates almost 57 percent of random rolls. The player will only bet on about 43 percent of the random rolls.
2. It gets the player on the controlled shooters (rhythmic rollers) at a higher frequency than *bet-all* players who wager on every shooter. If there is a controlled shooter at the table, the 5-Counter will be on him 11 percent more often than bet-all players.
3. It increases comp value because of "body time." The 5-Counter is often (though not always) given credit for 100 percent of the time he is at the table, although he is only risking money 43 percent of the time.

The 5-Count is the best method for deciding which shooters to bet on. It starts with a Point number on the Come-Out roll (Point/Box numbers are 4, 5, 6, 8, 9, or 10) and ends with a Point/Box number. Between the first Point number and the concluding Point/Box number, all rolls count.

So roll No. 2 can be an 11, roll No. 3 can be a 12, and roll No. 4 can be a 3, but roll No. 5 must be one of the Box numbers (4, 5, 6, 8, 9, or 10) for the count to be completed. Obviously, if the shooter sevens out, the count is over, the dice are passed to the next shooter, and the 5-Count begins again.

Let's take a look at the various scenarios of the 5-Count, how it works, and when to bet (the following charts are excerpted from my book *Casino Craps: Shoot to Win!*):

Example One: The Basics

Shooter's Roll #	Number Rolled	Count	Bet
1	7	0-count	0
2	*4	1-count	0
3	11	2-count	0
4	6	3-count	0
5	3	4-count	0
6	*8	5-Count	Betting begins

The above is the bare bones 5-Count. The shooter is on the Come-Out roll and rolls a 7, which is a winner but is not the start of the 5-Count, because it isn't a Point number. His second roll is a 4. The 4 is a Point/ Box number and is also his Point. He then rolls an 11, the 2-count; then a 6, the 3-count; then a 3, the 4-count; and then an 8, another Point/ Box number, which completes the 5-Count.

Example Two: The Holding Pattern

Shooter's Roll #	Number Rolled	Count	Bet
1	11	0-count	0
2	7	0-count	0
3	*6	1-count	0
4	5	2-count	0
5	9	3-count	0

Shooter's Roll #	Number Rolled	Count	Bet
6	11	4-count	0
7	3	4-count and holding	0
8	2	4-count and holding	0
9	*10	5-Count	Betting begins

Example Two shows what happens when other than Point/Box numbers are thrown after the 4-count. This causes a *holding pattern*. Roll No. 6, which was an 11, established the 4-count, but then the shooter rolled a 3 and then a 2—both of which are not Point/Box numbers—which causes the 5-Count not to be completed. The 4-count holds until a Point/Box number is rolled. Finally, the shooter rolls a 10, which is a Point/Box number, and the 5-Count is completed.

Example Three: Shooter Makes His Point

Shooter's Roll #	Number Rolled	Count	Bet
1	4	1-count	0
2	3	2-count	0
3	4 (shooter's point!)	3-count	0
4	7	4-count	0
5	11	4-count and holding	0
6	7	4-count and holding	0
7	11	4-count and holding	0
8	3	4-count and holding	0
9	*9	5-Count	Betting begins

Example Three shows what happens when a shooter actually makes his Point during the establishment of the 5-Count. His first roll is a 4, the 1-count; his second roll is a 3, the 2-count; and on his third roll, he hits his Point, the 4, which is the 3-count. Then he is on the Come-Out again. He rolls a 7. *Because it is a Come-Out roll, that 7 becomes the 4-count.* Then the shooter rolls a string of non-Point/Box numbers (the 11, 7, 11, 3) before he finally hits another Point/Box number, the 9. The 5-Count is completed.

How to Bet with the *5-Count*

How should we bet on the shooters who get through the 5-Count? The best way is to make *minimal* Come bets and take the full Odds. The Odds bet is a wash between the casino and the player. If you can afford to take the Odds, do so—if you are a frequent player, the Odds bet will wind up being an even proposition between you and the casino. And that is a very, very good thing.

Put up a Come bet after the 5-Count is completed. You have a 2-to-1 edge on this placement because you win eight times on the 7 and 11, and you lose four times on the 2, 3, and 12. If the shooter makes a Point/Box number, your bet goes up on the number, and you take the Odds.

Next you place another Come bet *if you wish*. There is no law of nature that says you have to bet more than one number, although most craps players like to do so—in fact, some players are maniacal bettors, some betting on almost every number and Crazy Crapper bet, and they give themselves very little chance to win over time. Keep in mind each number is a separate game against the house—the more numbers you bet, the more the casino's expectation is to beat you!

If the shooter sevens out when you place a second Come bet, you lose the bet on the number and win the bet just placed on the Come. If he rolls another Box number you go up on that number and take the Odds. If you wish to go up on a third number, you simply put out another Come bet. If the shooter has actually made his Point, then you make a Pass Line bet. We will use $10 betting units. You can translate these into your betting units.

Example Four: Come Betting

Shooter's Roll #	Number Rolled	Count	Bet
1	4	1-count	0
2	11	2-count	0
3	5	3-count	0
4	6	4-count	0
5	*8	5-Count	$10 Come
6	9 Come bet goes to 9		Take Odds on the 9 $10 Come bet
7	8 Come bet goes to 8		Take Odds on 8 Put up new Come bet if you wish to be on three numbers

You can also go up on the Come before the 5-Count is completed, doing so after the 3-count or 4-count, but only put Odds once the 5-Count is completed. The longer you wait, the better for your bankroll. However, many players don't feel comfortable waiting for the full 5-Count if they are going the Come-betting route. I prefer to go up after the entire 5-Count is completed.

Example Five: Place Betting

Place betting with the 5-Count is very simple. When the 5-Count is completed, you Place the 6 and/or 8.

Shooter's Roll #	Number Rolled	Count	Bet
1	7	0-count	0
2	8	1-count	0
3	12	2-count	0
4	6	3-count	0
5	4	4-count	0

Shooter's Roll #	Number Rolled	Count	Bet
6	2	4-count/h	0
7	*9	5-Count	Place Bet the 6 and 8 in multiples of six dollars. Be up on no more than three numbers.

What About Going Up on the Don't Right Away?

Some players think that going up on the Don't Pass or Don't Come before the 5-Count is finished is a way to play almost every roll with little risk. Not so. The very moment you put up that Don't Pass or Don't Come bet, the casino's edge is 8-to-3 over you, because the casino will win eight times on the 7 and 11 while the Don't bettor can only win three times on the 2 and 3. So you are just giving the casino more cracks at your bankroll going up on the Don't before the 5-Count is finished. In fact, going up on the Don't Pass or Don't Come right away is the same as betting on all shooters and all rolls. It is truly a waste of your money.

If you like to play the Don'ts, then wait until the 5-Count is finished, then bet a Don't Come (or Don't Pass) and, once up on a number, take full Odds. The 5-Count works the same for random Don't players as for random rightside players. Every player should use the 5-Count.

No Don't Pass: *As far as betting the Don't, I recommend only one bet per shooter, preferably a Don't Come bet and Lay full Odds. If the shooter hits the number and you lose, stop betting on this shooter. You never want one shooter to win more than one bet against you. Although it can happen, it is indeed rare that shooter after shooter after shooter will knock you off your number.*

What to Do When You Are the Shooter

We've talked about the "shooter" in all the above scenarios, but we have not discussed how to play and bet when *you* are the shooter. And you should definitely shoot, because that is one of the great joys of the game—rolling dem bones! (Oh, yeah, the origins of those dice were bones—sheep bones…and perhaps human bones too.) It feels as if you are taking fate into your own hands when you shoot the dice, although in truth, in a random game with no dice control, all you are doing is merely taking dice into your hands. Still, it feels good.

To shoot, you have to put up a minimal Pass Line bet, and when you establish your Point, put up the Odds. However, use the 5-Count on yourself and do not put up any other bets until the 5-Count is reached. Again, I recommend only using Come bets with Odds but, if you wish, you can also use the Place Bets of the 6 and/or 8.

If you are betting from the Don't, just use one Don't Pass bet, back it with Odds, and do not make any other bets. You do not want to be the shooter who loses you a ton of money because you got hot! You'll find it hard to live with yourself if you do.

What the 5-Count Isn't

Some ploppies mistakenly think that the Captain used the appearance percentage of the 7 to the other numbers as the foundation of the 5-Count. He wasn't looking at averages or short-term results…not at all. He was looking at the totality of the game to save us money over extended periods of time. These ploppies then state, "How stupid the Captain is. With five rolls or more before your bet, the 7 is more likely to occur."

No it isn't. These ploppies are, well, ploppies, and such thinking *proves* they are ploppies!

The 7 has about a 17 percent chance of occurring in a random game at any time—now and forever. There is no more likelihood of the 7 appearing on the ninth roll than on the first roll than on the 50th roll. Players who think a number is more likely to appear because it hasn't appeared in a while are mistaken. In a *random game,* a number does not have more of a chance to come up now because it didn't come up then, or not come up now because it did come up then. It takes some time to see that this is so...*but it is so*. When it comes to numbers at the random game of craps, probability wins out. Ploppy critics try to outthink the Captain, try to outthink the math, and try to outthink probability, which is all a total waste of their time—and ours—and their money when they bet based on their sad and silly suppositions.

The "due theory" of betting is based on the "Gambler's Fallacy," which advocates that something will occur if it hasn't occurred in a while. Sounds great, sounds logical, but it is not applicable to games of random chance. "Great" and seemingly "logical" don't always fit in with the real world of gambling...or the real world of life, for that matter.

CHAPTER 20
Dice Control

I opened my chapter "Card Counting at Blackjack" with this simple sentence: Blackjack can be beaten. I now add to that the following: Craps can be beaten.

For years craps was considered an unassailable game, falling into the independent trial mode, which meant that what happened in the past had no effect on what would happen in the future. The numbers and probabilities were set in stone. While such was indeed true for players who played the random game, such a belief was not true for players who could control the dice and change the probabilities of the game to favor them. New probabilities = a new game! Craps becomes a new game when dice control enters the picture.

I learned about dice control from the Captain in the late 1980s, and I was extremely fortunate to see the greatest dice controller of all time, the woman known as "the Arm." I was even more fortunate to play craps with the Captain. In those heady days of the 1990s, when the "Big Three"—composed of the Captain, Jimmy P., and the Arm—were hammering Atlantic City, there were very few accomplished dice controllers to be found. Most craps players were of the wild and wooly kind, throwing their money away on bad bets and often boozy losing battles with Dame Fortune.

The Big Three did not do this. They played the 5-Count—bet cautiously on the bets their skill could overcome—and they won so much money that some Atlantic City casinos passed their pictures around to alert other casinos to the "good luck" or magic these players seemed to have. Indeed, one casino executive wrote in his book about his admiration and fear of what the Captain had achieved.

The Basis and Basics of Dice Control

The two main ideas behind dice control concern limiting the appearance of the 7, thereby increasing the appearance of the other numbers. The second basis is to influence the dice in such a way that certain specific numbers (say, the 6 and 8) come up more than their normal probabilities indicate. The 7 might still come up more or less often, but the money will be made on the hitting of the specific numbers.

The non-7 approach to dice control is the best to take for new and intermediate dice controllers, because it requires little or no axis control of the dice. (I'll get to axis control in a moment.) The hitting of specific numbers does require strong axis control, which often takes quite some time for most dice controllers to develop.

The basics of a controlled throw are composed of the following:
1. Where and how you stand at the table
2. Setting the pips on the dice properly
3. Gripping the dice properly
4. Aiming at your spot
5. A proper backswing
6. A proper release of the dice
7. A backward spin on the dice when they are in the air
8. A soft hitting of the back wall

Where and How to Stand at the Table

The dice controller wants to get as close to the back wall as possible. Please note where the stickman stands at the table. You want to be right next to him or no farther away than the second position next to him, either on his right or his left. The farther away you are from the back wall, the harder it is to control the dice, because even the least imperfections in your throw will be magnified by distances. Use this saying to remind yourself of the proper position: farther = harder.

The best approach is for right-handed shooters to be on the stickman's left side and left-handed shooters to be on the stickman's right, because the shooter will be using a pendulum backswing.

You should stand flat against the table, your belly touching it (if you are overweight, it will flop over or under it, depending on how tall you are). Most people, even tall shooters such as the great Jerry "Stickman," prefer to stand on their tiptoes when they shoot, so they can get all the way out over the table. Like most athletic competitions—and dice control is a kind of athletics—being tall is better than being short...a sad fact.

Setting the Pips Properly

In the game of craps, you will run across individuals—both casino personnel and players—who talk about "dice setting" and "dice sets." This refers to those players who like to set the dice with certain pips in certain arrangements. Most craps players use some type of dice set, though almost all of them are *not* controlled shooters. For most players, setting the dice is a ritual, a style, and as such makes them feel good doing it. However, dice setting alone has no influence on the game; unless the player has control over where and how those dice wind up after hitting the back wall, a dice set is just a dice set.

Controlled shooters set the dice in various formations. The best dice set for avoiding the 7—and that is what you must learn to do first and foremost—is called the "Hardway Set." This set has the Hardway numbers set all around it. Here are the various formations of the Hardway Set:

Hardway Sets (T=top; F=face):

T5F4:T5F4

T4F2:T4F2

T2F3:T2F3

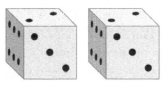

T3F5:T3F5

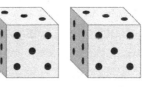

T5F3:T5F3   **T3F2:T3F2**

T2F4:T2F4   **T4F5:T4F5**

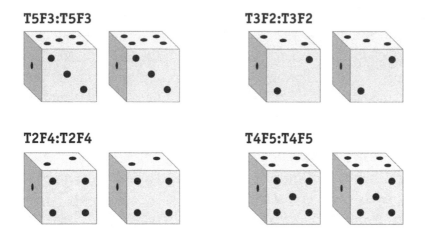

The axis on the Hardway Set goes through the 6-pip and the 1-pip; so the on-axis numbers are 2, 3, 4, and 5. If any one of these pips comes up after the throw, that die or those dice are considered to be on axis. If the 6-pip or 1-pip shows on one or both, that die or those dice are off axis.

The reason the Hardway Set is the best for avoiding the 7 has to do with the fact that no one pitch of the dice can bring that 7 to the fore. It takes two pitches of a die in relation to the other die for a 7 to appear. Without strong on-axis skill—a skill that might require a different dice set—the Hardway Set is the way to go in trying to avoid the dreaded 7.

Setting the dice has to be done quickly. The casinos are under the impression—often the correct impression, with many dice setters—that setting the dice slows down the game, and casinos hate when their games are slowed down, because they make less money that way.

So the very first thing you should practice at home is setting that Hardway Set quickly—in two to five seconds. Always set them the same way, with the same pips facing you, the same pips on top, with the 6-pip on the same side and the 1-pip on the same side. You do not want to think about what you are doing when you are setting the dice. You want to be on automatic pilot, allowing your muscle memory to handle the setting.

Gripping the Dice Properly

The objective of a proper grip is to make sure that the dice leave your hand together. You don't want one die lagging too much. We look to make as close to the perfect throw as possible—both dice together, spinning in exactly the same way. The grip is the key element in getting those dice to leave your fingers together. To have a chance at an excellent throw, your grip must be as close to perfect as possible.

After the dice are released, you have no control over them—so the better the release, the better chance you'll have of getting the edge over the casino. Any little deviation of finger placement will alter the flight of the dice—usually for the worse.

Gripping the dice too hard prevents the dice from rotating freely. Gripping too lightly might make the dice wobble in the air. You need a balance or, as the Greeks said, you need "moderation in all things," and that relates strongly to dice control. You should practice your grip every day, because it is the first big step in a controlled throw.

The grip should have the following characteristics:

- Very little finger contact with the dice
- Very little force needed to get dice to leave your hand
- Allows the dice to stay together in flight
- You have control, and the dice feel comfortable in your hand
- Both dice remain perfectly still in your hand during your pickup and swing
- There is no splitting of the dice
- All four sides of the dice are square with the table and walls
- The force that you apply to hold the dice is minimal
- The dice are released from your fingers with little drag
- Your fingertips are like a fulcrum
- The dice travel down the table in a perfect arc

Try to use the tips of your fingers on the front of the dice. Using the tips of your fingers gives you the least amount of finger contact, thus allowing for the smallest amount of drag upon release of the dice. If you grip the dice with the pads of your fingers, you obviously have slightly more finger contact on the dice. Still, use whichever is more comfortable for you.

Three-Finger Grip

The best grip, and the one that totally satisfies all the elements on the previous page, is the three-finger grip. In the three-finger grip, the index, middle, and ring fingers are straight across on the front of the dice, and the thumb is on the back of the dice. The pinky does not touch the dice at all during the pickup, grip, or delivery of the dice—that will interfere with the mechanics of the throw.

The holding of the dice with the three-finger grip is actually performed with the middle finger and thumb. The index finger and ring finger are simply placed along the front of the dice and act like wings of a plane and a fulcrum for the dice to rotate on as they are released.

The fingers have to be perfectly straight across the front of the dice, with no splits in the dice. A split will cause the dice to move away from each other in the air. The farther they separate, the less control exists. Freedom is good for human beings but very bad for dice!

Although we say that the middle finger and thumb are holding the dice, the pressure differences between the three fingers on the front are not that great. Softness is the key.

Picking up the dice for the three-fingered grip can be done in two ways: with the middle finger and thumb and then, during the aim, the ring and pointer are brought to their positions, or the dice can be picked up with all three fingers at once. Either pickup is fine.

The three-finger grip keeps those dice perfectly aligned and allows them to leave the hand together with an equal spin on the dice, and they'll move through the air together. This is not the easiest dice grip to learn, but it is, for just about all dice controllers, the best to use. It should be the first one you try to master. Give yourself time to learn it and use it. Do not get discouraged if you find that several days or even weeks are needed to really master this grip. Take your time and go for the best; beating the casino is worth it.

Thumb Placement

How should the thumb be positioned on the back of the dice? It really doesn't matter if the edge of the thumb is touching the dice or if the thumb is totally touching the dice, as long as the skin doing the touching is perfectly centered.

The important thing is that the thumb contact should be *equal* on both dice. How far up or down on the dice the thumb is can change the amount of rotations after the dice are released. Generally, the thumb should be about halfway down the backside of the dice.

Grip Adjustments You Can Consider

1. If the dice are slipping out of the fingers during the pickup or the follow-through, a little more contact on the dice is needed. Move the thumb down a little and perhaps move the fingers down a little as well.

2. If the dice are not coming out of the fingers without any backspin or are moving flat down the table, then adjust the thumb's position. Backspin keeps the dice together. Backspin will also remove some of the force of the forward momentum. So if more backspin is needed, move the thumb down the back a little lower than the fingers.

3. If the dice are spinning with too much rotation, then move the thumb up on the dice. Too much backspin will require more energy to be released as they land, and this could cause randomization. We want the backspin to almost cancel out the forward movement but not eliminate it, because we want the dice to softly touch the back wall.

4. Another problem could be that one die may be lagging behind the other or traveling higher than the other. Again this is a grip problem. Make sure that the fingers are square across the front of the dice, that the dice are square to the table and the walls, and that your hands are clean so that oils and perspiration don't cause the dice to leave your hand with lag.

Aiming the Dice

What does a hunter do when he sees Bambi in the woods and he's looking for a delicious dinner? Does he just fire the gun off and hope the bullet magically hits the poor deer? Of course not. He carefully aims the gun and makes sure it is his best shot. Then he blows Bambi's head off.

After you have gripped the dice and picked them up, you must pause, look at the back wall, and aim. You will probably want to hit the table between eight inches and six inches in front of the back wall. Because every table is different, your Come-Out roll(s) will give you an idea of where you have to land the dice so they hit the back wall softly. You do not want the dice to cascade all over the layout after they hit the back wall. That will more than likely be a random throw.

So the bottom line: To have a chance at a controlled shot, do not just pick up the dice and throw them. You must take a pause and aim them. This part of the controlled throw is often forgotten by some dice controllers, and they then wonder why their results are off. So, again, aim those dice!

The Proper Backswing

A right-handed shooter stands to the left of the stickman, while a left-handed shooter stands to the right of the stickman. The throw is like a short pendulum. After the aim, you gently bring back your arm about four to 10 inches and then bring it forward. The dice will come out of your hand naturally in an arc of about 45 degrees.

A right-handed shooter trying to shoot from the right side of the stickman or a left-handed shooter trying to shoot from the left side of the stickman is attempting a much more difficult throw. Because you can't really perform the pendulum swing when your body is positioned that way, more muscles come into play on the throw—the more muscles involved, the more difficult the throw will be. Can this kind of throw work? Yes, it can; but it takes a long, long time to master it. Stick with the pendulum swing in the beginning.

Proper Release of the Dice

If the grip is right and the thumb is placed properly and if the pendulum swing is there, the dice will come out of your fingers without any effort whatsoever. Even though we sometimes talk about throwing the dice, in reality we aren't throwing anything. The dice are simply reacting to the pendulum movement—they come out without you seemingly doing anything.

If the dice are not coming out correctly (they may just head down and slap the table right in front of you) or if the dice are not spinning properly or at all, then your grip is off or you are gripping those dice way too hard. You might also be trying to push the dice out of your hand as if you are throwing them.

The release problem can be a real pain in the neck, because some shooters just can't let nature take its course and allow those dice to do what they "want" to do as the pendulum swing moves forward. If you have this problem, it will take some work to train your brain to let those dice do what they would do if you allowed them to do it.

The Backward Dice Spin

If the dice are spinning forward, when they hit the table, they keep their momentum and hit the back wall hard. They will then bounce off and bing and bang and hop and skip all over the layout; certainly not much of a controlled throw in that scenario.

However, if the dice are spinning backward, when they hit the table, that spin slows down the dice and also allows some energy on those dice to be released into the table with a loss of much of the momentum in doing so.

The pendulum swing automatically sets up the dice for a backward spin of the dice. If you allow the dice to come out normally, you will find they sail into the air at around a 45-degree angle; they'll hit the table, lose energy, bounce to the back wall, hit it, and settle back softly. Such a throw is a controlled one.

Soft Hit Off the Back Wall

Power and speed are great in boxing, mixed martial arts, baseball, football, basketball, soccer, tennis, and horse racing. Power and speed stink in dice control. The harder you release the dice and the faster they zoom through the air to explode against the back wall, the worse it will be for your results—you'll be a totally random roller just like most of the other craps players in the world.

Those dice must hit the back wall softly. We do not want that back wall to rebound too much energy on those dice. It is the energy on the dice before they hit the back wall that determines how much energy will be released and rebounded by the back wall.

You want the dice to glance off the back wall, losing so much energy that they basically die several inches from the back wall.

How Do I Know I Have an Edge?

There are two types of dice control, as I stated in the opening of this chapter, and each can be proven using different tools. Because you are looking at avoiding the 7, you should look at how to prove to yourself you really do have the skill to beat the game.

In a random game of craps, the 7 shows up on average six times every 36 rolls. So a 7-to-rolls ratio (SRR) would be one 7 per six rolls or an SRR of 1-to-6. Anything over that would indicate that you are controlling the dice. Certainly you will need maybe 5,000 or more rolls to feel secure that your edge actually exists and isn't just variance in randomness. Most of the elite dice controllers I know have done between 10,000 and 20,000 rolls before they were confident they were actually changing the probabilities of the game.

What if you have an SRR of 1-to-6.2 or one 7 per 6.2 rolls? Is that a good SRR? The following chart will give you an idea of what Place bets you can beat, given certain SRRs. We will assume that all the numbers are equally filled in with the reduction of the 7, though that is not necessarily what happens:

Place Bet	SRR
6 and 8	1-to-6.2
5 and 9	1-to-6.5
4 and 10	1-to-6.7
Buy 4 or 10 for $25 with $1 vig on win only	1-to-6.2

Here is a sample of SRRs needed to overcome different Pass/Come bets with odds. The assumption is the Come-Out roll and first placement of Come bets are random and that all numbers are equally filled in while reducing the appearance of the 7 during the point cycle. The percentages in the boxes are your edges:

SRR	No Odds	1X Odds	2X Odds	5X Odds	10X Odds
1-to-6.5	1.6%	3.3%	4%	4.8%	5.2%
1-to-7	4.5%	7.1%	8.2%	9.5%	10.1%
1-to-8	9.5%	14%	15.8%	17.9%	19%

A second way to judge your dice-control skills is to use the software program SmartCraps, created by Dan Pronovost. This software will tell you not only what your edge is, but will determine whether you have poor, good, or excellent on-axis control. The individuals who pass the three tests in SmartCraps are often told to use other dice sets to increase their edges over the house on certain numbers.

As you can see, dice control is not a matter of belief. There are real methods to mathematically prove whether you have or don't have the skill. You can't fool yourself in this.

Also, keep in mind that once those dice leave your hand, powerful forces are working to randomize them, so your edge will not be huge. But an edge is an edge, and it is better to play with an edge over the casino than to play when the casino has an edge over you.

Betting With Dice Control

This isn't hard. You must make a Pass Line bet, take Odds when the Point is established, and then use the Come with Odds or place the 6 and 8. Don't be on more than three numbers at the start of your roll, and don't be afraid to be only on two or even one. You can increase your bets and the number of bets you have once you have made some good money. (What is *good* money? Make it three times your initial spread!)

How Much Money Can I Win With Dice Control?

Billions! Thousands of billions! You'll be able to pay off the trillions in debt of the United States, Canada, and Europe.

Come on, you'd think I was nuts if I tried to sell that idea to you! No advantage technique can promise millions of dollars in wins, because most players don't have giant bankrolls to start their advantage-play careers, and you win money in proportion to how much money you bet and can *afford* to bet without getting a heart attack from worrying about losses.

What kinds of downs can your emotions handle? Be honest with yourself. And you can safely count on plenty of downs and losing streaks, some quite long, even if you become an elite dice controller. No professional baseball team has ever had a perfect season; the best teams all have plenty of losses. You will not win every time you get the dice or every time you play a session. I am friends with the best dice controllers in the world and, believe me, there are times when they want to crawl into their rooms and go into hibernation after losing streaks.

The edges at dice control, while far higher than at blackjack, are not so monumental that you are going to turn a few hundred dollars into a few billion in a few trips. The time spent by even the best elite dice controllers in the casinos is not all that great either. A normal dice controller might go to the casinos about once per month. At my peak of play, I went to the casinos 130 times in a year. Now I go a third as much. (Hey, my wife, the beautiful A.P., and I would rather be with the grandkids than in a casino!)

I would recommend, strongly and even stronger than that, to make dice control and card counting and any other advantage-play technique an avocation, not a job.

And here is some advice from my own personal experience: don't get too greedy. I have been banned from casinos and from one whole state because I was hitting the casinos in those areas like the great white shark was eating those swimmers in *Jaws*.

Have some fun, win some money...but don't let it go to your head.

And for those of you who have an obsessive-compulsive gambling addiction, you will never become a good dice controller or card counter because you crave the action too much. You can never beat the casino if you can't contain your desire to throw your money away. For you, seek self-control, not dice control, before you ever set foot in a casino again.

Take the Next Steps in Craps Advantage Play

Dice control can get you good edges against the house, but there are levels to learning it. Much like going to school, you have elementary school, high school, college, and graduate school. You can win money just by going to elementary school, but if you really want to take it big time to the casino, consider taking further steps up the ladder of your dice-control avocation. The following are books, DVDs, software, and other resources, including the Golden Touch website, where dice controllers and other serious craps players meet and mingle and talk to each other about the game they love.

Books:

Casino Craps: Shoot to Win! by Frank Scoblete with Dominator ($19.95)

This book comes with a DVD showing the great Dominator rolling the dice, and it will open the door to all aspects of savvy craps play and skilled dice control by showing you multiple dice sets, proper techniques, and betting styles in pictures and words. You'll learn how to "push the house" to get better games than the casino advertises and even how to get a monetary edge without using dice control.

Learn money-management systems for aggressive and conservative players, in addition to team play and camouflage. Enjoy reading the full story of the greatest roll in craps history and join the Five Horsemen—Jerry "Stickman," Nick@Night, John "Skinny," the Dominator, and me, Frank Scoblete—on one of our extended trips to Las Vegas. (Available at bookstores, Amazon.com, or by calling 1-800-944-0406.)

Cutting Edge Craps: Advanced Strategies for Serious Players! by Frank Scoblete with Dominator ($16.95)

This book contains information about craps that has never been written about before, including dice correspondence, double-flips, the V-Spread, and how the back wall can react as if it is flat with double-point hits and single-point pops. This book analyzes the highest levels of on-axis dice control and includes radical, mathematically proven betting styles.

Discover the Hardway Set anomaly; learn how to handle various types of layout surfaces, some requiring radical changes in shooting styles; and how to keep yourself calm and relaxed as you take on the casinos. Also enjoy the stories behind Dominator and Frank's amazingly wonderful, then awful weekend in Las Vegas. And finally, experience the Captain's 147-roll hand, the longest roll ever recorded for a controlled shooter. (Available at bookstores, Amazon.com, or by calling 1-800-944-0406.)

DVD:

Beat Craps by Controlling the Dice, written and narrated by Frank Scoblete ($299)

Seeing is believing! In this unedited professional DVD—yes, *unedited*, meaning *all* throws are shown!—watch four of the greatest dice controllers in the world do their thing: Dominator, Jerry "Stickman," Bill "Ace-10" Burton, and me. You'll see our dice rolls from all angles, also in slow motion, and you'll be able to go step by step through the mechanics of the throw with the world's elite. (Available from Amazon.com or by calling 1-866-SET-DICE.)

Software:

SmartCraps, created and developed by Dan Pronovost ($129)

All aspects of craps can be analyzed using this software, including whether you have an edge, what that edge is, and what dice sets to use in order to exploit that edge. Available by calling 1-866-SET-DICE or via download from http://www.gamblersoutpost.com/?p=687&c=32&cn=Computer+Software&pn=Smart+Craps+Professional%2C+download.

Website:

The Golden Touch private website at www.goldentouchcraps.com has more than 5,000 members, with message boards about craps, get-togethers, other games, and much more.

Dice-Control Classes:

Golden Touch dice-control classes are usually given five or six times each year in the following venues: Atlantic City, Las Vegas, Tunica/Memphis, and Chicago. These two-day classes will teach players everything they need to know to go into the casino and play with an edge. The instructors are the best dice controllers in the world. Call 1-866-SET-DICE or go to www.goldentouchcraps.com for more information.

CHAPTER 21

Goodbye to the Legends: The Captain, the Arm, and Jimmy P.

I am obviously a strong advocate of dice control, the ability of some players—through skill and training—to influence the dice, reduce the house edge, and even get the edge over some bets at the game of craps.

As I wrote earlier in this book, I learned about this in the late 1980s from the Captain, who first developed a method for shooting the dice with control in the modern casino, where the back wall is lined with foam-rubber pyramids to randomize the game.

Along with his friends Jimmy P. and the amazing woman known as the Arm, the Captain made a fortune playing craps from the late 1970s to 2008, when he retired at the age of 87. The Captain died in 2010 at the age of 89. When the great legends of history are born or die, nature seems to reflect their passing—there was a brutal snowstorm in New York City on the morning of his peaceful passing.

Although Atlantic City casinos are not allowed to ban players, these three had Tropworld (now Tropicana) so upset at their wins that the Trop executives sent out a flyer announcing the trio's substantial wins and how good they were at beating the game. Indeed, Tropworld told the Captain and his two mates that they were not welcomed, even though they couldn't ban them outright, and that he and his trio would no longer get any comps—which were in the tens of thousands of dollars.

The problem Tropworld had—but didn't realize that they had, for some unknown reason—was the fact that the Captain had a crew of 22 monstrously high rollers who were not dice controllers but "wild and crazy" gamblers who were losing far more than Jimmy P., the Arm, or the Captain were winning. When the Captain decided to switch casinos, his high-rolling crew moved with him.

With the exception of Satch, now a dice-control instructor in Golden Touch Craps, and me, the Captain's crew are all gone to that craps game in the sky.

The Arm was the greatest dice controller I have ever seen, even better than the greatest dice controllers playing today. She had a unique throw and a consistency that was amazing. She had the uncanny ability to hit the same number over and over again. In those days, we did not count the actual number of rolls before a seven out; we only counted the time the roll took. Sadly I'll never know how many numbers she hit on her greatest rolls, but she did have many that went much longer than one hour.

I wrote about the Captain and the Arm beginning in 1990. And boy, did I take a beating from skeptical craps players, other gambling writers, casino executives, and even some dealers.

I felt like John the Baptist "crying out in the wilderness" when I wrote about their technique for beating the game. Except for a small group of players, dice control was considered ridiculous, and I was considered if not an outright scammer, a complete dolt for believing in it and writing about it.

Times have changed. Now there are many gambling writers who have witnessed the success of the Golden Touch dice-control shooters and have seen just how effective this technique can be in the hands of a skillful player. Many different schools have opened up that teach their versions of dice control. Some of these schools are teaching a competent throw; some of these schools, run by bloated windbags, are cut-rate and totally incompetent. Golden Touch teaches the best throw based on the Captain's throw, a technique that can be learned and executed with practice and discipline.

Even the casinos have seen some of the good dice controllers beat them. Indeed some of the casinos have reacted—that is, totally *over-reacted*—to this new phenomenon that has hit their tables. They have harassed and even banned some of the better players.

That is a shame for a couple of reasons. I am guessing that only about 10 percent of the people who attempt dice control get good enough to beat the casinos. And what percentage of the millions of craps players even bother? Maybe a fraction of a percent of that total number. Most craps players have the loser's mentality: *I enjoy playing even if I lose money.*

Sorry, most craps players are completely wrong in their approach to the game. The Captain believed the following statement: "Winning is the *most* fun!" Indeed it is.

Is the throw so hard to master that only 10 percent of those who try actually succeed? Not at all. Just about anyone—with time, discipline, and patience—can develop a good enough throw to overcome the low-house-edge bets at the game.

Sadly, an overwhelming majority of would-be dice controllers just can't stop making the worst bets at the game of craps, bets even a decent amount of skill can't overcome. Other dice controllers, those with the hearts of gamblers, just can't get themselves to practice on a regular basis to get their skill level into the *competent* range. They want everything to come easily. It isn't going to happen.

So casinos that have reacted proactively have hurt their bottom lines the way Tropworld hurt its bottom line. Many shooters who try to look like dice controllers at a table are not really capable of winning in the long run.

In fact, when players see a dice controller have an amazing session, those players don't walk away with their wins, never to play again. Instead they play more and more in order to duplicate such an exciting experience, ultimately failing miserably as the math of the game eats them up. Indeed, good dice controllers might even be considered a new kind of shill for the casinos, inspiring the losing ones to play the game even more than they would have normally.

Yes, the three we have to thank for this dice-control revolution in the game of craps are the greatest craps players of all time: craps master legend the Captain, along with his first mate Jimmy P. and the greatest dice controller who ever rolled dem bones—the amazing woman known as the Arm.

We won't see their like again. May they enjoy the great eternal craps game in the sky.

CHAPTER 22
Spin Roulette Gold

It probably all started this way: Maximus the Murderous stood on yonder high hill holding his golden shield and eyeing the village down the slope in the valley, known as the Meadows.

He haughtily looked at the sniveling leprotic slave who was bowing and scraping before him. "Spin my shield, oh stinking, slovenly, unpleasant, leprous one, so that I mighteth understandeth the will of the supreme gods." The bellowing Maximus then handed his shield over to Hopelesseebus the Horrible, who bowed even lower, took the shield, and spun it with all his might, losing part of a decayed finger as he did so.

Around and around the shield spun as the legion of battle-scarred soldiers watched Maximus, wanting to know what he would do when the spinning golden shield stopped. On the golden shield was a pointed crown. When the shield stopped spinning, if the crown's point faced the village of Meadows, the legions of Maximus the Murderous would attack the Meadows, laying everyone and everything to waste; but if the crown's point faced toward the opposite side, the rugged mountains, Maximus would still attack the village, laying waste to everything, but he would also slaughter the disgusting one, Hopelesseebus the Horrible, for spinning the wheel wrong! The soldiers were rooting for the shield to face the mountains, because they were all grossed out by Hopelesseebus the Horrible and his erupting skin sores. Hopelesseebus the Horrible was also the legion's cook.

No matter how you sliced it, spun it, or analyzed it, the Meadows' villagers were screwed royally because the murderous one had greedily eyed them, and that spinning golden shield became the instrument that dictated their fate—in this case, death.

And so roulette was born...or maybe not, but the game certainly came to us from ancient times and places.

The game of roulette has wiped out the money of many more villagers, both peasants and aristocracy, than any single casino game. Over the centuries, aristocrats fell to peasantry by playing it. Medieval times saw casinos built in France where the hanky-sniffing Europeans tried out their various systems to beat the game as the game hammered them into poverty.

Today roulette is the third-most-popular table game in the casinos, behind blackjack and craps, and its popularity seems to be steadfast. In both Las Vegas and Atlantic City, roulette pits have many wheels—and many players risking their money at those wheels. It is a rare casino that does not have roulette tables.

So why does roulette have a strong following? I think there are five reasons.

1. **Tradition:** There is little doubt that when you play roulette you get a feeling that you are a part of a long tradition. While all casino games have histories, roulette players seem to plug into roulette's history more than do craps, blackjack, or baccarat players.

2. **Elegance:** The game is leisurely; players are given time to think about what they are going to do. There is a sense of civility when playing this game, although there are some uncouth players who push, shove, and throw tantrums during the game—but these players are considered the peasants. Also, even in low-limit games, there are so many special roulette chips filling the layout that the game appears to have tons of money being wagered on it.

3. **Systems:** If you want to test or play your system, roulette is a great game, because you have so many "even-money" bets that feel as if they are close contests, allowing such systems to work. (They aren't close contests, but truth has never stopped a gambler.)

4. **Opportunity:** Many gamblers like the idea of huge payoffs, and certainly roulette offers such payoffs on a host of bets. With

payouts as high as 35-to-1, you can see why many roulette players are in dreamland when they think of this game.

5. **Anticipation:** All gamblers at all games experience the delight of anticipation before the dice are thrown, the cards are dealt, the reels are spun...but roulette players seem to have anticipation in spades! Because the game is leisurely, because the players are given plenty of time to make their decisions (you'll rarely see roulette dealers rushing players as they often rush them at blackjack and craps), the adrenaline can flow freely through the body, giving the player that delicious sense that *something important is about to happen*. I think a part of the thrill of gambling and the thrill specifically of roulette is just such anticipation. If a player didn't care about what was about to happen, he probably wouldn't play.

Can Roulette Be Beaten?

Back when, yes. Now, probably not.

When roulette wheels were strictly mechanical devices whose performances were not analyzed very often, biased wheels—that is, wheels that caused certain numbers to come up more than probability indicates—existed, and really smart players could get substantial edges at such wheels. Such biased wheels had deep pockets, so once the ball was settling in, it settled in quickly. The stories you hear of banks being "broken" in Monaco and Las Vegas and Atlantic City are all stories based on the existence of biased wheels in those venues.

Sadly for the players, and happily for the casinos, today's roulette wheels are superb machines, with shallow pockets so the ball tends to bounce around like crazy, and these wheels are constantly being analyzed to make sure they have no defects. No defects = good for the casino, bad for the advantage player.

Biased wheels might still exist at times here and there, but spending countless hours "tracking" wheels to find that needle in the haystack isn't going to be appealing to most roulette players or readers of this book. It is just too time-consuming for the casual player. Actually, it is probably a severe waste of time.

There is a belief, which I tend to give credence to, that some dealers can hit segments of the wheel they are aiming for. Lately, seeing the youth of the dealers, I am beginning to think this "skill," if it ever did exist, is not one to be found in casinos today. Well, maybe somewhere out there are dealers who can still do this. I haven't run into any lately. So while this could be an advantage-play technique, you'd have to find a dealer who could do it and one who would want to do it *for you!*

The Game

There are two types of roulette wheels—the "American wheel," which was developed in Europe, and the "European wheel," which was developed in America. No, I didn't screw up the above sentence. What they use in Europe, America invented; and what is used in America, Europe invented. Such is the way of the world. The American wheel has two green pockets labeled *0* and *00*, along with pockets labeled *1* through *36*; the European wheel has only one green *0* but also has pockets labeled *1* through *36*. The European wheel is the preferred one because the house edge is 2.7 percent or an expected loss of $2.70 per $100 wagered; while on the American wheel, the house edge is 5.26 percent or an expected loss of $5.26 per $100 wagered.

The table and wheel of roulette resemble a sperm...no kidding...with the large wheel on top and a long layout connected to it. The wheel is divided into three sections:

1. The backtrack, with the groove where the ball is spun
2. The bottom track, where the ball falls when it leaves the backtrack
3. The wheel head, with the pockets in which the ball lands

Roulette balls, like dice in craps, come in different sizes, and modern roulette tables often have two balls assigned to them—a large one and a small one. Note that when the ball is spinning on the bottom track, there are "bumpers" that make a clean descent into the wheel head almost impossible. These bumpers are to prevent any manipulation of where the ball will land, and they help keep the game random.

Unlike the other casino games, roulette has its own chips. Although you can use regular casino chips at roulette, the casino prefers the special roulette chips, which come in an assortment of colors and have no denominations printed on them. When you buy in, you tell the dealer what size denomination you want your chips to be, and they will make a note of it as they give you whatever color is available. You'll be the only player at the table with that color. This makes paying out all the bets easier for the dealers.

The players make their bets, and at a certain point the dealer starts spinning the ball. As the ball goes around and around the wheel, players can still make bets, but then the dealer will say, "No more bets!" and all betting must immediately stop.

Once the ball lands in a pocket, the dealer calls out the number and its color, puts a marker on the winner, and then collects all the losing bets. Once the losing bets are collected, the dealer will pay off all the winning bets, and the process begins again.

The Wheel Isn't What You Think

One, two, three, four, five, six, seven, eight...sorry, that's not how it goes on a roulette wheel.

Take a look at the American Double-Zero Wheel, and you'll note that no numbers run in normal strings; now take a look at the betting layout, and all the numbers run in their correct strings. Huh? What's going on here?

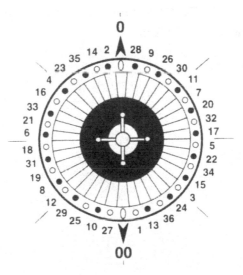

The American Roulette Wheel
Taken from "Action Play Roulette Tracker" Card

Through the generations, roulette proprietors worried about players discovering biased numbers and sections of the wheel and then playing them. Many roulette players really enjoy playing groups of numbers, and many players actually think the group of numbers they are playing are on the wheel as they are on the layout...you know—one, two, three, four, five, six, and so on...but playing groups of numbers on the layout is meaningless if the intention is to see the ball land in a specific area of the wheel where those numbers congregate, because there is no area of the wheel where these groups of numbers congregate.

Let's take a look at how the Double-Zero Wheel is numbered:

- There are 38 pockets numbered 1 to 36 and 0 and 00.
- Half the numbers are red (open *o* on diagram) and half are black (black *o* on diagram).
- The 0 and 00 are green or sometimes blue.
- Almost directly across from an even number is the next odd number. You can see this by looking at the diagram.
- The 19 and 18 are the closest consecutive numbers on the wheel, separated by the number 31. So if 18, 31, and 19 are hitting frequently, maybe this is a biased section.
- Pairs of even numbers alternate with pairs of odd numbers, except when split by the 0 and the 00.
- The colors of the numbers on the wheel correspond to the colors of the numbers on the layout.

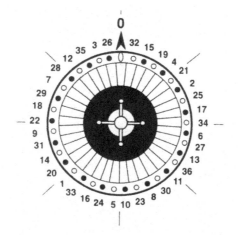

The European Roulette Wheel
Taken from "Action Play Roulette Tracker" Card

The European Single-Zero Wheel is structured somewhat differently than the American Double-Zero Wheel, because it has only one green or blue 0. The numbers on the wheel do not correspond to the numbers on the layout, and their actual placement on the wheel is somewhat different. Just take a look, and you will see that some of the numbers are closer together than on the American Wheel, but they aren't so close as to make it easy to spot biased wheels.

The Bets of Roulette
Inside Bets

The Straight-Up Bet (French: *En Plein*): You bet one or more individual numbers. If your number hits, you are paid 35-to-1, meaning $35 for every $1 wagered. If you bet other numbers as well, these would be losers. The house edge on the Double-Zero Wheel is 5.26 percent, and on the Single-Zero Wheel it is 2.70 percent.

Split Bet (French: *A Cheval*): You place your wager on the line between two numbers, and if either of these numbers comes up, you are paid 17-to-1. The house edge on the Double-Zero Wheel is 5.26 percent, and on the Single-Zero Wheel it is 2.70 percent.

The Street Bet, also called **Three-Number Bet, Side Bet,** or **Trio (French: *Transversale*):** You are betting that any one of three numbers hits. You place your chips on the outside border of the three numbers. If you win, you are paid off at 11-to-1. The house edge on the Double-Zero Wheel is 5.26 percent, and on the Single-Zero Wheel it is 2.70 percent.

The Corner, Square, or **Four-Number Bet (French: *Carre*):** You are betting that one of four numbers will hit on the next spin. This wager can only be accepted on those numbers that form a square. You place your bet on the intersection where all four numbers meet. A winning bet pays 8-to-1. The house edge on the Double-Zero Wheel is 5.26 percent, and on the Single-Zero Wheel it is 2.70 percent.

The Five-Number Bet (French: *Les Monster-o-So-Awful!*): Okay, okay, there is no French word for this bet, because it can only be made on the American Double-Zero Wheel. You are betting that one of the top five numbers—0, 00, 1, 2, or 3—will hit on the next spin. You place your bet where the line between the 0 and the 3 meets the border of the layout. The bet pays off at 6-to-1. The house edge on the Double-Zero

Wheel is 7.89 percent, and on the Single-Zero Wheel it is time for a coffee break, monsieur.

Word of Advice: *If you want to bet those specific five numbers of Les Monster-o-So Awful, do each one individually, and you bring the house edge back down to 5.26 percent.*

The Line Bet, Six-Number Bet, or **Sixline Bet (French: *Sixain*):** The bet is placed on the outside borders of the six numbers you wish to bet. It is placed on the line that separates the two sets of numbers. This bet pays off at 5-to-1. The house edge on the Double-Zero Wheel is 5.26 percent, and on the Single-Zero Wheel it is 2.70 percent.

Outside Bets

The Column Bet (French: *Colonne*): This is a single bet that one number within one of the three columns will hit. You place this bet at the bottom of the column you wish to wager on. The 0 and 00 are not considered part of any column. The bet pays off at 2-to-1. The house edge on the Double-Zero Wheel is 5.26 percent, and on the Single-Zero Wheel it is 2.70 percent.

The Dozens Bet (French: *Douzaine*): You are betting that within a dozen consecutive numbers on the layout, your number will hit. Mind you, this does not mean a dozen consecutive numbers on the wheel—just those on the layout. You make the bet in the area that says *First Dozen* or *Second Dozen* or *Third Dozen*. You are paid off at 2-to-1. The house edge on the Double-Zero Wheel is 5.26 percent, and on the Single-Zero Wheel it is 2.70 percent.

The Odd and Even Bets (French: *Impair et Pair*): Place this bet where it says—come on, take a guess—correct, *Odd* or *Even*. There are 18 odd numbers and 18 even numbers. On the Double-Zero Wheel there are 18 ways to win and 20 ways to lose, while on the Single-Zero Wheel there are 18 ways to win and 19 ways to lose. The 0 and 00 are two numbers against you, giving the house its edge. The bet pays off at 1-to-1. The house edge on the Double-Zero Wheel is 5.26 percent, and on the Single-Zero Wheel it is 2.70 percent.

High or Low Bets (French: *Passe et Manque*): This bet is placed in the boxes marked either *1 to 18* or *19 to 36*. You are betting whether the high numbers or the low numbers will hit. There are 18 ways to win and 20 ways to lose on the Double-Zero Wheel, while there are 18 ways to win and 19 ways to lose on the Single-Zero Wheel. The house edge on the Double-Zero Wheel is 5.26 percent, and on the Single-Zero Wheel it is 2.70 percent.

Red or Black Bets (French: *Rouge et Noir*): This is an even-money bet (1-to-1) with the same odds of winning as the High or Low bets. This bet is placed on the area of the table that shows...all right, seriously, where would the bet be placed? On the head of the person sitting next to you? Or on the layout that shows *Red or Black?* I vote for Red or Black. The house edge on the Double-Zero Wheel is 5.26 percent, and on the Single-Zero Wheel it is 2.70 percent.

Two Helpful Additions to the Game

There is good news for those of you who were sick of reading the following sentence about the above bets: "The house edge on the Double-Zero Wheel is 5.26 percent, and on the Single-Zero Wheel it is 2.70 percent." Some casinos—perhaps inspired by divine providence—offer an element that really reduces the house edge on the outside bets of Even-Odd, High-Low, and Red-Black.

Some casinos will return half your bet if the 0 or 00 hits. This is called "Surrender." This option reduces the house edge in the Double-Zero game to 2.63 percent—not so great, but still twice as good as the 5.26 percent on all the other bets. Many casinos that have this option do not advertise it, so always ask the casino dealer if this option holds true for their game. Then never, ever, make any other bet at roulette except the ones mentioned in the previous paragraph.

The Single-Zero Wheel, as played in Europe, has a variation of the Surrender option called *en prison*. When the 0 hits, all the bets on the Even-Odd, High-Low, and Red-Black are imprisoned. They are not lost, but they cannot be won. That's the European haiku that translates thusly: the next spin of the wheel after the bet is put in prison either liberates the bet for the player to take back, or it loses the bet (which means the casino takes the bet). If the 0 should hit while your bet is in prison, nothing happens, but then the bet must hit two consecutive times for it to be liberated. The en prison rule lowers the house edge on the Single-Zero wheel to 1.35 percent, and that is a good bet—the best one you'll probably ever find at a roulette table.

CHAPTER 23

Getting the Best of Roulette

The system most favored by ploppy gamblers is to bet with the trend; their next-favorite system is to bet against the trend. One of the great enjoyments of my casino playing career is to watch two players at the same table playing each of the above systems—one player going with the trend, the other player going against the trend. One player will think his system works (at least for that session), and one player will feel deflated (at least for that session). In some sessions, both players lose! That's the most fun.

Trend bettors are rife in all casino games, and they are rife in roulette too. Human beings want to know what the future holds, and so we tend to look at the past as not only a prelude to the future but as a prophetic event heralding the future. In random games there is no prophecy going on, just the working out of probability. There is no fate, only numbers working themselves out in their cold, hard fashion.

Trends can only be "predicted" for past events, but sadly none of us can go backward in time to bet on what has already happened. We're all going forward in time, and nothing has yet been set in stone to give us confidence in our future bets. Randomness in casino games doesn't give you a chance for accurate predictions. In such games, you gamble based on hope and nothing more. But hope does spring eternal in the gamblers' chests, and it also drains their bankrolls.

Let me give you a little reversal on my trend-betting skepticism. I think trend betting is great at random games, and I really don't care if you are betting with the trend that has just occurred or against it. *Wait,* you think, *has Scoblete just gone crazy?* No, no, just follow my reasoning. I'm crazy like a...like something that seems crazy but isn't.

If you use my positive trend-betting system, you will reduce the hit on your bankroll from roulette's powerful 5.26 house edge on the Double-Zero Wheel and its far better, but still bad, hit of 2.70 percent on the Single-Zero Wheel. You will use trend betting to *reduce* the number of total spins you wager on. Fewer spins wagered = better for the player.

Here's how to do it.

Because just about all casinos today have scoreboards that show you the last 16 to 20 numbers that have hit, you don't even have to use pen and paper anymore.

First let's take a look at outside betting. You can use the following on High-Low, Odd-Even, or Red-Black. I'll use Red-Black as an example.

Buy in, and then wait to see which color comes up (the green 0 or 00 does not count—except to add to your losses over time), then bet that color.

If that color comes up again and you win your bet, continue to bet that color. The moment you lose the bet, sit out the next spin. Wait for the next color and then bet that color. You always wait one spin before betting the color after losing a bet. We'll make your bets $10.

Let's take a look at how this would work:

Positive Trend Betting

Bet/Color	Color	Win or Lose	Total
0	red	0	0
$10 on red	red	win $10	$10
$10 on red	red	win $10	$20
$10 on red	black	lose $10	$10
0	red	0	$10
$10 on red	black	lose $10	0
0	black	0	0
$10 on black	black	win $10	$10
$10 on black	black	win $10	$20
$10 on black	black	win $10	$30

Bet/Color	Color	Win or Lose	Total
$10 on black	red	lose $10	$20
0	black	0	$20
$10 on black	red	lose $10	$20
0	black	0	$10
$10 on black	red	lose $10	0
0	red	0	0
$10 on red	red	win $10	$10
$10 on red	black	lose $10	0
0	red	0	0

Let's take a look at my "negative" trend-betting system. You wait for a color to come up, and then you bet *against* that color. If you win the bet, you continue to bet on that same color until you lose. Then you wait out a spin, and on the next spin you bet against whatever color came up on the spin before that.

Negative Trend Betting

Bet/Color	Color	Win or Lose	Total
0	red	0	0
$10 on black	red	lose $10	- $10
0	red	0	- $10
$10 on black	black	win $10	0
$10 on black	black	win $10	+$10
$10 on black	black	win $10	+$20
$10 on black	red	lose $10	+$10
0	black	0	+$10
$10 on red	black	lose $10	0
0	black	0	0
$10 on red	red	win $10	+$10
$10 on red	black	lose $10	0
0	red	0	0
$10 on black	red	lose $10	-$10

Bet/Color	Color	Win or Lose	Total
0	red	0	-$10
$10 on black	black	win $10	0
$10 on black	black	win $10	+$10
$10 on black	red	lose $10	0
0	black	0	0

Finding Biased Wheels

There was a day when I could safely put roulette players on the path to finding real biased wheels, thus giving them a real mathematical advantage. That day is no longer *this* day. While some biased wheels may still exist in out-of-the-way casinos hidden in the backwoods of areas where there are a lot of backwoods, I truly doubt that today's casinos have biased wheels.

However, do not let that stop you from playing wheels by using bias-identification principles. As Shakespeare's Macbeth stated, "Nothing is but what is not."

Yes, I am telling you to look for biased wheels, even if biased wheels don't exist, for a simple reason—you have to have some reason for betting what you are betting and, who knows, maybe by using bias-identification principles you might just stumble on a wheel that is actually biased. (That is a big *maybe,* I agree.)

So how do you look for biased wheels? In the past you would watch thousands of spins and clock the numbers—you might spend a couple or more days doing this. If you found a certain number or numbers coming up way out of proportion to their probability, you would wager on these numbers.

Most casino players are not going to drive or fly to a casino and spend a couple or more days clocking wheels to see if they are really biased. But you can do a modified version of this technique.

Check out the scoreboard and see if any one number or series of numbers in the same area of the wheel is hitting. Sure, you only have 16 to 20 examples, but so what? If you're playing a random game, which you probably are, you would use some selection principle even if it were only, "Um, I'll bet, ah, 16 for the hell of it!" Unthinking selection in a random game of roulette is the same as thinking selection. So use thinking selection, as it makes the upcoming results more exciting because your anticipation will be greater. Anytime you think, you want verification that your thinking is correct.

What we want to find on the wheel are numbers that congregate together—say in four-to-eight-number groupings or numbers that are repeating and/or numbers that are repeating within the four-to-eight-number grouping.

Check out the bold and italicized numbers in the following scoreboard examples. The bold shows numbers within an eight-number frame, the italics show repeating numbers, and the bold/italics show repeating numbers within an eight-number frame. I've also put stars next to repeating numbers as well.

I'll get into how to bet these groupings or repeating numbers and/or repeating numbers that are in these groupings. You'll have to give serious consideration to bankroll requirements, because you will be betting on more than one number and perhaps as many as eight numbers.

Okay, let's take a look of some scoreboards and what numbers came up:

Scoreboard No. 1:	Scoreboard No. 2
*13	*22
1	*7
27	*0
*25	31
26	*14
*25	*22
5	6
6	*15
10	17
00	*0
35	*14
30	26
11	*7
17	*22
4	*15
*13	*7

On scoreboard No. 1, we have a strong grouping of six numbers—13, 1, 27, 25, 10, and 00—with two repeating numbers: the 25 and 13. Break up your betting as follows: one unit on the nonrepeating numbers in the group and two units on the repeating numbers. If you do not want to bet that much, you have two choices: go to one unit on all the numbers or just bet the two repeating numbers.

On scoreboard No. 2, we have several repeating numbers but not a strong enough grouping of numbers. Therefore we would only bet on the repeating numbers.

Number	Appearances	Betting Recommendation
22	three	two units
14	two	one unit
15	two	one unit
7	three	two units
0	two	one unit

As play continues, at some point these groups might disappear, and/ or the repeating numbers might disappear as well. That would be the time to quit and go to another table and check out the numbers on the scoreboard there. However, if the groupings continue to show and/or the repeating numbers continue to show, then continue playing.

Obviously, you'll have to decide how much you can afford to bet in this system. If betting all the numbers in a group is too much, then bet four or three or two. The same holds true for the repeating numbers. Because this is really not an advantage-play system, do not overextend your betting amounts. Stay contained.

Handling Those Other Bets at Roulette

Certainly there are many other bets at roulette, but they are all—as I call them—"layout bets." Not one of them is looking for anything other than a quick hit of luck. Okay, my strategies above are also looking for a hit of luck too, but...agree with me on this...they just seem more powerful (even if they aren't). The trend betting I advocate on the outside bets reduces the hit on your total bankroll by quite a lot.

The other outside bets, such as the Dozens and Columns, can also be trend-betted (is that a phrase?). Just follow the numbers; so if a number from the First Column appears, bet that column—or bet against that column. You decide. Then sit out a spin and see what column comes up next and bet for or against that column. Betting like this will also save you a lot of money. The same betting scheme works for the Dozens. You'll save money, have some fun, and not fall into the roulette trap that destroyed all those European aristocrats down through the ages.

Some Legendary Roulette Wins (All in Dollars)

Person/Team	Year	Venue	Amount Won
Joseph H. Jagger	1873	Monte Carlo	$325,000
"The Italians"	1880	Monte Carlo	$160,000
W. N. Darnborough	1911	Monte Carlo	$415,000
Hibbs and Walford	1947–48	Las Vegas and Reno	$40,000
Helmut Berlin Team	1951	Mar del Plata	$420,000
"Jones Boys"	1958	Las Vegas	$32,000
Dr. R. Jarecki	1971	Monte Carlo and San Remo	$1,250,000
P. Basieux Team	1981	Bad Wiesse	$153,000
Billy Walters	1986–89	Atlantic City and Las Vegas	$4,810,000

CHAPTER 24

For Two Days I Was the King of Casino Gambling!

When my kids, Greg and Mike, were growing up, they looked up to me. As little kids, they thought Dad knew everything—at least Dad knew everything that they asked about, which is all the important stuff in a little kid's life. Yes, I strode through their little lives as a god among mere mortals.

Somewhere in their early teenage years it started to dawn on them that Dad didn't actually know everything; in fact, Dad *didn't* know a hell of a lot about everything. As happened with the American education system, Dad became "dumbed down." I lost the entire aura I had when I was that striding god. It was a long tumble. I went from knowing everything to knowing almost nothing. It was remarkable that I even knew how to feed myself, so low I had fallen in their esteem.

Now both Greg and Mike are adults. Yes, I am smarter now in their eyes than I was when they were teenagers, but I will never be as smart as I was when they were little kids. That's the way of the world, specifically the way of parenting. Start off big, fall a long way, then slowly climb as your children age, until you aren't dumb but you aren't a god either. At some point your kids look at you as a human being, which is, frankly, only what you are. There are no humans who are gods, despite what the Romans believed concerning their Caesars.

Ahh, I do have a shot at being in the divine intellectual category again—for a few years anyway—as my little grandson John Charles and little granddaughter Danielle look up to Grandpa Scobe and seem to listen to everything I say with rapt attention. Of course, I know that when they get older, they too will realize that Grandpa Scobe doesn't know very much about everything.

That is all a prelude, dear readers, to my gambling confession, which is—I don't know *everything* about gambling either.

Early in my gaming career, I thought I would tackle horse racing—but do it in a smart way by getting inside information. A certain individual who had "inside knowledge" started me off with a great pick for one of the Triple Crown races. "This horse can't lose. He'll blow away the field," said my source. I was convinced I would win a lot of money if I bet on this horse, so I bet *a lot* of money on this horse—with my wife, the beautiful A.P., saying, "I don't think you should bet that much on a horse. You don't know anything about horse racing."

"Honey," I said confidently, "this horse is going to blow away the field."

My horse did not blow away the field. Instead he broke his leg midway through the race and had to be put to sleep. He had been a superb animal but a miserable betting choice.

My inside source gave me two more "can't lose" tips, and I bet heavily on both. I explained to my wife, the beautiful A.P., "Don't worry, these horses can't lose!" when she fretted about how much I was putting on my horses' heads.

In the first of the two races my horse came bolting out of the starting gate and looked like he would destroy the field. However, at the first turn he decided he didn't want to continue the race and headed for the stables. All the other horses went around the track, but my "can't lose" horse just ran to the right and into the barns. The jockey was whipping him, yelling at him; the fans were jeering him merrily—and I lost the first of two very big bets.

Okay, two races, two horses that didn't finish. My third horse had to at least make it around the track, didn't he?

Don't bet on that.

My third horse looked a little weird—if horses can actually look weird—as he walked to the starting gate. He didn't want to go into the starting gate, but that is not unusual, as many horses don't like to go into the starting gate.

But when the race started, my horse leaped out of the starting gate and ran in a small circle, around and around as if chasing his tail, foaming at the mouth, bucking and kicking, and trying to throw the jockey, who was hanging on for dear life. The horse looked as if he had taken a massive dose of LSD. It took a whole bunch of people to settle the horse down and save the jockey. The horse then walked meekly back to the stables while the race proceeded without him.

Three horses, three nonfinishes, three big losses.

My horse-racing career was over. It is one thing to lose a race, but my horses couldn't even finish them. That had to be God telling me, "Scobe, no more betting on horse racing for you."

I am not sure anyone can beat the horses in the long run, although I have heard tales of some long-term winners, but I remain skeptical. Too much is involved in horses running around the track, not the least of which is the enormous vig you have to pay when you win those races. You also have no idea if the race is fixed, to put it bluntly. Obviously my horses didn't need to be "fixed," because they couldn't even get around the track, but horse players always talk about how the smaller races might actually be more like professional wrestling than real competition.

I have no idea, really. I don't want to have any idea, really. Because I really know that while horses are really the most beautiful of animals, betting on them racing around a track is not really in my cards. When it comes to horse racing, I am the father of teenagers—I have no glory, no glow, and no godliness. I am really just a dumb loser.

And that brings me to my professional roulette career—perhaps the shortest professional career in history—that saw me giving free rein to a budding, though short, hubris.

This was in the 1980s at the Sands Casino in Atlantic City—a casino that is now just a sandy stretch of empty lot, which could perhaps be said about my professional roulette career too.

I had never been in a casino before. I was waiting for my costar, Alene Paone (now my wife, the beautiful A.P.), to arrive in Atlantic City that Monday night. We were going to study the game of craps, because we

were both starring in a play, *The Only Game in Town*, about a degener-
ate craps player and the chorus girl he loves—which is when the two of
us fell in love, which is, surely, life imitating art. I knew nothing about
craps, and I had long monologues about the game. It's hard to give oomph
on stage to something you know nothing about. We decided to go to
Atlantic City to do research.

I arrived on Friday, so I had until Monday to beat roulette before my
lovely costar met me. I knew just how to do it. I had considered different
ways to bet, and I came up with one that I absolutely knew would work.
It couldn't fail.

After I checked in, I immediately went to the roulette tables to see if
any other players had discovered the secret of destroying the game. No
one—not one single person!—played the way I would play.

I walked around and scouted the players and realized my moment of
winning millions would start right then.

I went to a $5 roulette game. The maximum bet was $500.

I placed $5 on red. I won! My professional gambling career had started.
(Total: +$5.) Had I quit right then and there, I would be one of the few
players to ever beat the casinos at roulette in his career. But what gambler
stops when he is ahead after winning the very first bet? Probably none.

But my plan was not to make $5 bet after $5 bet after $5 bet and
winning all of them. I knew that I would not win on every spin of the
wheel. My winning plan was far cleverer than that. I didn't have to win
on every spin to come out ahead. I didn't even have to win on a majority
of the spins to finish ahead of the house.

I bet on red again, and it lost. (Total: 0)
I then bet $5 on red, and it lost again. (Total: -$5)
I bet $10 on red, and it won. (Total: +$5)
I bet $5 on red. I won again. (Total: +$10)
I bet $5 on red, and it lost. (Total: +$5)
I bet $10 on red, and it lost. (Total: -$5)
Then I bet $20 on red, and it lost. (Total: -$25)

I wasn't the least worried. I could not lose so many wagers that I
would end up losing my money. I would just keep doubling my bet until
I won. No one can lose every bet he ever makes, can he? Of course not.

Although I knew there was a limit to what I was allowed to bet, it would take a monstrous losing streak, one that would rarely happen.

My betting would go: $5, $10, $20, $40, $80, $160, $320. I would have to lose seven bets in a row to be a loser. I couldn't see that happening.

So I bet $40 on red, and it won! I was up $15! My brilliant plan was working like a charm. I would win even if I lost the majority of my bets. I was amazed that no one else had discovered this system before. It was foolproof. Maybe I discovered it because I was new to the game and, being new, could look at it in a different way. New eyes = new game.

I was up $15 when I looked at the scoreboard on the wheel across from me. There were nine blacks in a row on that scoreboard. Damn! I didn't expect to see that. Had I been betting black I would have lost.

Right then and there, the genius of Frank Scoblete was revealed, and I would become the king of roulette by modifying my system to fit the fact that nine of one color could indeed come up in a row, as that other scoreboard showed. But could it come up 10, 11, 12 times in a row? I doubted it.

I would not start betting on any one color until I saw a color come up five times in a row. I would then bet *against* the streak continuing. I knew that I could bet another seven hits against that color before I would lose. *No color is going to come up twelve times in a row!* My genius was in high gear at how quickly I had modified my wonderful system to take into account the fact that I had misjudged how long streaks could be. That was certainly my naivete; I just hadn't seen the game in action—only in the movies. I knew a lot more now. Oh, man, no wonder hubris (overweening pride) goes before the fall!

So I was $15 ahead, and I stopped playing at that table and walked around the roulette pit until I saw five of one color appear. I then bet $5 against that color appearing again.

My infallible system worked brilliantly all weekend long. The longest streak was 10 reds in a row, but I bet $80 against that red color coming up the 11th time, and I won. *Of course I won!*

I was ahead by about $300 come Monday afternoon. I decided I'd play one more session and then take a nap and wait for A.P. to arrive. I would treat us to a fine gourmet dinner with my winnings—the best food, the best wine, the best of everything. This gambling was easy and fun too.

And then the bolt from Zeus came from Mount Olympus to put this strutting peacock in his place. The gods love shooting you down when you stand atop a mountain and think you can challenge them.

I saw five blacks in a row, and here is what happened when I bet against black:

Color	Appearance	Amount Bet	Total Won/Lost
black	6th time	$5	-$5
black	7th time	$10	-$15
black	8th time	$20	-$35
black	9th time	$40	-$75
black	10th time	$80 (gulp)	-$155
black	11th time	$160 (choking)	-$315
black	12th time	$320 (angina)	-635
My face was red	Sweating forehead	Way too much	Way, way, too much

I was a little shook on that $80 loss because that had been the most I had wagered all weekend until that point, and I had won the previous $80 bet. But then I lost the $160 and the $320 bets, and I felt weak-kneed. How could my infallible system lose? And look at how much I lost! More than twice as much as I had won in the previous two days. How could that be? How could that be? I started the day up $300 and suddenly was down $335.

My professional roulette career ended then and there. That's when I learned, *There must be more to this gambling thing than I thought.*

The "Wonderful" Martingale Betting System

The system I used in my fledgling career as a roulette master is called the martingale system and was named after a man named Henry Martingale [the spelling of his name was actually Martin*dale*] or after a series of islands known as Martin, or some such, whose natives were very, very poor gamblers. They are now extinct.

It doesn't matter what the origin is. What does matter is that the martingale is usually the first gambling system "discovered" by new gamblers as they begin their flirtation with Lady Luck.

Let's take a look at what doubling one's bet at roulette actually involves (you can apply these concepts to all games) and why the martingale is such a dangerous system to use. Remember, the casino wins on 20 hits of an even-money bet, while the player only wins 18 times, so the odds of hitting various streaks has to be changed from streaks without a house edge.

Also keep in mind you are not betting one bet on whether a number or color will come up *X* number of times and then being paid off at the true odds for that one bet. No, with each number in the streak, you are making separate bets, and these bets are getting larger and really larger. And that is where the killer nature of the martingale comes into play, just as it did for me. Long streaks, larger and larger bets, tiny win if you do win = economic disaster waiting to happen.

Game with No House Edge

Consecutive Hits	Probability of Hitting	True Odds
1	1 in 2	1-to-1
2	1 in 4	3-to-1
3	1 in 8	7-to-1
4	1 in 16	15-to-1
5	1 in 32	31-to-1
6	1 in 64	63-to-1
7	1 in 128	127-to-1
8	1 in 256	255-to-1
9	1 in 512	511-to-1
10	1 in 1,024	1,023-to-1

Double-Zero Wheel

Consecutive Hits	Probability of Hitting	Roulette Odds
1	1 in 2.11	1.11-to-1
2	1 in 4.45	3.45-to-1
3	1 in 9.39	8.39-to-1
4	1 in 19.82	18.82-to-1
5	1 in 41.82	40.82-to-1
6	1 in 88.24	87.24-to-1
7	1 in 186.20	185.2-to-1
8	1 in 392.88	391.88-to-1
9	1 in 828.98	827.98-to-1
10	1 in 1,749.14	1,748.14-to-1

Single-Zero Wheel

Consecutive Hits	Probability of Hitting	Roulette Odds
1	1 in 2.06	1.06-to-1
2	1 in 4.22	3.22-to-1
3	1 in 8.68	7.68-to-1
4	1 in 17.83	16.83-to-1
5	1 in 36.65	35.65-to-1
6	1 in 75.31	74.31-to-1
7	1 in 154.77	153.77-to-1
8	1 in 318.05	317.05-to-1
9	1 in 653.59	652.59-to-1
10	1 in 1,343.13	1,342.13-to-1

My grownup children are right. I now know a lot about a few things and practically nothing about most things, but I do know one thing for certain—avoid using the martingale! It is a horse running around trying to bite its own tail, and when it does, it hurts...badly.

CHAPTER 25

To the Slots Go the Spoils

Casino gambling and/or racinos are in more than 80 percent of the United States. They are in Canada and throughout Europe and the Middle East. Casino gambling is almost as popular with the human race as warfare.

Casinos would never have spread like wildfire had it not been for the slot machines. There just aren't enough table-game players to make casino gambling popular enough to warrant such an amazing industry growth throughout the country. With slot machines, it is a totally different story. In some venues, 90 percent of the revenue the casinos make comes from the slots, without which there would be no casinos in those venues.

Go into any casino, and you will note seemingly endless aisles of slot machines with a small area reserved for table-game play. Slots are the No. 1 attraction in the home of Dame Fortune, and slot players are the true kings and queens of the casino world.

When I was young and foolish, I once joked that the world would end when I saw slot-machine advertisements on television or if I saw a movie in which the dashing hero played the machines. I mean, picture James Bond strolling haughtily into a casino and saying in that suave way of his, "I just love Blazing Sevens!"

And now advertisements on television are almost strictly for the slot machines, and the movies and television shows are following suit. The grand days of table games have long since ended. In 1984, for the first time in the history of modern casino gambling, slot machines made more money than the table games in Atlantic City and Las Vegas, and now casinos are more associated with slots than with any other form of gambling.

Today's casino industry *is* the slot machine.

Check out the billboards as you go into casino towns. It is doubtful there are many extolling table games or the winning of a few hundred dollars ("Look at me, everyone, I just won $57 at blackjack!"), but there will be countless ones singing the praises of their slot machines and slot winners ("Jaime March won $2,000,000 on our super hot machines!").

At Tropworld in Atlantic City, posted over the urinals were pictures of happy slot players, most of them women, holding those outsized checks and letting you know they had experienced a really big one in the casino. I never saw a picture of a craps player, a roulette player, or a blackjack player hanging above a man's urinal.

Today's Slot Machines

In the old days of saloon slots that paid off in gum and cigars, which then would be bought back by the bartender (that's how these clever entrepreneurs got around the gambling laws), the slot machines were just gears and pulleys, and their payouts were marginal. Then the technology morphed the slots into electromechanical devices. This was after World War II, and this electronic morphing allowed for big jackpot payouts and caused the beginning of the "dream big" fantasy of today's slot players.

Today the slot machine is a computer-driven marvel of modern technology. Everything is decided by the pesky computer, just like the computers that rule so many other aspects of our lives.

Players might still think that the spinning of the reels is an independent event and that the reels are the devices that decide whether you win or not. Sorry, that is no longer the case. The reels have nothing to do with whether you win or lose. They merely *tell you* whether you won or lost.

Here's how it all works.

Inside the slot machine is a computer program known as the "random-number generator" (RNG), which selects a series of numbers at random, and these numbers will relate to the symbols on the slot reels. When you play your credits, the RNG is working. Once you press the *play* button, the RNG will tell you what symbols it has selected at that moment. It tells you that by showing you the symbols on the reels.

Here's the kicker: even when the machine is not being played, the RNG is in a continual process of selecting number sequences. When you play your credits, it has nothing to do with what sequences are being chosen, which then means it has nothing to do with what the reels will be doing. That RNG figuratively spits out a decision, tells the reels where to land, the reels land there, and you either clap or moan.

Because the RNG is creating its number sequences in less than a second, there is no way to know what will come up or when it will come up. There is no way to jiggle the handle, if the machine even has a handle, or press the *play* button with this or that strength to turn the game in your favor as clever slot cheats were able to do more than 100 years ago. That was then, this is now. The computer age is the age all slot players now live in.

Inside that cold, hard exterior of those slots is a computer brain that only does one thing—it picks what will or will not appear on the reels. The reels are not the deciding factor—they are no factor, as many slot machines don't even use reels anymore but have animated figures of animals, people, and things. There are slot machines that have more than 100 lines of possible wins going in every direction at once. Such a machine could never have existed without the computer revolution that gave the world the RNG. With the RNG came the computer-revolution payoffs that could never have been made in the past but are now being made daily in casinos all over the world.

How the Machines Are Programmed

Slot machines do not pay out their wins smoothly. It isn't as if the player wins one, the slot machine wins one or the player wins two and the slot machine wins two or any type of sequence based on close to a 50/50 game. For slot players, such a 50/50 game would be boring. If they wanted that, they would play baccarat.

Instead, slots are explosive. The player can lose a long sequence of decisions (which is usual), win a little and lose a little here and there (which is also usual), and then *kaboom!*—a big win appears (which is what the slot player has longed for). It is the promise, the dream, of a big hit that drives the slot players' fantasies.

But how does the casino allow these big hits and still make money? In fact, how do the slots make *so much* money for the casinos?

The slots are programmed to keep a certain percentage of all the money put into them. Let's say that percentage is 10 percent, which means the machine will keep $10 for every $100 bet by the player, thereby returning the rest of the player's $90 in wins. The actual rate of return can be as little as 83 percent (casino keeps $17 out of every $100 played) and as high as 98 percent (casino keeps $2 of every $100 played).

So the machine is going to pay back $90 in our example. How does it do that? Sporadically.

Most of the decisions—the overwhelming majority—will be losers for the player, a few spins will be little wins, even fewer will be medium wins, and every once in a while the machine will pay off big. But...and this is an important *but*...the machine is only returning, on average, $90 of the $100 the player put into it. Those little, medium, and big payouts will simply equal $90 in the long run. And that is how the casino makes its money; it gives you back less than what you originally put into the machine. You get the thrill of playing and hoping you can win; the casino gets the pleasure of taking your money over time.

Obviously the amazing amount of money the players put into the machines allows for monster jackpots in the millions and tens of millions of dollars. But the idea above, while simple, is actually what occurs; only it happens in a bigger and more complex way when you deal with the masses of people playing the machines.

As I wrote, slot machines pay off in explosive ways. The slot player has been trained to handle long losing streaks in the hopes of winning a big one. And most slot players have won enough big ones over time that they are satisfied with losing streaks to get to those big wins. What is a big win? I'd say any win that makes the casino give you a W-2G IRS form is a big win. Going from a $1,200 win, the minimum for a W-2G IRS form, the player can sail into the multiple thousands, tens of thousands, hundreds of thousands, millions, and tens of millions of dollars. And those numbers, across that monetary continuum, are the bread and butter the casino serves to its slot players. And the slot players find such a meal delicious.

Paybacks and Denominations

There are some general traditions in the slot world. These aren't laws of nature, but in the casino world they come somewhat close.

- Lower-denomination machines keep a greater percentage of the players' money. The lowest paybacks to the players are usually found on penny and nickel machines. You are probably looking at an 85 percent return on your money. What makes that even more horrible is the fact that the penny and nickel machines can be played with so many multiple lines that in reality the player is not a penny or nickel player but a 25¢ or dollar player without the benefit of getting a 25¢ or dollar return. Players think they are saving money on these machines when, in fact, they are being suckered.

- Twenty-five-cent machines will return between 88 and 92 percent of the money put in them, depending on the venue and casino. Any machines that encourage the playing of more than three coins are doing to the 25¢ players what the penny and nickel machines are doing to their players—something quite unpleasant.

- Fifty-cent machines usually come in around 89 to 92 percent.

- $1 machines usually come in between 89 and 94 percent.

- $5 machines usually come in between 92 and 96 percent.

- Machines that are higher than $5 can go from 94 to 98 percent.

There is an interesting caveat to the above numbers. Progressive machines keeping a large percentage will actually lower the average percentages. If you are a $1 player *not playing* an interlinked-progressive slot machine, your return will probably be higher than the average returns cited above, because those interlinked progressive machines keep a huge percent of the money played in them, thus lowering the average for all machines in that denomination.

The Deadly Machines: *Don't play those large progressives! You are giving the casinos way too much money, hoping to hit a monster jackpot.*

Hit Frequencies

How often a machine pays is called its "hit frequency." Some machines have hit frequencies as high as 25 percent, which means one-fourth of the time something will be returned to the player—a win or less than a full loss, such as getting two quarters returned for three quarters played.

Then there are slot machines that have hit frequencies as low as 7 percent. These machines will have many more big wins associated with them, because they do not pay smaller wins with any frequency.

As a general rule of thumb, the more big jackpots a machine shows, the lower the hit frequency. That does not mean two machines, one with a low hit frequency and one with a high hit frequency, can't return the same exact percentage of the money played in them. They will just return that percentage in different ways—one with many smaller hits, one with fewer smaller hits but more big hits.

Which Machines Should You Play?

I have my own philosophy of which slot machines people should play. You might have your own ideas. If your ideas are similar to mine, well, then you obviously have given this question deep, careful, and intelligent consideration. If your ideas are radically different from mine, then...come on, come on...rethink those ideas and realize that I am right.

The machines that give back the worst overall paybacks are the intercasino-linked monster progressives, such as Megabucks. The casinos will keep about 17 percent of all the money played in these machines—and that is a tremendous amount of money. Short of hitting some really big ones, you are essentially throwing your money down the drain playing these big progressives. Yes, those big wins are the stuff of dreams, and an infinitesimally small percentage of players have hit those big ones—the key words being "infinitesimally small."

Just keep this in mind: very few slot players will ever get their pictures plastered over the urinals at Tropworld!

Games Within Games

Machines with games within games, usually called "bonus rounds," are not paying back any more money than machines that are straight-paying ones. Machines that give you bonus rounds when you hit certain symbols will have a slightly lower hit frequency during the regular rounds of play, but that hit frequency zooms up during the bonus rounds, which makes these machines pay back somewhere within the normal averages for those denominations.

As an example, take the Wheel of Fortune, an in-casino-progressive machine. When you hear the Wheel of Fortune song, you know someone is about to watch the wheel spin and spin. To your eyes, it looks as if every possible bonus segment on the wheel has an equal chance of showing, but that has nothing to do with the truth of the matter. The big hits are programmed to hit rarely, while the little wins will occur time after time.

In almost all types of Wheel of Fortune slot machines you must bet full coin in order to be eligible for the bonus rounds. Such machines tend to have strong house edges—around 12 percent. I am going to be redundant—again!—and say these machines are just not worth playing. Looking to win the big one is almost always associated with substantial losses over time.

"Zillion" Line Machines

Some people find these machines hard to fathom. The more coins you dump in them, the more potential winning lines you have. The confused players can't follow which lines are paying what and when. The players just play the maximum credits allowed and pray for the best.

Of course, there is a steep price for playing these multi-multiline-machines. Penny machines can grab 25¢ to 50¢ per round. Nickel players can actually bet as much as $5 per round. But the killer is this: the monster multiline machines only return the same percentage of what normal penny and nickel machines return; thus they keep much, much more of the players' money than the normal quarter and dollar machines.

You are probably looking at house edges hovering around the 15 percent mark. Said another way, these horrors are probably returning 85 percent—just not worth it.

One caveat here: If you are only going to play a couple of pennies or nickels, then we aren't talking about much of a long-term hit on your bankroll. But it will take tremendous discipline in the face of all those other lines showing winners for you to just ignore them. I have seen players start off conservatively on these machines and in a short while play like deranged dervishes. These multi-multiline machines are the sirens of the slot aisles and are soaking players who believe they are getting a good game.

Progressive Machines

There are three types of progressive machines in the casinos:

- Intercasino-linked progressives, such as Megabucks, where the jackpot can be hit at any casino using these machines. These machines will offer huge winning potential, and they are the machines of which dreams are made.
- In-house progressives, such as Wheel of Fortune, where the jackpot is strictly based on the money played in the machine by players at that casino. The possible wins are nowhere near what the intercasino-linked machines pay out, but they are still life-changing amounts.
- Single machines with progressive jackpots. These machines are within the realm of understanding, as the jackpots are more pedestrian.

Playing the intercasino-linked progressives is a total waste of money, as they can have edges approaching 17 percent (83 percent payback). Check out the example of the intercasino-linked $1 slot machine, like Megabucks. The player must bet full coins or credits ($3) to be eligible to win the jackpot. Each session is one hour long.

Session on Progressive Intercasino-Linked Slot Machines; 83 Percent Return	Expected Loss Per Session, 800 Decisions	Expected Cumulative Losses
1	$199.20	$199.20
2	$199.20	$398.40
3	$199.20	$597.60
4	$199.20	$796.80
5	$199.20	$996
6	$199.20	$1,195.20
7	$199.20	$1,394.40
8	$199.20	$1,593.60
9	$199.20	$1,792.80
10	$199.20	$1,992
11	$199.20	$2,191.20
12	$199.20	$2,390.40
13	$199.20	$2,589.60
14	$199.20	$2,788.80
15	$199.20	$2,988
16	$199.20	$3,187.20
17	$199.20	$3,386.40
18	$199.20	$3,585.60
19	$199.20	$3,784.80
20	$199.20	$3,984
21	$199.20	$4,183.20
22	$199.20	$4,382.40
23	$199.20	$4,581.60
24	$199.20	$4,780.80
25	$199.20	$4,980
-------------------------	Total Losses in 25 Hrs	$4,980

Just look at a player's expected losses in a 25-hour period—a massive $4,980. True, some players could be ahead in such a short time period, but given someone who frequently goes to the casinos, short of hitting the big one and overcoming those 50,000,000-to-1 odds, the losses will be staggering.

These machines have to keep such huge percentages in order to occasionally pay out their big jackpots. Every player gambling on such machines is paying an added "tax" for the jackpot, but only a chosen *infinitesimally small* few ever win. You might think of such machines as taxation without compensation. What are the approximate odds of hitting the big jackpot? As I wrote above, almost 50,000,000-to-1 (that's 50 million–to-1)! That's more than most state lotteries and, worse than that, you are not just playing one or a few tickets at such horrifying odds, you are playing thousands upon thousands of spins!

And here's another thing to chew on with these big jackpots: they are not paid out in one lump sum but are paid over a 25-year period *and* are subject to taxes.

Taxes: *There was a time in American casinos where gambling wins were not taxed as if they were income. Gambling was considered a hobby and, as such, any money generated by it was yours, not the government's. Evidently the current hobby of the government is to take as much money from the citizens as it can without creating a second American Revolution.*

The in-house-linked progressives aren't much better either; certainly they take a strong double-digit slice of all the money dumped into them in order to build the jackpot. Keep in mind that those jackpots have to be paid for by the money put into the machines by the players of that particular casino. To do so, the machines have to keep enough to make hitting those jackpots possible.

I guess we can, by a process of elimination, look at the single-machine progressives as the best kind to play—if you are looking to commit suicide slowly. Here the single machine itself is building a progressive jackpot only for the person playing that single machine in that single casino. There are no links to any other machines. The progressives obviously hit on rare occasions, but they are not monster jackpots and are easily fueled by the individual players at those individual machines. I'd say most of the jackpots range from $1,099 to $9,000—give or take some.

Once again, to be eligible for the top jackpot you have to play full coin in the machines, and they are just not really worth the effort or, more important, the expense.

Today's "Typical" Slot Machines

The casinos are filled with slot machines of every character and type, denomination and appearance. Some are reel spinners, many are video slots that give you an actual show—perhaps with singing and dancing or exploding pigs—when you hit certain symbols, and some are even based on table games such as blackjack, craps, and roulette. Some machines are based on game shows, movies, television shows, comic-book characters, and famous actors and actresses.

Still, almost all machines follow general patterns and principles, despite what their outside appearances might suggest. There are machines that take one-two-three-four-five (and perhaps more) coins/credits, clearly highlighting the fact that you will win more money on the jackpot line when you play maximum credits.

There are also machines that pay off equal percentages on all their lines. These are known as "equal-distribution machines." You'll play one coin/credit, and the jackpot is $200; two coins/credits, and the jackpot is $400; three coins/credits, and the jackpot is $600. Extra coins/credits will not offer you more in winnings—just the same multiple of what you bet. There is no advantage to betting three coins, because you get no reward for doing so when you hit the jackpot. You are just risking three times more money.

Obviously these are the *perfect* machines on which to bet one coin or credit, allowing you to play your normal amount of time but reducing the hit on your bankroll by 66 percent. These are machines I *highly recommend* you play. Because they are not offering extra money, the paybacks will fall in the higher range for their denominations.

Above-Average Paybacks: *Just because the average of a certain denomination is a certain figure does not mean all machines in this denomination conform to that figure. If you have 25¢ machines averaging 90 percent paybacks, you will have some machines, such as progressives, coming in really low, maybe 83 percent, and some machines coming in quite high, maybe 95 percent. Equal-distribution machines can come in with paybacks far above that 90 percent average, so playing them is a smart move!*

Now there are machines that offer you a reward on the jackpot line for playing maximum coins or credits. If you have a three-coin or three-credit machine that pays $200 for one coin or credit, $400 for two coins or credits, and $1,000 for three coins or credits, you can see that hitting the full-coin or full-credit jackpot wins you more money; thus the house edge on such machines is definitely lower when you play three coins or credits. On equal-distribution machines, the house edge is the same no matter how many coins or credits you play.

Most players looking at this reduction in the house edge and the increase in the jackpot line—and indeed most gambling authors assessing this fact—jump to the conclusion that playing maximum coins or credits is the way to go. It is if you are thinking strictly in terms of percentages; it isn't if you are thinking of total amount lost, even over an extended period of time.

First, if you are playing three coins or credits, the reduction in the house edge is marginal, no more than some-tenths of a percent. If I give the increased-jackpot machines a 0.5 percent reduction in the house edge, let's take a close look at what your losses really mean when comparing playing one coin or credit in an equal distribution machine at 95 percent return; playing one coin or credit in an increased-jackpot machine with a 92 percent return and playing three coins in an increased-jackpot machine at 92.5 percent return.

Just as we did with the intercasino-linked progressive slot machines, the player will play for one hour per session, and we'll see what happens after 25 such sessions in terms of bankroll. We shall use 800 spins/decisions in that hour (approximately 13 spins per minute) to come up with the average loss. We will use $1 machines.

Session on $1 Machines	Equal-Distribution Machines (95 Percent Return)	Total Cumulative Loss	Reward One Credit (92 Percent Return)	Total Cumulative Loss	Reward Three Credits (92.5 Percent Return)	Total Cumulative Loss
1	-$40	$40	-$64	$64	$180	$180
2	-$40	$80	-$64	$128	$180	$360
3	-$40	$120	-$64	$192	$180	$540
4	-$40	$160	-$64	$256	$180	$720
5	-$40	$200	-$64	$320	$180	$900
6	-$40	$240	-$64	$384	$180	$1,080
7	-$40	$280	-$64	$448	$180	$1,260
8	-$40	$320	-$64	$512	$180	$1,440
9	-$40	$360	-$64	$576	$180	$1,620
10	-$40	$400	-$64	$640	$180	$1,800
11	-$40	$440	-$64	$704	$180	$1,980
12	-$40	$480	-$64	$768	$180	$2,160
13	-$40	$520	-$64	$832	$180	$2,340
14	-$40	$560	-$64	$896	$180	$2,520
15	-$40	$600	-$64	$960	$180	$2,700
16	-$40	$640	-$64	$1,024	$180	$2,880
17	-$40	$680	-$64	$1,088	$180	$3,060
18	-$40	$720	-$64	$1,152	$180	$3,240
19	-$40	$760	-$64	$1,216	$180	$3,420
20	-$40	$800	-$64	$1,280	$180	$3,600
21	-$40	$840	-$64	$1,344	$180	$3,780
22	-$40	$880	-$64	$1,408	$180	$3,960
23	-$40	$920	-$64	$1,472	$180	$4,140
24	-$40	$960	-$64	$1,536	$180	$4,320
25	-$40	$1,000	-$64	$1,600	$180	$4,500
Amount Lost	-----	$1,000 Loss	-----	$1,600 Loss	-----	$4,500 Loss

In just 25 sessions of one hour's length, you can see the immensely different outcomes using these three different betting styles. Playing one coin or credit in the equal-distribution machine gives the player a losing expectation of $1,000. The player using only one coin or credit on the increased-jackpot machine has an expected loss of $1,600. However, the player going for the gusto on the increased-jackpot machine by playing three coins or credits faces an expected loss of $4,500—and that is just the expected loss in 25 hour-long sessions.

Yes, in the real world of casino play, the expected losses don't necessarily come out as I have shown in 25 hours—that's too few decisions for probability to work itself out. Some players might be ahead on any of these machines, but other players will be substantially behind. Naturally, more players will probably be down than up at any time in their playing. But as time wears on, the slot player will reach close to his or her expectation, and those players dumping three coins or credits into these machines thinking they are getting a greater game will merely be getting greater losses.

Can those of you who intend to go the casinos, say, six times per year or more, playing four or more hours each day, really want to face such horrible expectations by using the traditional thinking of betting full coin or credits? Play equal-distribution machines for one coin or, of you can't find those, just play one credit in the increased-jackpot machines. That's the sensible thing to do. The expected losses in the previous table should tell you everything you need to know.

Machines with Entertainment Features

On the video slots, you will find entertainment features such as songs, small video shows, and the like when certain symbols are hit, and because these "and the likes" take up some time in trying to entertain you, the machine is not actually being played during the show, and thus the casinos will often buy tighter machines from the slot companies to make up for the entertainment features. Although I can't say this is a universal pattern, it probably is a strong pattern; after all, when a machine is not being played, it isn't making any money for the house.

I recommend you stay away from these machines and stick to my recommended slots above.

Hey, She Stole My Jackpot!

You are sitting at your favorite machine and you decide to take a deep breath to smell that delicious casino smell—a combination of booze, adrenaline, cigarette smoke, and pheromones. There are no credits left in the machine because you have—sadly—lost them all. You do have more money to dump into the machine because you have taken a second mortgage on your house, but first you want to pause and think about the nature of reality.

Suddenly a woman with severely dyed red hair with blue streaks in it, wearing dark eye shadow and ruby red lipstick, head swollen from multiple botox injections and a facelift that has made her mouth look like Mr. Sardonicus, rushes in and dumps her credit slip into the machine. You are aghast. Hey, this is your machine! Can't she see that through her eye shadow?

The credits register on the machine, and she pushes the *play* button. The reels spin and spin and—oh, my Lord!—the *big* mucho-magnificent jackpot symbols all appear, one after another, and this horrifying hag has just won 10 million dollars!

Your eyes grow big, your mouth tenses, and then...

[...*you leap on the woman, grab her neck and start choking her with every ounce of strength your adrenaline-soaked system contains. As she utters gurgling sounds and struggles to pull away from your death grip, you keep the pressure on until her botoxed forehead explodes in a shower of pudgy pieces of pink pus*...]

...you feel terrible because you believe that woman stole your jackpot, and you slink away into the casino as dozens upon dozens of people applaud the good luck of this supersmiling satanic Sardonicus.

Well, let me make you feel happy right now. No one can steal your jackpot because with each tenth of a second *or less*, the RNG is selecting number sequences after number sequences that relate to the symbols on the reels. Even if you were about to press the *play* button, and this monstrously made-up woman pushed your hand aside and pushed the play button instead of you, the time between her pushing your hand aside and her pushing the button is more than enough time for a completely new set of symbols to be selected. Had you pushed the *play* button, you probably would not have won the jackpot. So you can drop the desire to kill this woman.

Manners at the Slot Machines

Unlike some games—such as blackjack, in which some players think they are obliged to tell you how to play your hands, even if these "experts" have no real idea of the correct basic strategy; or craps, in which some players dislike it when players take care with their rolls; or roulette, in which players bump your hand as you are trying to make your bets so they can make their own bets; or baccarat, in which players stare and fume if they are playing the opposite of the hands you are playing, because you are winning your hands and they are losing their hands—the slot world still does have its manners and unwritten rules.

Here are some:

- Do not play more than one machine if the casino is crowded and people are waiting to play. Doing so is rude. It is also stupid, because you are possibly doubling the casino hit on your bankroll.
- Do not ask a player, "Are you finished playing that machine yet?"
- Do not try to strike up a conversation with a player who seems to be intently watching the screen. It is more than likely that this player does not want to talk to anyone.
- Do not ask a person how much money they have won or how much money they have lost. That's really bad manners, just like asking someone what their salary or earnings are.
- Do not jump onto a machine that has a *saved* sign on it. Until the casino attendant frees the machine, it is taken—otherwise people couldn't go to the bathroom, and my fear is that casino carpeting could get very, very messy.
- Do not complain about your losses. Other players might be polite, but no one really gives a damn if you lost money. They are concerned with their own money.
- Do not brag about your wins. Aside from making someone who was just hammered feel even more awful, winning has nothing to do with your greatness as a person or as a player. Slots are random, and an ape who knows enough to push the *play* button could win too. So do not display your wins on your wings as if you were a peacock.

Money Management at Slots

Does this sound right? The bartender pours your favorite drink. You sip it in a leisurely fashion. You are adult and cool, calm and considered, as you imbibe slowly. In fact, you are feeling somewhat philosophical as you nurse your drink. Other folks are at this trendy bar as well. It is a truly nice atmosphere for a mature and calm adult such as you to do some serious thinking.

After a while you order your second drink. You can feel the warmth of the first one starting to go through your body. It feels good—a slight buzz, almost undetectable. You drink this second drink down just slightly faster than the first one. Ah, the buzz is feeling stronger.

You order your third drink. This you drink slightly faster than your second drink, which was slightly faster than your first drink. Your sense of humor is intensifying as you start to finish that third drink. You make some witticisms. There are some slight smiles from the others at the bar.

Then you order a fourth drink, take four or five gulps, and the drink is finished. You immediately go for the fifth drink, which you swallow down in three breaths. Then a sixth, a seventh...

You slap the guy sitting next to you at the bar after he said something that you really didn't quite hear. "Hey, mahn," you blurt, "you are one fununnee guy! Ha! Ha! Ha!" The guy sitting next to you becomes livid as he tells you that he isn't a guy but a woman, and what is so funny about how her husband died? You slap her on the back again and laugh uproariously, allowing spit to fly into the air and into the drink of the guy sitting next to her.

On your eighth drink, this woman storms off, saying you are the most disgusting human being she has ever encountered. You chortle as a booger goes in and out of your nose. You are socking those drinks down so fast, the bartender can barely keep up. You scream out that you will treat everyone in the bar to a drink, as you fumble with your wallet. Everyone takes you up on it. And then...

The next morning you wake up in the alley wondering what the hell happened the night before.

Here's what happened: you are the typical slot player.

Even when most slot players think they are going to play in a leisurely fashion, the longer they stay at the machine, the faster they play. It's just like the drinking. The first drink is sipped; the last one is chugged.

With such high house edges, the last thing you want to do is play the slot machines as fast you can. Note that when I set up the slot tables, I used 13 decisions per minute as our benchmark. And that is not a ridiculous speed—it's a totally reachable speed and one that will kill a slot player's bankroll, as evidenced by those total expected losses.

So the first rule of money management at slots is to *slow the pace* by not allowing the natural tendency to play faster overcome your good sense. You must think your way through your playing sessions. A slot player who just goes on instinct is a slot player looking to get hammered and one who *will* get hammered.

How many decisions per minute should you strive for? No more than six—one decision every 10 seconds. Even if it means counting to 10—and I mean using the one-thousand-one, one-thousand-two, one-thousand-three method—you have to make sure your pace is a reasonable one.

Do not give yourself unlimited funds to play a given session of slots. For every session you intend to play, give yourself enough money to handle a loss on every spin! That's right: if you are playing six decisions each minute, you will be playing 360 decisions in an hour. You should be able to lose all 360 decisions. On a $1 machine, you'd bring $360—because you are only going to bet $1 per spin. On a 25¢ machine, you would bring $90, because you are only betting one quarter per spin.

If you are going to the casino for a vacation of several days, then divide up your bankroll into the number of sessions you intend to play, and make sure you have enough to play all those sessions even if every one of them winds up being a disaster.

If you intend to play four sessions of one hour each on every day of a three-day trip, you are looking at 12 sessions of play—12 hours—so the one-dollar player should have $4,320 as a bankroll; the quarter player should have $1,080. Obviously, short of a murderous losing streak that sees you lose every single spin in three day's time, you cannot lose all those session dollars.

Will it take discipline to play as I suggest? Absolutely. But money management at slots is the key ingredient for giving you a chance to win and also the benefit of not going home broke and embarrassed.

I wrote about this before, but it is absolutely essential to set up a 401(g) account, preferably a money-market account that gives you interest. The G in the 401(g) stands for *gambling*. This is money you have put aside strictly for gambling purposes.

On slot machines, the longer you play them, the better chance you will be a loser, so you are going to have to feed your 401(g) with money on a regular basis. Take some money from every paycheck or some money from the profits of your business or some small percentage from your retirement income, and keep socking it into the 401(g). Always do this on a regular basis. If you have a nice, healthy 401(g), you can conduct your playing sessions as I recommend and never worry about losses, because any losses are covered by your total gambling bankroll.

Do not use household money to gamble—because you can get yourself into trouble, and some of you might be the type to overdo it in the heat of the moment, even if you aren't a problem gambler.

Join More Than One Slot Club
Slot players are often quite conscious of the kinds of comps they get based on their play. Casinos will rate your play based on how much you put through a machine, and then they will comp you accordingly. I recommend you join several slot clubs at various casinos based on the following factors:

- Decide what level of comps you want. Are you interested in being RFB (meaning a really big shot), or are you content to get a free or reduced-rate room, some buffets, some free-play coupons, and reduced tickets to shows?
- Play only the amount of money needed to get the comps you want.
- Once you have fulfilled the requirements for that casino, go to another casino and do the same thing. If your 401(g) allows, you can have several casinos that welcome your play and reward you for it at the levels you want.
- There are some casino empires that have a player's card that can be used at all their properties, but the comps are doled out based on

the level of the property at which you're interested in staying. If you want to play and stay at their best property, you might not get the top comps. However, if you stay at their secondary properties, you can play at the premier property but use the comps for your stay at the secondary property. You'll get better rewards that way.

- Slot play is not affected by using your player's card, and it is stupid not to use one. You want to get as much from the casinos as your normal play allows.

Some Serious Questions About Slots

Question: *I heard that if machines have not given out a jackpot in a long, long time, they are overdue. That's because they are programmed to pay out a certain amount, and if they don't pay it out regularly, the machine backs up and programs a jackpot win.*

Answer: Not so. Every spin is an independent event. If you are facing odds of 50,000,000-to-1 on the very first spin, you are still facing odds of 50,000,000-to-1 on the 50,000,000[th] spin. Yes, the longer a machine is played—say, some thousands of trillions of times—those 50,000,000-to-1 shots will likely come up, but all spins still face odds of 50,000,000-to-1. Nothing is ever due.

Question: *Don't slot attendants know when machines will hit and can lead you to those machines?*

Answer: They don't know any more than you do. They lead you to machines hoping you win big so that you give them a nice, big, fat, juicy tip.

Question: *I heard that machines that are dented will mispay, and you can make a fortune on them.*

Answer: They are probably dented because a player became so outraged at losing he punched the machine. Any dents you see are just dents, nothing more.

Question: *Aren't airport machines looser because they want to get people to play when they go into the city? If they win at the airport, they will really go into the city pumped up and ready to play all day and all night, right?*

Answer: Many slot players want to play all day and all night, but it has nothing to do with airport machines being loose. In fact, the airport machines are probably the tightest in the city! Most people play these machines as they wait for their planes to go home. It is rare someone comes off a plane and heads to an airport machine. These machines are the last scavengers before the player goes back to his or her normal life.

Question: *If a machine is paying out because it is broken, aren't you entitled to the money you got out of the machine?*

Answer: There's usually a little sign on or near the machines that state unequivocally that a malfunctioning machine voids all pay. If the machine is "broken," the money belongs to the casino.

Question: *There are some people who will give you—for free—a system that is guaranteed to work on the slots. When you win, you just give the seller a percentage of your wins as payment. You have nothing to lose!*

Answer: This is one of the oldest scams in the books. It is used at every single game. The scammer is right; his system costs no money. He is right; if you win, you just give him a percentage of your win. Now comes the bad part: does his system really give you an edge? No, it doesn't. You will win and lose based on the probabilities of the machine, but when you win—a difficult enough task—you give away more money than you give away to the house edge. You lose it all when you lose, but you lose when you win by dividing up your money. The scammer can just tell you to twirl your finger in your ear and that will help you win. So in one session you do win. Has the twirling of the finger really influenced the machine? No. Has the scammer really scammed you out of your money? Yes.

Question: *So what other scams exist in the world of slot play?*

Answer: Here are the ingredients in all scams: Scams promise the player extraordinary wins: You can have your own island. You'll have servants happy to make your every wish their command. You'll be loved and idolized by all the people you know who now wish they could be like you. The methods are simple as one-two-three. The scammer tells you he is tired of playing his method now that he owns an island paradise or an estate in the country or estates in many countries. But there is a rush.

He will only sell his secret, developed by a brilliant physicist who lives in seclusion, for the next several days, weeks, or months. Get in on it now, or you will lose out forever.

Question: *You mentioned that the martingale is a dangerous way to play the table games. But is it dangerous to play at the slots? If you lose a certain amount at quarter machines, why not go up to $1 machines, or $5 machines? Sooner or later you have to win a spin that gets you back all of your losses and then some.*

Answer: Because the expectation on all those machines is negative, adding one negative to a bigger negative to an even bigger negative adds up to? Yes, a negative. You are asking to have your head pulverized by using a martingale on slots. In a negative-expectation game, the results, over time, will be negative. It's a fact you cannot escape.

Question: *Didn't you write a book more than 20 years ago that said exactly where the loose machines are? But you aren't doing that in this book. Why not?*

Answer: The times have changed. What was true long ago is no longer true today. Are there machines that are so loose at times that players can get a real edge? Yes; see further reading at the end of this chapter about such machines. Are loose and tight machines placed in casinos the way they used to be? No, not at all. If everything in my old book were true, I wouldn't be writing new ones. Even in casino gambling, things change—sometimes even for the better...and the bettor.

Question: *They used to be called the "Big Bertha" machines. I haven't seen many of them lately. Isn't it true they were really loose?*

Answer: Just the opposite; they were as tight as tight could be. Because they gave you a thrill just watching those huge reels spin and all those people watching you play, there was no need for the casino to offer "looseness" as an incentive. They are still around, although perhaps not as abundant as before.

Question: *I have heard in craps that the casinos bring in what are called "Saturday night dice," which cause more 7s, so the players lose more money. I also heard that for slots it is just the opposite; they reprogram* *the machines so players win more jackpots, which then encourages more people to play. There are a lot of people in the casinos on the weekends, and even though the slots are looser, the casino makes much more money from all those players playing.*

Answer: There are plenty more people in the casinos on the weekends. The casinos do make more money on the weekend. There are even more jackpots hit on the weekend. But the machines are not reprogrammed to be looser (or tighter); that would be a waste of time. Players come to the casino motivated to play. With all the players playing on the weekend, it stands to reason more jackpots will be hit because the number of decisions goes through the roof. As far as "Saturday night dice," there are no such things.

Question: *Why do the casinos bring in so many new themed slots each year?*

Answer: Slot players are a restless breed. They will play a machine for a while, but when the losses mount up, they break up with that machine and move on to another in the hope the new one wins them some money. It is an ongoing process, and the casino has to replace the slots that are underperforming with new slots to keep the players interested. It is much like dating. Most of the people you dated, you broke up with (or maybe all of the people you dated!), and slot players subconsciously think of the slot machines as their dates. These relationships are usually doomed to failure.

Question: *Does using a player's card make the machines tighter or looser?*

Answer: Using a player's card is a good thing because the casino will give you back some of your money in the form of comps. These comps can actually be for cash and free or reduced rates for rooms, food, and shows. Many casinos will also give you presents for playing their machines. There is just one thing to watch out for—do not play to get these comps. They will come based on your normal betting; do not bet more than you planned in order to get a free buffet that could cost you hundreds of dollars in losses. The use of a player's card has no effect on whether you win or lose.

The 10 Commandments of Slots

Let's go over it all now. These are the 10 commandments I have brought down from RNG Mountain to help make your slot experience as winning as possible, given the probabilities.

1. Avoid all intercasino-linked progressive machines. The house edge is around 83 percent—just awful.
2. Avoid all those mega-multiline machines that can make a nickel player into a $5 player. These machines are bankroll killers.
3. Avoid machines that offer entertainment features. To pay for dead time, the machines have to be tighter.
4. Play one coin in equal-distribution machines or, if you must play enhanced-jackpot machines, also play just one coin.
5. To have a better chance of winning a given session, play machines that have a lot of small wins as opposed to machines that concentrate on big wins.
6. Slow down the pace to no more than six spins per minute.
7. Give yourself a session stake equal to the number of decisions you will face in the amount of time you will play.
8. Always use your player's card when you play.
9. Develop a 401(g) for money that is used strictly for gambling.
10. Obey the mores and manners of slot-machine play.

More on Slot Machines

This chapter is a great introduction to playing the slot machines correctly, but there is much, much more to know if you really want a strong chance to beat the house—enough to fill an entire book! Indeed, there are actual machines at some venues and casinos that can be beaten. For further investigation:

Slots Conquest: How to Beat the Slot Machines! by Frank Scoblete ($16.95)

In unique copyrighted material, you can learn how to recognize and play advantage slot machines that give the players a *real* mathematical edge! You'll learn when to play them and what bankrolls you'll need. These are not expensive machines found in high-roller rooms! Just about all slot players will have the bankrolls necessary to get the edge over the house on these advantage-play machines.

Also, *Slots Conquest* explains why you can't quit while you're ahead, and you'll discover the relationship of slot machines to sex. You'll also enjoy weird and wacky true slot adventures that I have experienced. And is there a place for psychic experiences in slot-machine play? Some players think so. All aspects of the slot machines are explored in this groundbreaking book! (On sale at bookstores, Amazon.com, or by calling 1-800-944-0406.)

CHAPTER 26

Casino War

I t was called War, and you probably played a version of this as a kid or in a bar to determine who bought the next drink. Hopefully you weren't a kid in the bar. It's really just simple, as in you get one card, your opponent gets one card, and whoever has the highest card gets the free drink. Or if there is a tie, you go to war.

It's probably the easiest card game the casino offers, but it looks to me as if more and more players are gravitating to it for some reason. Casino War has the same underpinnings as War, with some interesting variations, none of which will cause your brain to freeze any more than a brain usually freezes when in a casino.

The game is usually played with six decks, but you can find casinos that play with more or fewer decks as well. The ace is the highest card, and all the other cards are ranked based on their faces...so a king beats a queen, a 3 beats a 2, and so on.

As in the standard game of War, each player gets a card and the dealer gets a card. If the player's card wins, he gets even money for his bet (a $10 bet wins $10). If the dealer wins, the player loses his bet.

Should the dealer and the player have the same card, a tie, that can be war or surrender, where the player can surrender his hand and get back half his bet or say, "Bring it on, big boy. I never surrender!" Okay, the player might not say it that exact way, but you get the idea. Surrender is the poorer of the two options, so never surrender. Make war not peace. Or as the Marines say, "Surrender, hell!"

Making war is as easy as, well, making war. The dealer will burn three cards (no, it doesn't mean he puts a match to them; it means he discards them) and then deal the player another card after the player has doubled his bet. If the player wins or ties with that second card, the dealer will pay him for his second bet, but the first bet will be considered a push. But here is the sneaky part: if the dealer beats the player, the player loses both his original bet and his second bet. Yuck!

Some casinos offer a "Tie bet" that usually pays 10-to-1. That bet, just like the Tie bet at baccarat, is a waste of money, coming in with double-digit house edges, depending on the number of decks being used. Don't ever make it.

The house edge at Casino War hovers around 3 percent, depending on the number of decks. Although this edge is somewhat better than many other table games, Casino War is fast-paced, and that pace is highly dangerous, again similar to the speed of mini-baccarat. With many decisions, a small casino edge can become a deadly casino edge over the player.

The War Room: *If you decide to play Casino War, consider sitting out the hand after you lose one. Tell the dealer you worry about negative streaks. Or sit out a hand after you win a hand, saying that negative results come after positive ones. By reducing the hit on your bankroll using this technique, Casino War will not be as dangerous.*

CHAPTER 27
The Big Wheel

Gamblers who want to be "big wheels" usually lose all their money and are looked down upon by all who know them. They should be. There are very few really big wheels in gambling. That's a fact. Check out the millions of casino gamblers around the country *and* the world, and you find a recurrent theme—the player loses, the casino wins. That's a fact too.

Nowhere is this statement truer than at a device variously called the Big Wheel or Big Six. You have no prayer of ever becoming a big wheel if you play the Big Wheel. That is also a fact.

The Big Wheel is the original wheel of fortune and could be found in carnivals all over the world. Bleary-eyed townsfolk would bet on each spin, hoping they would never have to slop the hogs again.

The game is simple. There is a large wheel, and on the betting table, under glass, there are various denominations of money: $1, $2, $5, $10, $20, along with a joker and a logo—the two highest-paying bets. Here is the usual payout scheme. Note that in Atlantic City the Big Wheel pays out more for the hits on the joker and the logo.

Bet	Payout	Ways to Make It	House Edge
$1	$1	24	11.11 percent
$2	$4	15	16.67 percent
$5	$25	7	22.22 percent
$10	$100	4	18.52 percent

Bet	Payout	Ways to Make It	House Edge
$20	$400	2	22.22 percent
Logo	$40-to-$1	1	24.07 percent
Joker	$40-to-$1	1	24.07 percent
A.C. Logo	$45-to-$1	1	14.81 percent
A.C. Joker	$45-to-$1	1	14.81 percent

The Big Wheel does have one thing going for it: the game is super slow. Very few players stand at it and play for long periods of time. The action is truly intermittent, because most players tend to be touristy types who know almost nothing about casino games. For them the Big Wheel is easy and fun, and most of these tourists don't live in areas where the hogs need to be slopped.

So if you decide to actually play the Big Wheel, just bet $1, so you are facing the smallest house edge. Relax and take your time. It's the only way to go when it comes to the Big Wheel.

CHAPTER 28

Sic Bo

I f you have a checkbook handy, now would be a good time to take it out and write a check to your favorite casino that offers the game of Sic Bo. The game is that bad; so if you are flirting with playing it, save yourself the heartache and just write a check.

"Sic Bo" means "dice faces." It is extremely popular in Asian casinos and in the Asian-games rooms of American casinos, but it is also quite popular in mental-health hospitals, where security personnel had to drag those poor deluded players who tried to beat the darn game, couldn't, and went away foaming and screaming, "Where did all my money go?" The house edges, even on the best bets, are ridiculous. And on the worst

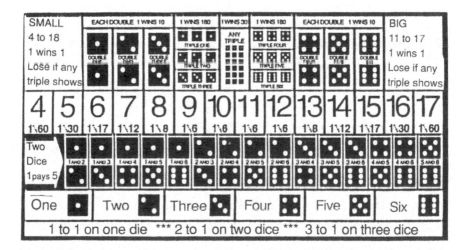

bets, which are legion, they are ridicu-lousy and ridicu-lousier! My advice, even before I discuss this game, is really simple: ignore it.

Strangely enough, there are many variations in payouts for Sic Bo, which makes writing about it a real pain in the...you know what. But the game stinks in all its forms, so I will use just one basic Sic Bo game, and you can take it from there. Why would a game that is so awful have so many versions?

Sic Bo is played with three dice. Okay, that's it, now on to the next game...okay, okay, I was just kidding.

The object of the game is to bet on what faces show when those three dice land.

The three dice are in a cage, which is rotated so the dice land randomly. The game's layout will show the winning combination because the winning combination will light up. Many of the players are probably lit too, or why else would they play this game?

Dice Faces: The player wins if any one of the dice faces he bets on appears. If one die has the face, he is paid off at even money ($1 for $1). If two dice have that face, he is paid off at 2-to-1 ($2 for $1). If three dice have that face, he is paid off at 3-to-1 ($3 for $1). The house edge is 7.87 percent.

The Two-Face Combination: You are betting that a given two-face combination will appear. The bet is paid off at 5-to-1. Sound good? Don't get excited; the house edge is a monstrous 16.67 percent!

The Three-Face Combination: You are betting that a given three-face combination will appear. The casino pays the bet off at 150-to-1. Wow! No, actually ouch, as the real odds are 215-to-1. Because the casino is paying off so little, the house edge is 30 percent! Ouch is right.

The Couplet: You are betting that a pair will be thrown—like 3:3— and if that should happen, the casino pays you off at 8-to-1. Ouch, ouch: the house edge is 33.3 percent.

The Triplet: If any three of the same face show, the player wins 24-to-1. The true odds on this bet are 35-to-1. The house edge is 30.5 percent.

The Totals Wager: This wager is the total of the three dice. The house edges vary widely, based on the totals. Check out the chart—some of the edges are really, really, really bad, and some are worse.

Total	Payout	Casino Edge	Loss Per $10 Bet
4 or 17	60-to-1	29.1 percent	$2.91
5 or 16	18-to-1	47.2 percent	$4.72
6 or 15	14 to 1	30.5 percent	$3.05
7 or 14	12-to-1	9.7 percent	$0.97
8 or 13	8-to-1	12.5 percent	$1.25
9 or 12	6-to-1	18.9 percent	$1.89
10 or 11	6-to-1	12.5 percent	$1.25

I saved the best bets for last.

Small: You win on a total of 4 to 10 but lose on anything higher than 10 or on triples (2:2:2 or 3:3:3) appearing. The payment is even money, $1-to-$1, and the house edge is 2.78 percent.

Big: You win on a total of 11 through 17 but lose on anything less than 11 or on three of a kind (4:4:4 or 5:5:5). The payment is even money, $1-to-$1, and the house edge is 2.78 percent.

Betting and Bankroll: *Only bet Small or Big, and make sure you only play about 40 to 50 decisions per hour. Bet table minimum.*

CHAPTER 29
Keno and the Lottery

Keno

Keno is a game in which the player gets to pick one to 10, 15, or 20 numbers from a total of 80. Many casinos will limit how many numbers a player may choose, and often it peaks at 15. The house then picks 20 numbers. Wins are based on how many of the casino's numbers the player matches.

The casino gives you a small piece of paper with all 80 numbers, and you color in which ones you wish to have. Every 15 minutes (or so), the Keno ping-pong balls are put through a randomizing machine for the casino to choose its 20 numbers. This machine is often called a "bubble" because the numbered balls are mixed with strong air currents that push them into the winning tube.

That's the game, pure and simple. Here is what isn't pure and simple: the house edges, which range from 20 to 35 percent. Yikes! However, Keno has a major thing going for it—the slowness of the game. Those 20 to 35 percent edges can only hit you when those balls are recorded, which happens infrequently.

Oh, No: *There is a second type of Keno game that is far deadlier than live Keno, and that is video Keno. This is a slot machine that acts just like a Keno game but is far, far faster. While the edges hover around the 10 percent mark, many more decisions are reached in such short periods of time that video Keno is far more dangerous to your bankroll than is regular Keno.*

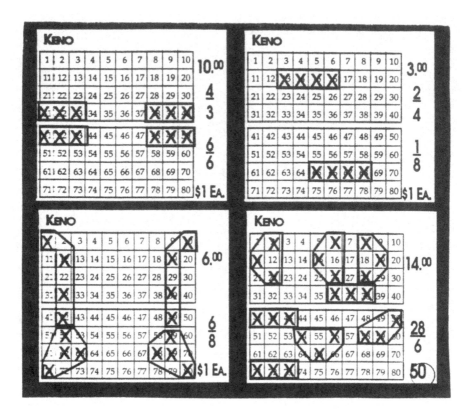

The Lottery

There probably isn't a person in the country who doesn't know what a state lottery is. You pick numbers—usually five or six out of 49 to 56—and attempt to match the numbers that the state picks. Why, it's just like Keno!

The house edges on lottery tickets can run upward of 50 percent, and there isn't a single state lottery that is truly worth playing until the jackpots reach enormous heights—usually in the $30 to $300 million range, depending on the game. Indeed, the best and only advice for such games is simple: don't play them. And if you must, only bet $1. This way you get to dream about a big win until you find out someone else, who didn't deserve it like you did, won it.

Most games also have a special number picked from a different "real-life" random-number generator (usually those ping-pong balls again), and if you pick the correct numbers on the original game and also the special number, you win the mucho-biggo jackpot.

But, as always, there is a catch. You have two choices in how you take your winning jackpot. You can take it as 20 equal installments over 20 years, or you can take a "cash value" of 50 percent of the jackpot immediately. The government gets to keep the other 50 percent. Believe it or not, the cash option seems to be the better choice, because you can invest that money, and in 20 years it should come out to more than the yearly payments.

Scratch-Off Tickets

As always, the state has a big edge on scratch-off tickets—usually much higher than 25 percent. Nevertheless, there are two methods of trying to pluck the golden tooth from the dreaded scratch-off dragon. The first is to go to the lottery pages of your state lottery and check the scratch-off results. Usually games that are finished, meaning all the top jackpots have been won, will be in red or otherwise noted. Obviously, you don't buy these tickets if you should see them in the local store, as they are being recalled.

Your best chance of winning the scratch-off lottery tickets is on the very *first* day these tickets are released to the public. All the jackpot numbers are in play, and therefore the odds of winning are at their best for the player. That's about the best you can do when it comes to the state scratch-off tickets.

PART 3:
Everything Else About Casinos

CHAPTER 30

The Amazing Colossal Vegas

I n 1957 many of Las Vegas' casinos were destroyed or at least seriously damaged when the movie giant the Amazing Colossal Man rampaged through the city. Most of you will not recognize the Vegas that Glen "Big Boy" Manning rampaged through in 1957, and that is to be expected.

Manning was a colonel in the army who received 80 trillion godzillion megadoses of plutonium radiation that caused him to grow to taller than 60 feet and then go bananas because his one-cell heart (yes, in those days *his doctors* thought the heart was a one-cell organ) could not pump enough blood to his brain.

So as a nutty lark, Manning kidnapped his small girlfriend and went on a monstrous tear through the Vegas of yesteryear. Yes, he was bigger than any building in town. He was colossal!

I know most of you did not visit the Vegas of 1957 unless you were born in 1936 or earlier, so let me tell you what Vegas was like in those good old days.

Except for a few big high-rise buildings—or rather what they *called* "high-rise buildings"—the Las Vegas "hotel casinos" looked more like *motel* casinos. The amazing colossal man could be seen from every vantage point in the city because, frankly, Vegas was not really a city as we know cities today. Vegas was a bunch of motels with nice swimming pools and a few stars singing and dancing in what today would be considered cheesy lounges, all of this in the middle of an unforgiving, dusty desert. Some of the air-conditioning systems supposedly still blew air over ice to cool things down during the blistering summers.

The Amazing Colossal Man, crazed and foaming at the mouth by the end of the movie (and finding it hard to keep his oversized diaper on too), fell off the even bigger Hoover Dam and—except for a truly horrendous sequel, in which his eye had been poked out and his mouth ripped apart—was thankfully never heard from again.

Same with the Vegas of those times, because from 1957 through 1987, Las Vegas went through a building boom unlike anything seen previously. Iconic casinos such as Stardust, the Dunes, the Landmark, Caesars Palace, the Sands, a revamped Flamingo, the Aladdin, Vegas World, Imperial Palace, the Desert Inn—which was the Mecca for sedate and wealthy high-rolling golf players—and the MGM Grand all shot upward. Buildings even taller than the Amazing Colossal Man were evident all over town—even in downtown Vegas.

This was the Vegas that everyone celebrated as the true "Sin City" of Sinatra, Dean Martin, Elvis Presley, Sammy Davis Jr., George Burns, Liberace, and a host of singers and comedians too numerous to mention. Vegas was the adult playground, with real air-conditioning in the summer and even larger pools and bigger shows than ever before. Instead of a dozen showgirls at the typical glamour stage shows, there were sometimes hundreds of spangled, sparkling young lovelies. And if these beautiful showgirls made a man...well, you know...he could always go out to the Mustang Ranch and ride a metaphoric mare.

So that was that for Las Vegas, right? It lived happily ever after.

Well, no, not really.

What was thought to be the uber building boom from 1957 to 1987 was merely the insemination by a seed of what would grow into one of the most fabulous cities in the world. Liberace's death in 1987 signaled a change of direction for Las Vegas. And that direction was, sadly, economically downhill.

And Vegas had Atlantic City to thank for that.

Yes, Atlantic City, the Queen of Resorts, started to hammer Vegas in the pocketbook department. Vegas tourism was slowing down, and it looked as if Atlantic City would win the war of the slot machines as they became the dominant form of gambling in both Las Vegas and Atlantic City in 1984.

It appeared Vegas could do nothing to turn things around.

Then in stepped Steve Wynn, who built the fabulous Mirage—a new style of casino that out–Caesars Palaced the original Caesars Palace. Wynn bought the Castaways, a property that could have been crushed by the foot of the Amazing Colossal Man, and erected the most expensive and attractive casino ever built—the Mirage.

How important was the Mirage to the establishment of a new Las Vegas? Until its opening in 1989, Atlantic City was taking tourists away from Sin City in droves, and none of the icons of Vegas could figure out how to get those tourists back. Why travel more than 2,000 miles from the East Coast when you could pull the handle of a slot machine by the beautiful Atlantic Ocean just as easily?

Sure, Atlantic City was really just a strip of casinos inhabiting a city of slums, where steely-eyed brutes prowled the streets and the nights, but most gamblers didn't care what was going on outside. They just wanted to play!

But the building of the Mirage did the trick. With its exploding volcano in front, its island-themed hotel-casino, amazing shows, and superb restaurants and other amenities, the Mirage became *the* place to see and be seen. Celebrities flocked to the Mirage, and where there are celebrity sightings, there are hordes of hopeful celebrity sighters.

The Vegas of the 1950s, '60s, and '70s tended to cater to an older crowd—but the new influx of megacasinos suddenly struck a responsive chord with the 30-something crowds, and the current Vegas has more nightclubs than ever before—many of them way up on the rooftops of those magnificently colossal hotel-casinos.

The growth of the new Vegas started with the Mirage, and from that point until...well, it still hasn't stopped...the Las Vegas architecture has been zooming up, up, up, and away—and not just the casinos! The building boom is scratching the sky with dozens of large—and I mean *New York City*-type large—condominiums and casino/shopping/hotel/condominium projects that cost billions of dollars. Look at the Vegas skyline, and it now actually has the feel of the big city because it actually is now a real big city—a big city whose growth has been staggering.

In the mid-1980s, the Clark County population figures hovered around the half-million mark; now they are scratching 2 million—a fourfold increase.

Vegas was no longer just the gambling capital of the Wild West (and of Western civilization), it became a top-drawer tourist attraction as well, even for people who rarely or never gambled. Today, Vegas welcomes roughly 40 million visitors each year.

So why do so many tourists from all over the world go to the diadem of the desert? The casinos bring them in, yes, but the legion of spectacular stage shows and famous headliners, the incredible gourmet restaurants with world-famous chefs, the awesome nightclubs, and the elegant shopping venues right inside the casino-hotels have caused tourists from everywhere to look at Vegas as a first-class resort town. And, brother, do tourists flood into the desert.

Just look at the casinos that came into existence after 1989 to compete with the surrounding mountains, touch the sky, and make the Amazing Colossal Man look diminutive ever since Steve Wynn's Mirage made its stunning appearance: Rio Suites, Excalibur, Union Plaza, Treasure Island, the new MGM Grand, Luxor, Stratosphere Tower, Hard Rock, the Orleans, Monte Carlo, Harrah's, Paris, New York–New York, Bellagio, Venetian, Mandalay Bay, the new Aladdin (now Planet Hollywood), Palms, Aria, Cosmopolitan, *M*, and the Wynn. Add to these casinos the absolutely beautiful "locals" casinos, such as the Station group, and we see an explosion in casino development that makes the pre-1989 "boom" look more like a bust.

Even downtown Las Vegas got into the act by building a spectacular light show called "the Fremont Street Experience."

To cause such drastic changes to Las Vegas, some other properties had to be exploded—or rather imploded. Say "bye-boom" to the following hotel-casinos: Castaways, Desert Inn, Boardwalk, Hacienda, Dunes, Silver Slipper, Landmark, Sands, and the original Aladdin.

But it isn't enough to have brilliant hotel-casinos, because *A*-level properties also need *A*-level entertainment. And Vegas has now matched New York City as the town with its finger on the entertainment pulse of the nation, with such spectacular stage shows joining permanent star vehicles. Even many New York productions and Broadway shows are now playing to sold-out audiences in Vegas.

And, yes, while Vegas temporarily tried to position itself as a "family town" in the 1990s (what maniac suggested that?), wiser heads prevailed, and now Las Vegas is once again the true Sin City of the United States, and some of the shows playing the casino venues are certainly not PG-rated, that's for sure. And if you want strip clubs, well you can trip over them as you take a walk for your evening exercise.

Finally one has only to scan the skies over the Strip and other areas to see the phenomenal condos that have rocketed into space. I'm guessing that at night an astronaut can see the brightly lit Las Vegas surrounded by darkness as he orbits space.

If the Amazing Colossal Man were ambling about the new Las Vegas, very few people would see him, because the city now stretches upward and outward, dwarfing him.

So welcome to today's Las Vegas. Who knows where it goes from here?

CHAPTER 31

Ghosts, Demons, and Larger-Than-Life Tales

A re the tales of ghosts, demons, and larger-than-life individuals in this chapter actually true? Some are; some might not be. Real, definitive truth often has little to do with myths and legends. If some of the information that follows is not true, although thousands believe that it *is* true, then it *should* be true to make the world of casinos just that much more fun.

So what's coming up is probably composed of some truth, lots and lots and lots of hyperbole, and a strong smattering of myth. Enjoy them, because we habitués of the casinos need our miracles and legends too.

The Mormon Will

How would you like to receive $156 million for doing a good deed for a broken-down old man? Melvin Dummar almost did. The great movie *Melvin and Howard*, directed by Jonathan Demme, recounts the tale.

Gas-station owner Melvin Dummar of Gabbs, Nevada, picked up an elderly man on a highway in the desert in the early 1970s. The unkempt old man seemed nuts, with long fingernails and an odd glare. Dummar figured the guy was probably a homeless bum and gave him whatever spare change he had as he took the guy to the Sands casino. Sadly, the old nut insisted that he was the billionaire Howard Hughes, who owned airlines and numerous casinos. Of course, Dummar didn't believe that this hopeless, wacky, perhaps totally mad individual could be one of the richest businessmen on the planet. Just look at him!

Some time passed, and then one day Dummar got a letter with instructions to bring it to the Mormon Church in Utah. Dummar followed the directions. After Howard Hughes' death, the letter was unsealed, and it seemed to be a will of the billionaire Howard Hughes, leaving $156 million to Dummar simply for being so kind as to give Mr. Hughes a ride and some spare change.

Then the villains appeared to ruin Dummar's great windfall. What is now the Howard Hughes Corporation contested the validity of the will. Handwriting experts, paid for by the Hughes Corporation, proved the "will" was forged by Dummar. The Hughes Corporation won, and Dummar lost—another example of how Vegas ultimately defeats the average person.

Dummar might have had the last laugh when director Jonathan Demme immortalized his story on film.

Mister, Can You Spare a Nickel?

Have you ever found cash on the casino floor or at least wished to? I have found cash, chips, and slot tokens on the floors over the years, and my windfalls would probably total roughly $18.50.

How about finding a brick, which means $5,000 in $100 bills, wrapped in paper? There it was, right on the carpet, right in front of anyone who looked down. That certainly puts my $18.50 to shame!

Andrew N.S. Glazer, author of the excellent book *Casino Gambling the Smart Way*, was the man who discovered that brick at Bellagio.

Here's how Glazer relates it:

As we walked towards the very fancy cashier desk, there was one couple in front of us. I also noticed, on the floor in front of the couple, lying up against the desk, a brick. The couple moved off to the side, and I walked to the window. I put one of my very large feet on top of the Five Large while I decided what to do. Clearly, there was a chance the money belonged to the people who had just cashed in, mostly because $5,000 doesn't get left on the floor for very long in a casino, even at 3:30 a.m. But it also could have been there for a *while, because people don't always look down—my two friends were right next to me, and they hadn't seen it—and the place was pretty empty. So, I had a few things to think about: how to figure out if there was a rightful owner, and how to get the money for myself if there wasn't. I didn't want someone else to see me pick it up and then yell 'hey, that's mine!' So my size-13 foot helped buy me some time.*

Glazer finally lifted his elephantine foot, stuffed the money into his pocket, and then watched the people in the area of the cashier's cage. He immediately saw a couple searching through their bags for something. They looked very upset. Glazer then confronted a true moral dilemma— one that would reveal what kind of character he had. The $5,000 brick of money was in his pocket. He could walk out of Bellagio with five big ones. Here's what he did: he asked the couple, "What are you looking for?" They told him they were looking for the $5,000.

How would he handle this moral dilemma?

Glazer gave them back the brick. The man gave Glazer a $100 bill for his honesty. For being so honest, we should all buy Glazer's book to help him make up the $4,900 he gave up in winning the moral back-and-forth of that evening.

Monster Winners and Monster Losers

If an article appears in the newspaper or on the Internet about someone who won a monstrous amount of money gambling in the casinos, most people read about it with some envy in their hearts. Stories of people who lost monstrous amounts are profoundly interesting too—and most people feel comfort that they are not as stupid as to do the stupid things that the stupid people did in order to lose all that money. Here are some of the big winners and losers in casino gambling's lore.

In 1992 Archie Karas from Greece claimed he cared nothing for money. One night he wanted to play some "betting" pool and proceeded to borrow $10,000 from his friends. After doubling his initial stake at pool, Archie made his way to the Horseshoe in downtown Las Vegas, a casino where the top poker players could be found. Karas then played one-to-one against 15 of the world's best players, and he won millions. After a very short time, no other poker players wanted to get wiped out by Karas, and they all refused to play him.

With no one left to play, Archie went to the craps tables. Lady Luck continued to be his muse, and he stayed hot, winning millions more. He had won $17 million the toughest way—beating good pool players, beating good poker players, and beating the purely random game of craps (Archie was not a controlled shooter).

Lady Luck is a fickle mistress, and Archie began to lose and lose ever more. He lost the entire $17 million. Archie had been an amazing colossal winner and then became the incredible shrinking man.

One Bet in a Lifetime?

Ashley Revell was not considered a religious man by any means, but he still sold everything he had. Instead of giving his money to the poor, he headed to Las Vegas to place one single bet at roulette. He would either lose everything he had or double his money. He went with his parents who, wild as this scheme was, gave him the moral support he needed.

Ashley went to the Plaza Casino in downtown Las Vegas, and with reporters from all the media alerted, a circus followed. Everyone wanted to see what would happened when Ashley put his whole monetary life on the line—and what line on the roulette table that would actually be.

Ashley slowly placed $135,300 on red. The legions in the audience chanted, "Red! Red! Red!" Then everyone held their breath as the dealer spun the ball.

Ashley watched the ball, which was metaphorically his money, go around and around and around. The ball descended into the pockets. It popped in and out of the pockets—red, red, black, red, black, black, and then...the ball settled into the number 7—the *red* number 7. Ashley Revell suddenly had $270,600. Members of the audience wondered if he would take another shot at the wheel. After all, gamblers find it hard to leave the tables. But Ashley stuck to his word. He tipped the dealers $600 and flew back to England. He had $270,000 to spend as he wished.

He had gambled it all on one thing...and won!

Shoeless Joe, the Million-Dollar Bum

It was 1995 at Treasure Island Casino (now called TI) that a filthy, odorous, slimy man now known as "Shoeless Joe, the Million-Dollar Bum," staggered into the casino several hours after his long-suffering wife had thrown him out of their humble Las Vegas abode. He cashed his $400 Social Security check and proceeded to sink the Treasure Island treasury for almost $1.6 million. It took him almost a week of blackjack play to accomplish this amazing feat, but he stuck to it, and Lady Luck turned her gaze his way.

I know this story is true because I interviewed the dealers, pit personnel, washroom attendants, waiters, and waitresses who dealt to this man, served this man, and watched this man, and every single one of them said that they hated the Million-Dollar Bum! Obnoxious, disgustingly crude, with hygiene habits nearer to a beast than a civilized man, Shoeless Joe actually went shoeless at times, his feet dirty and somewhat gnarled. But as he constantly won, he just kept playing and getting smellier and smellier because he never bathed.

And that strumpet Lady Luck can really do the unthinkable. The Million-Dollar Bum played an awful game of blackjack, hitting and doubling and splitting on hands where he should have stood and taking insurance every time the dealer had an ace showing. But Lady Luck made everything he did wrong come up right. He was a disgusting man, disliked by all, but loved by Dame Fortune, Lady Luck's other name.

Shoeless Joe, the Million-Dollar Bum, did not lose all the money he won. Steve Wynn, the owner of Treasure Island at that time, had security escort the Million-Dollar Bum to the door. According to some people in the know, Shoeless Joe was last seen in the Gold Coast Casino's parking lot drinking from a bottle in a paper bag. He hasn't been seen, heard from, or smelled since.

The Suitcase Man

There are six different versions of this story. Here's the one that I believe is the most accurate.

William Lee Bergstrom arrived at the Horseshoe casino in downtown Las Vegas with a suitcase filled with $777,000, which he put on the Don't

Pass Line at craps. The shooter then sevened out after establishing his point (said to be the 6). Bergstrom took his original $777,000 and his win of $777,000 and left. Had he never come back, he would be a winner without peer—a man who took the casino's money and ran!

Ah, but he couldn't stay away for long. He returned and won a $590,000 bet; then he returned again and won a $190,000 bet; then he returned once more and won $90,000. The legend was already spreading throughout the gambling world about the Suitcase Man. When would he return? Had he finished his gambling career with $1.5 million in his pocket?

But he eventually had one too many flirtations with Dame Fortune, it seems, because he came back in 1984 and made a $1 million bet—one of the most famous bets ever made in a casino—and he lost! Three months later, Bergstrom killed himself at a Strip hotel. He blew his head off.

One thing is certain: all the tales have Bergstrom ahead when he unheaded himself.

Packer Deflates the Texan

He was casino gambling's real-life Amazing Colossal Man—a giant who actually owned casinos but still played in Las Vegas, with a bankroll that could have helped the United States pay off its debts. His wagers would be in the hundreds of thousands of dollars. He would win or lose millions in a single weekend of blackjack and baccarat play.

In short, he could bring a casino to its knees if he got lucky. That was the late Kerry Packer, a billionaire from Australia, who won $40 million dollars at the MGM Grand one weekend.

More wild stories currently circulate about him than about any other high roller in recent casino history. And the stories just get bigger with time, as myths should. His generosity was heralded as much as his awesome wins. His tips often equaled a waitress or dealer's yearly salary. Packer was once reputed to tip a waitress a house, or he paid off her mortgage, depending on which version of the story you hear. In another tale, Packer gave $125,000 in chips to a dealer because he didn't want them. Gee, I wish people would tip writers like that!

But here is a great story about Kerry Packer. It is my favorite of all the stories about him.

A loud and obnoxious Texas high roller in a cowboy hat, wearing those Western pants and with the big buckle on his belt, was playing at the same table and drinking up a storm. The man was belittling the dealers and the waitresses. Finally, Kerry told the man to stop tormenting the personnel. The man got even louder and more obnoxious and put his mug into Packer's face, saying, "Do you know who I am? I am worth $60 million, pardner!" The Texan paused to let this sink in, then said, "Sixty million dollars, pardner. That's what *I'm* worth." Packer eyed him, paused, and then calmly said, "I'll flip you for it!" [For different Kerry Packer stories, read Barney Vinson's book *Ask Barney*.]

The Challenge of Chance

Play against a house edge and, over time—sometimes a short time, almost always a long time—the player gets his behind handed to him. That's the problem with playing games in which the casino has the edge: your expectation is to lose—that is, unless you are an advantage player who can get the edge over the house. Advantage players are few and very far between.

But the world of probability is not always a straight and ordered path where everyone strictly fits into the proper mathematical mold. Not all gamblers *must* lose; indeed, some players have faced overwhelming negative probability and still won. Probability exists on a continuum, with some people all the way on one end when it comes to good luck and some other people all the way on the other end when it comes to bad luck, with most people squeezing toward the middle, having some good luck and some bad luck. But those at the extremes are the outliers; and when an outlier has remarkable good luck, it makes us all wish deep inside ourselves, *Couldn't that have happened to me?*

So what people and events have seemingly defied math and gone to the outlying extremes of the probability continuum?

The longest streak for a single number in roulette was six in a row, and this occurred twice—once in San Juan, Puerto Rico, in 1956, and once in Las Vegas on July 14, 2000. On that latter day, the number 7 came up six times in a row at Las Vegas' Caesars Palace.

What are the odds of a selected roulette number hitting six times in a row? They are 3,010,936,383-to-1! Did Caesars casino lose a boatload of money on such an amazing streak? No, it didn't. The players played as they always played, and the casino lost—hold your breath—a paltry $300 during this out-of-the-world event. The record is hard to believe, but the amount of money the casino lost and the piddling money the players won is even harder to believe. [Barney Vinson, an eyewitness to the "Caesars' Six," writes about it in his book *Ask Barney*.]

And what about craps?

On Saturday evening, May 23, 2009, at Borgata Casino in Atlantic City, Patricia DeMauro played craps for the second time in her life and rolled 154 numbers before sevening out. This epic roll eclipsed the great legend of Atlantic City, the man known as the Captain, who previously held the world record of 147 numbers.

DeMauro's roll lasted four hours and 18 minutes and, in terms of time, also eclipsed Stanley Fujitake's record length of three hours and six minutes (Fujitake rolled 118 numbers before sevening out). DeMauro is now the new champ in terms of time and, more important, in terms of the total number of rolls before sevening out. "The king is dead; all hail the queen!"

The Captain's roll lasted two hours and 18 minutes, but he had a secret weapon that Fujitake and DeMauro did not have. The Captain wasn't overcoming the odds by luck. He was a controlled shooter, so his achievement, while still highly unusual and unexpected, is not as wild a ride as DeMauro's or any random roller who takes it to the house using nothing but luck. What were the odds of DeMauro rolling 154 numbers before sevening out? A mere 5,600,000,000-to-1 (5.6 billion–to-1), give or take a little! But here is the stunner: because so many people at the table were new players—three of whom had never played—and most were red-chip players, the casino lost approximately $180,000!

Editor's Note: *The full story of Pat DeMauro's world-record roll is in Frank's book* Casino Craps: Shoot to Win! *and the full story of the Captain's roll, which Frank witnessed, can be found in* Cutting Edge Craps: Advanced Strategies for Serious Players!

As far as I know, the longest sustained winning streaks in craps belonged to the late Arm. The Arm played weekly with the Captain through the 1980s and 1990s. Those who played at the same table with her, a group known as "the Captain's Crew," vouched time and again that she almost never had a losing roll. She might have had poor rolls now and then, but she could be relied upon to blaze a winning trail when she hit the tables. The Captain of craps had this to say about the Arm: "She was completely focused when she rolled. I'd say her *average* rolls lasted 15 to 20 minutes, but she has strung together back-to-back 45-minute and one-hour rolls that I witnessed. She was a master of avoiding the 7."

The Arm was the greatest rhythmic roller I ever saw, and I have seen just about all of the great ones in my career.

The Golden Touch Craps website at http://www.goldentouchcraps.com/worldrecords.php4 has a list of craps players who have rolled more than 50 numbers before sevening out, in addition to a whole host of other records. At this moment, here are the 10 top rolls (No. 10 is a tie) the Golden Touch website has recorded. Each of these rolls had eyewitnesses verify it. There could be other monster rolls that have occurred, but none of those have been recorded and verified.

The Top 10 Verified Craps Rolls Before Sevening Out

1. 154 rolls: Patricia DeMauro
2. 147 rolls: The Captain
3. 118 rolls: Stanley Fujitake
4. 100 rolls: The Captain
5. 90 rolls: Charlie "Sandtrap"
6. 89 rolls: Frank Scoblete
7. 88 rolls: Timmy
8. 86 rolls: CharlieF
9. 84 rolls: CharlieF
10. 79 rolls: Dominator
10. 79 rolls: Metafast

The greatest sustained wins at blackjack occurred in a small stretch of time between late 2010 and into the spring of 2011 by Pennsylvania's Don

Johnson, who won $15.1 million from Tropicana, Caesars, and Borgata. Johnson made a deal with these casinos that they pay back 20 percent of any losses he had during his playing sessions. This deal was to his benefit and allowed him to overcome the very low house edges on the Atlantic City blackjack game.

Slot Monster

The largest jackpot ever won at slots was $39,713,982. It was achieved in Las Vegas at the Excalibur Casino on March 21, 2003, during the NCAA tournament, by a player who had only gone to Vegas to watch some basketball and put some coins into the machines. He certainly hit a three-pointer by overcoming almost 50,000,000-to-1 odds!

Happy New Year?

I am not sure of the exact date when this happened, but it was probably in the late 1980s. A player at Caesars Palace, so the story goes, had one of those amazingly lucky nights at both the slot machines and the craps tables, winning millions. To make it even better, it was New Year's Eve. What a nice way to end the year—winning a fortune.

Having had quite a bit to drink, he toasted the casino at the big New Year's Eve party and went to his room to sleep it off and count his millions the way some people count sheep.

He woke up the next morning slightly hungover, but how can you not be happy being a newly minted millionaire? Yes, he would have to pay taxes on the money he won, but so what? There was money and more money left over.

He decided that his luck would continue, and he hit the machines and the tables on New Year's Day. He hit them hard...and lost every penny he had made the night before! Do you think that's a horrible beginning to a New Year? Come on, the stories of gamblers losing all their wins are nothing new.

Here is what's new: Because he had won his money in one year and lost his money in another year, he was still responsible for the taxes! And those taxes were on millions of dollars. The moral of the story? Happy New Year isn't always so happy.

Nasty, Nasty, Nasty

Boxing and buffets, martial arts and marriage—that's the Vegas many of us know and love. The greatest evening of eating and boxing occurred at the exact same time on the night of June 28, 1997, when Mike Tyson tried to eat Evander Holyfield's ears in their World Heavyweight Championship match. Tyson did not enjoy the taste of the first ear and spewed it out into the audience. Then he took a chunk from the other ear and coughed that out too.

The fight was stopped because of Tyson's strange eating habits, but the Tyson fans, upset by their top chef's disqualification, ran wild through the MGM Grand—perhaps looking for other ears to eat.

Eyewitnesses said that gunshots were fired, but the official report claimed the rampagers were just popping corks of champagne bottles— probably a vintage that went well with earlobes. Young men, perhaps future chefs, with golden teeth along with dripping gold chains, decided to borrow various brightly colored chips as they smashed tables and goose-stepped their way through the casino. If a fleeing casino patron passed their steely gazes, the patron was belted out.

But the biggest mystery of the evening has little to do with rampaging fans popping champagne corks and pummeling casino patrons. Everyone wants to know in the past decades what actually happened to those pieces of Holyfield's ears? Were they pocketed by the custodians? ("Hey, Jim, look at this gooey thing! It's the big piece of Holyfield's ear.") Discarded? ("Oh, man, throw that damn thing out, Paul.") Were the various pieces saved as mementos? ("These are gonna be worth a fortune someday. Let me have them.")

There is some speculation at the Nevada Culinary Institute that one of Tyson's fans picked up the biggest piece of Holyfield's ear, dried it, and now wears it at the end of a gold chain hanging from his neck.

The Greatest Crossroader

Crossroaders will steal chips from unsuspecting craps players by just reaching next to them and swiping the chips at the end of the rail. They will try to steal money that has been rejected by slot machines. They will try anything but actually going out to work like a normal human being. Yes, they are scum, but the great ones are fascinating scum.

The Encyclopedia of Gambling, a great book by Carl Sifakis (Facts on File Books), lists Glen Grayson as the "king of the crossroaders." Grayson was the leader of a team of thieves who stole from the casinos in Las Vegas and other parts of the world. Grayson did, however, have an affinity for Las Vegas and loved to switch in "loaded" or "crooked" dice when he was the shooter.

He also enjoyed stealing slot machines from casinos. He would walk into a casino dressed like a slot technician and, with his fellow "technicians," put the machine on a hand-truck and take it out the front door, where their "service truck" was waiting. Glen Grayson stole these machines in the Mafia-controlled casinos that were owned by far bigger crooks than he. (For more information on Glen Grayson, read John Soares' book *Loaded Dice*.)

A Most Disgusting Crossroader

If you have the least bit of human sensitivity, you might want to skip this part. But if you like something gross to make your scalp tingle and your mouth scrunch, this is for you.

This happened at Bally's in Las Vegas more than two decades ago. A man with a heavy Greek accent—history now refers to him as "the Greek"—was playing craps, and one of the security officers who worked the eye in the sky noticed that this particular player was stealing black chips from the player next to him.

The guy was pretty good too, and he only stole the chips when the other man was shooting. If the guy hit some numbers, our Greek patted him on the back and cheered and slipped his fingers into the player's rack of chips, quickly taking a black chip. He occasionally did this when the player was reaching down for the dice too. He'd put the black chip he had stolen down the back of his pants where, thought the security officer, he probably had a sock bag to hold it.

This kind of ploy had been worked many times before; it was part and parcel of the crossroader's handbook. Even thieving dealers had used a variant of the sock-bag trick—usually the bag was in the sleeves of their shirts, and as they swiped chips now and then from the chip tray, the chips would go into the arm bag. I saw a live demonstration of this and, believe me, the dealers who did the arm-bag theft were really good. I never saw the chips being stolen.

But the hubris-endowed Greek was merely a stupid pigeon thinking he was nailing an even stupider pigeon, and when he had stolen enough chips to make the theft a big one—big enough to put his fat ass in prison—the Bally's security team had the Clark County Police arrest him.

In a holding area at the police station, the Greek was told to drop his pants and turn around. He did as he was told. "Pull down your underwear," the cops instructed. There was no bag in his underwear or wrapped around his waist. There were no black chips to be seen.

"Oh, God," said one officer.

"Oh, crap," said another officer.

"Damn," said still another officer.

If the Greek had not used a bag to put the black chips in, what had he put them into? He had definitely stolen a lot—and I do mean *a lot*—of black chips from the player who was next to him at the craps table. So where were they?

Yes, he had shoved those many black chips up his...well, you get the unsavory picture. Whichever police officer had to dig out those chips should have gotten hazardous-duty pay.

The Greek spent some time in jail and was finally sent back to his native country and told never to return to America. I wonder if he listened? To be protected, protect your chips.

Another World

Books, television shows, and movies have an enthusiastic audience for tales of the supernatural and of the otherwise strange. I think many of us also have just such a fascination. I know I do. Casino gambling lore has plenty of stories about those weird things that can happen in the world of luck—and I am talking *really weird*.

Is God in the Numbers?

Think of 9/11—of course, without explaining it, you know what those numbers mean—the worst terrorist attack on the homeland of the United States in our history. And it has now been imbued with mystical import.

On Sunday, September 11, 2011, which was the 10th anniversary of the terrorist attacks on America, the first three winners at the Belmont Race Track in New York were 9, then 1, then 1—yes 9-1-1.

Adding to the strangeness of this event is the fact that this particular raceway was a staging area for rescue crews working the World Trade Center site.

The Ghosts of Las Vegas

Don't be terrified, but I am going to rip the lid off a problem that has been haunting Las Vegas for years now...ghosts! That's right, ghosts.

Las Vegas is home to great singers, comedians, hypnotists, magicians, beautiful showgirls, gambling, fine food and drink...but it also has sometimes bubbly spirits that have not come out of a champagne bottle.

I am sure that most of us might think, *Oh, well, those old-time miners are probably still haunting the caves and valleys. No need for me to worry about that. I stick to the hotels.* Sorry, the hotel-casinos, even the new ones, have plenty of ghosts. No need to gamble on that fact.

Okay, so I cannot prove that any of the tales I am about to present are absolutely true. But I can say that I received this information from reliable sources, which is to say, from sources other than my imagination. Make of it what you will. Are my sources merely nuts who seem reliable or reliable sources that are called "nuts" once they relate what they know? You'll have to decide.

The great musician and comedian Liberace is still floating around Vegas. He loves to appear at the Tivoli Gardens, where he plays jokes on the customers. He once owned that venue, and he obviously doesn't want to leave. Sometimes he is seen with the ghost of Elvis—the old Elvis, that is, of the star-spangled, flaming suits.

Elvis also likes to make occasional appearances at the Las Vegas Hilton, where he performed in his last years. Sometimes some audience members get a glimpse of him on the stage when another singer is performing. Are these audience members really seeing Elvis? Or have they imbibed a little too much in the way of spirits?

Another great entertainer, the late Danny Gans, has a seemingly haunted bathroom near the former Danny Gans Theatre at the Mirage. It seems a wall fell down there, and cold spots are felt when you use the facilities. Is it the ghost of Gans returning to his old venue to imitate a ghost? Or is it just bad pipes?

Mandalay Bay and Luxor seem to have Native American ghosts wandering their grounds dressed as workmen. Could they be the ghosts of construction workers who passed away but didn't want to leave the job undone?

Luxor also has a problem with two ghosts who walk the balconies over the registration area. Both are young men who seem distracted. Who wouldn't be, with all the action under them? It is whispered that one of these ghosts was a suicide who probably still thinks he's on vacation.

Those of you who follow ghost stories know that most ghosts are pretty stupid. They walk up and down stairs and in and out of walls, make noises, and cause cold spots, but they don't seem to have much in the way of IQ or humor. Not so with the ghost of the old Stardust Hotel. This one—dressed in the formal style of the late 1950s, including a bowler hat—showed up when guests came off the elevator. He would dance, doff his hat, laugh, and walk right through the wall. He seemed to be totally aware of what he was doing, perhaps more so than some of the people staggering off the elevator.

Okay, so these stories aren't too scary, right? Fine, you asked for it. Planet Hollywood Las Vegas, which took over the new Aladdin, which was rebuilt on the ruins of the old Aladdin, has a legendarily haunted room. Stay in the Panorama Suite on the seventh floor, and see what you see, feel, and hear. The reports are that *several* ghosts haunt this room.

Cheating on your wife can have dire consequences, as some of you men know. Several conventioneers a few decades ago, who were staying at the late Sahara Hotel, told their lovely wives that they were going golfing but went to a house of ill repute instead. On their way back to the hotel after all that illicit fun, they got into a crash and were killed. Not such a bad fate, considering their wives would have killed them anyway—very *slowly*—had they found out about their preferred entertainment.

Here's the kick: These conventioneers didn't just fade away into lore. No, sir; they just keep going to the rooms where they were staying and knocking on the doors to be let in. They are *still* knocking on those doors to this day. So if you hear someone knocking on the door, and when you look through the peephole no one is there...those husbands have returned and are coming home to roost.

Many of you might know the story of the haunted craps table at Caesars Palace. Casinos judge the amount of money they should make based on a formula that uses number of decisions multiplied by the amount wagered to come up with an estimate of how much they should win each month.

But this craps table lost month after month after month for 13 months straight. That is unheard of. One month, yes; two months, okay; three months, maybe...but 13? No way! So the superstitious casino executives took the table out back and set it on fire. No table since has ever lost money for such an extended period of time. Oh, yes, casino executives can be just as superstitious as anyone else.

The Ghosts of Atlantic City

There are some psychic researchers who believe that ghosts are house-specific as opposed to land-specific. They maintain that a stretch of land that houses so many new buildings, a stretch such as the Atlantic City Boardwalk casino area, just doesn't have the necessary ingredients for entertaining ghosts or entertaining ghost tales.

Well, behind the exterior walls of some of our beautiful Atlantic City casinos are buildings with real histories—and interesting ghost stories as well. Obviously I can't vouch for the validity of the tales I'm about to share with you, but if you like fun ghost stories, hang on to your lantern and enter the dark world of Atlantic City's spirits.

The very first casino to open in Atlantic City was Resorts International. But the building Resorts used to gain a foothold in the land of Lady Luck was actually built in 1868 as the Chalfonte Hotel. This hotel was moved twice to get it closer to the water.

In 1903 the Chalfonte merged with the Haddon-Hall building to form the Chalfonte–Haddon-Hall Hotel. And that was when the first ghosts were recorded.

This 1,000-room hotel was 15 stories high, and guests constantly reported the top floors had areas of supreme cold—a signal of the presence of ghosts, according to ghost hunters. Although the building was brick and steel, it seemed to move with the wind, which also was said to howl through the halls.

Some psychic researchers, who would not allow me to name them, say that those winds and howls can be heard to this day. If you ride the elevators, you will sometimes hear sounds that are—as one ghoulish expert stated—"the knocks and pings of a disincarnate spirit trying to escape." What is this spirit trying to escape? I have no idea, nor does anyone else. Maybe his luck is as bad as many of the gamblers on the casino floor?

During World War II soldiers were quartered in the building, which had become a hospital as well. There are reports that, on many nights, ghosts of hospitalized air corpsmen were seen walking the hallways of Resorts, and some have even entered the hotel's registration areas. Although some areas of Resorts were knocked down in 1980 to make room for a parking lot, enough of the old building remains to make a good environment for many spirits and infernal nocturnal manifestations.

The casino has also had its share of spectral anomalies, like the wraith in the Charlie Chaplin "Little Hobo" costume who hangs around the darkest area of the casino, flipping his hat at passersby. Only a fraction of a percent of passersby catch a glimpse of the movement, and an even smaller number really see the ghost.

One former Resorts dealer stated, "I saw him. He seemed to notice people, but only a few of the people ever noticed him. Some people just thought he was an entertainer, and many smiled and just walked by him."

There are also a spectral bride and groom who are occasionally seen on the second floor, where Resorts restaurants can be found. These two only have eyes for each other and walk through walls, strolling arm-in-arm and smiling into each other's pale faces. Who are they? Why are they walking the property? Again, no one seems to know.

On the beach outside of the casino are many cats, and early in morning—as the sun is coming up over the horizon to herald the start of day—a woman all in black walks the sand just beyond the boardwalk. The meowing of cats heralds her presence, as she appears to be feeding them.

Perhaps the strangest visions in the Resorts area are those of children, some very young. Glowing nurses can be seen wheeling children in ghostly carriages and wheelchairs. Young boys and girls slowly walk outside the front of the hotel, many being helped by nurses in uniform. This seems to have its zenith near the valet parking. These spectral children will often just disappear in a puff of pale light. Some of these children look dazed and confused, others look sad, some look hostile and angry. Where do they come from, and why are they there? Who are these children?

Are these ghosts really real? Does Resorts have a lingering population of the spirits of the dead who have not gone to their eternal rewards? Or are these but tales "told by an idiot, full of sound and fury, signifying nothing," as Shakespeare's Macbeth said?

Real or imagined? True or fictional? As I said, you'll have to make that decision.

CHAPTER 32

Casinos Are the New High Schools

Casino gambling is about more than casino gambling. It's the closest thing to high school, short of driving America's roads, where any ploppy can get a license. In a casino, you rub shoulders with every type of human imaginable, some of whose shoulders you wish they'd kept to themselves.

You can go from nice, friendly, clean, presentable, pleasant, and successful folks down to the dissipated, disgusting, obnoxious, whiny, drunk, slurring, stupid, loud, smelly, and disheveled creatures that just might not be humans.

There are peasants and paupers, kings and queens, walking the floors, aisles, hallways, and restaurants of almost any casino.

Yes, just like high school, where all manner of kids are dumped together to more or less fend for themselves, casinos essentially invite the public in, and the public is, unfortunately, the *public*. As anyone whose job it is to deal with large swaths of the public will attest, "Many of them are idiots."

Think about that other high school analogy, namely driving on the roads. It's rare that you hear someone scream out the window, "You are a good driver; I commend you!" No, what you hear on the public roads is usually, "You are a fucking idiot!"

High school is dominated by dopes. Indeed, there are more kids fighting to be the stupidest kid in school than are fighting to be the smartest, and there are only a handful of students who have a shot at being the valedictorian. In fact, when I was a teacher I recommended to the school that we set up a new award called the Dumb-Dick-Torian for the absolutely stupidest student in the school.

For some reason this idea was frowned upon by the administrators, many of whom were former teachers who had fled the classroom like rats leaving the Titanic because they realized they couldn't handle the dumb-dick-torians of America.

But when it comes to nice people, you don't hear too many complaints, do you? "Oh, my, my, Mrs. Jones is just too nice! She gives to charity, helps the poor, goes to church, and has a smile for everyone. Isn't that disgusting?"

No, the Mrs. Joneses of the world don't elicit our scorn. But Mrs. Jones' cousin, Elmer the Drooling, sure does. He's loud and dirty and pushes his way into your life, whether you want him there or not. All his conversations are loud and in your face. He has no capacity to whisper or even talk in a normally pitched voice.

On the beach, Elmer the Drooling plays loud music; in his car, the *thump, thump, thump* of the bass can shake the foundations of a skyscraper. He smokes in nonsmoking areas, drinks too much and is often seen and/or heard regurgitating in the alleys of life. When in a restaurant, he spits when he eats because he talks with stringy food loaded in his wet mouth that has more cavities than he does teeth. He's a poor tipper too and loves to degrade waitresses with what he thinks is humor.

Elmer the Drooling is the creep who jumps ahead of you in the buffet line and handles the rolls and desserts with his hands instead of using the tongs. He also analyzes pieces of these foods and puts back the ones that are too small—after bringing them up to his mucus-dripping nose to smell them.

At the gaming tables, he is loud and wants everyone to share in his misfortunes as he laments with foul language his inability to win. Or he wants the entire world to know he is a winner as he shouts out his simian challenge: "I can't lose!"

Of course, nice people try to ignore him, but he figures if he can't attract attention by screaming, he will attract attention by screaming *louder*. No experience is so refined or delicate that he can't ruin it.

In truth, most people are nice or, at the very least, tolerable; but the Elmer the Droolings just dominate the human landscape as hordes of ploppies dominate the high school experience.

Casino gambling is fun, and most of us try to push the beastly ones away from our remembrances of casino visits from the past. Unfortunately, I don't have that capacity. I remember the casino ploppies.

I remember the California heart surgeon who threw over a black-jack table at the Golden Nugget because he was losing. I remember the drunken woman at the Silverton who passed out onto my lap and then slid to the floor in a heap. I remember the player who threw a towel into the dealer's face at the Maxim after purposely dumping a drink onto the table. I remember the player who relieved himself onto the leg of a dealer at a craps table at a casino that will remain nameless.

I remember the young lady who went on a cursing spree because she thought all the games were fixed against her (duh) at Mirage. I remember the two elderly women—one with blue hair and one with weird-looking red hair—fistfighting over a slot machine and pulling out each other's somewhat thinning, dyed hair by the roots. This was at Showboat in Atlantic City. And they were sisters!

I remember the blackjack player at Tropicana in Atlantic City who abused an entire table for causing him to lose because none of them played correctly. I've seen craps players heave-ho onto the craps layouts at several casinos. "I'll take a yooooooooooooo...*splash!*"

I am sure every casino gambler has his or her own list too. After all, the public is the public. You can't escape the roads, and the casinos are nothing more than high school students all grown up. But, sadly, most of them are as stupid as ever.

CHAPTER 33
Cruising for a Bruising

I have never given much thought to cruising on the ocean. That's never been my idea of a vacation—rocking, rolling, and perhaps "losing it" on the wavy waters. On occasion in the past two decades, I have been invited to speak on this cruise or that, and my wife, the beautiful A.P., and I have always turned down such proposals. Being on a cruise ship was never on the top of my fun list, even though I had never been on a cruise ship.

Such is prejudice.

However, ever since seeing the HBO documentary *Braving Alaska* in 1993, the beautiful A.P. and I have been fascinated with our 49th state. So we've always wanted to visit Alaska—which is a long, long way from our home in New York. Still, it never occurred to us that going on a cruise would be a great way to see this fabulous state.

But things changed this past summer. My good friend and fellow writer, Jerry "Stickman," and his wife, the sainted Tres, gave us a proposition—let's go on an Alaskan cruise and, better still, let's invite six other Golden Touch Craps members to come along: our good friends Skinny and Jean, the Goddess and Sandtrap, and the Raging Baritone and Betty. That would make 10 of us heading for the high seas.

Six of us are controlled shooters: Stickman, Skinny, the Goddess, Sandtrap, the Raging Baritone, and me. We all thought confidently that, given seven days on the ship, we would be able to recoup the expensive cost of the voyage and have a free sailing vacation, compliments of the cruise line.

Such is hubris.

The first disappointment I had was the fact that the ship's single craps table did not open until 9:00 PM (which was 1:00 AM New York time). I am not really a nighttime shooter, because my bedtime is—don't laugh—between 9:00 and 10:00. My best rolls come in the afternoon, especially after I swim. I didn't think of this as a problem, because the others were more than capable of holding their own at night, and I would just have to keep my eyes open in order to rack in the casino's chips.

So that first night on the ship, we headed for the craps table and had it all to ourselves. This was not a cruise with many craps players; indeed, this ship's casino never really got hopping as I've been told other cruise casinos do. The craps table rarely had more than three other players on it, aside from our contingent.

My second disappointment came in the form of the odds allowed on the Pass Line and Come bets—they were 2X. Okay, no problem; I would bet in units of three, to capitalize on the maximum amount in Odds. This is called "pushing the house," a way to get a better game than the casino advertises. So I could bet $30 and back that up with 2X (or $60) on the 4 and 10 in Odds, but I could back up the 5 and 9 with $80 and the 6 and 8 with $100.

"Sorry, sir, you can't do that," said the box lady when I first put $100 in odds on my $30 Come bet.

"Can't I go 60, 80, 100 in Odds on a three-unit Come bet?" I asked. I had not been in a 2X casino in a decade that did not allow pushing the house this way.

"No," said the box lady. The dealers and the box lady were not native English speakers, and Skinny thought that maybe they didn't understand what we were saying. Each had a heavy accent, and it took them time to understand what we said. As the beautiful A.P. would tell us, "They are conversational in English but not fluent." This turned out to be true for almost every worker we met on the ship, except for the bosses.

So Skinny called over the director of the casino, who was British, and asked him about the three-unit bet. "No, we don't do that," said the director.

So we pumped up the bets to $50, so we could take $100 in odds.

Once the initial disappointment wore off, which it did rather quickly, our team took the dice...and stunk. The Raging Baritone rolled a 17 before sevening out, the best roll of the night, but Skinny, Stickman, and the Goddess just didn't have it that night. I took the dice once, made my point, established another point, hit a number, and sevened out. Not an auspicious cruise-casino debut.

By 10:00 we ended the session.

"We'll get them tomorrow," we sung in unison.

Sadly, we didn't get anything on the morrow, either. The ship had activities all day, in addition to the incredible scenery right off our balcony, and by 9:00 PM we were all tired. We had to force ourselves to play.

So that second night, we stunk as well. I again took the dice once, made three numbers, and then sevened out. The only interesting thing on that second night was that the dealers, box lady, and casino director had figured out who I was—the writer who teaches people to beat the game of craps. I could imagine the guffaws on their breaks, as I had come tumbling down before their very eyes.

After the second night, Stickman and I decided it was a waste of our time and money to play the ship's craps game. We were too tired, and our shooting was awful. In truth, we knew we just couldn't perform under these conditions, and so we stopped playing. I was in bed by 9:00 and enjoyed the trip immensely—even though I had to actually pay for it.

Had Stickman and I continued to play craps, well, we would have been cruising for a bruising.

CHAPTER 34

Eat...Me?

By the time you read this, I will be skinny. Okay, maybe not skinny as in "My God! Frank Scoblete is so skinny now!" but more like, "He dropped a lot of weight and doesn't resemble a float in the Macy's Thanksgiving Day Parade anymore."

You see, I have a bone to pick with casino gambling—and it's not a bone with juicy steak on it or fried chicken on it or pork with delicious barbeque dressing dripping all over it or...uh, excuse me, I've been dieting, and I am thinking about food a lot.

My bone has to do with the fact that when I started my casino eating career—sorry, I mean my casino *gambling* career—more than 20 years ago, I was 5'7" tall and weighed a mere 145 pounds. Yes, having just come from my life in the theater, as a leading man who always got the girl, I could also run 10-mile races at six minutes per mile, I could do 100 pushups and 100 pull-ups and 1,000 sit-ups, and I could see that my wife, the beautiful A.P., is eating this delicious apple crumble that she makes... Ohhhh! There I go again.

I am not good on a diet. These past 24 hours have been hell on my nerves. And by my calculation I have another 4,800 hours to go on this darned thing. If my local pizzeria took so long to deliver their incredible, scrumptious pepperoni pizza just dripping with grease and cheese and...

Sorry. I am now 5'6½" tall and weigh in at more than 200 pounds... okay, much more than 200 pounds. I am a huge Chunky candy bar. Yes,

I have gained an unsightly number of pounds and somehow lost half an inch in height. Maybe gravity is weighing me down.

When I went to my doctor—a nice attractive woman about 55 years old, skinny, a yoga teacher too, and…really, no casino is offering her free booze, free food, free shows, and…uh, sorry—she told me that right now all my blood work is okay and my prostate is "perfect" (that's her quote! My quote was, "Can you *stop that* now!")

"Get control of your weight. I want to see you lose 40 pounds in the next year," she said.

That is so easy for a skinny woman who teaches yoga to say. If I told her to lose 40 pounds, she would disappear and cease to exist. But I didn't tell her to do that. I am too nice a guy.

Okay, now some of you are guffawing, "Yo, Scoblete goes to a woman doctor! Ha ha!"

Okay, fella, who is smarter, you or me? I say me, and you know why? Because when I hit 50 years old, I did have a male doctor. He was 6'4" and said to me, "It's time for you to have *that* exam." And *that* exam is the one mentioned above, where I am "perfect," mind you. He held up his hand with the latex glove on it, and his hand looked just like those giant hands they sell at sporting events with the one finger pointing, and I knew an absolute truth then: *that thing* is not going into me.

So I switched to a woman doctor who is maybe five feet tall and has very small, delicate, feminine fingers. I figure with so little meat on those fingers, even as she ages, the finger she uses for *that* exam will always be thin.

Bones, yes…I forgot my bone to pick with the casinos. The casinos thought they could get me to forget that, but I remembered.

The casinos made me fat because they *forced* me to eat all those comped buffets and gourmet meals and to drink all those comped drinks. And they *forced* me to play those table games for endless hours instead of going to the gym, where the treadmill waited to torture me with the loss of about 100 calories per mile.

My word! Only 100 calories per mile! You eat a brownie, and there are maybe 300 or 400 calories in it. You have to run three or four miles just to get rid of one stinking brownie. And what if you like to put some vanilla ice cream on the brownie? That's another 300 to 400 calories. Then I love nuts when I have ice cream, and those are loaded with calories. I also prefer brownies that have nuts in them, because I like their crunchiness.

So let's see, just for a stinking brownie I have to run maybe a half marathon. The main meal at a buffet is composed of many important elements—like seven or eight different meals. How can you go to a buffet that is comped and not eat everything in sight?

You can't.

So you have to figure that I would have to run for several days without sleep just to work off my lunch. So, okay, when would I play the casino games that got me the buffet comp in the first place? I wouldn't.

Without playing the games, I would not get the comps! You see the dilemma I'm in? I'd be in the damn gym all the time working off brownies and ice cream and steak and chicken and pork and rice of different varieties and Chinese food and pizza and the occasional salad my wife forces me to eat so it looks as if I eat a balanced diet.

Forget about it, working out for 72 straight hours is not fun, and I refuse to do that. Why would I fly to Vegas or drive to Atlantic City just to work out endlessly in the gyms? You'd have to be nuts to do that—like a pecan nut or a walnut or a peanut slathered with fudge.

I *want* those comps! I mean, I *deserve* those comps, after all, for my play. I am only getting what I deserve.

Also, come on, let's be *honest* here: those people who do nothing but work out in the gyms all the time, there is something seriously wrong with their skinny selves. Their minds are gone. All they do is look in the mirrors to see how good they look. I never look in the mirror, not since I transcended the 180-pound mark a few years back. I am not vain!

What the heck am I talking about here? You see how confused I am? The casinos have done this to me, wanting to force me to work out for days straight in the gyms without eating anything. How crazy are those casino people? They should ban the gyms from the casino hotels. There should be a law. Yes, I want a new law that no casino properties are allowed to have gyms, because gyms are inhuman!

And they should loosen their comps even more so that we can eat for 24 hours straight if we want to.

That's my bone to pick with the casinos! There, I said it.

Now I could use a brownie.

CHAPTER 35

Are You Going Overboard?

Drinking, eating, running, and gambling all have one thing in common, which is that you can get so hooked on them that they become obsessive negative endeavors instead of positively fun endeavors.

Obviously, a glass or two of wine at dinner or a cocktail of two at a party are enjoyable, but if you become a stumbling drunk, it isn't good for you. If you eat too much and become one of the hordes of heavies in this land of milk and lard, that too is not a good thing, as any doctor will tell you. Yes, there are even long-distance runners who have damaged their bodies so much that their doctors caution them to cut back or cut out running altogether. I know one long-distance runner who damaged his kidneys with his crazy daily workouts.

Gambling, casino or otherwise, is now enjoyed by about 54 million Americans, most of whom have it in complete control—they win some, they lose somewhat more. No big deal, it's the price of entertainment. Yet there are some gamblers who have taken their joy into the realm of the ridiculous.

Now I am not speaking of the totally addicted gambler, one who ruins his or her life and relationships because of an insane urge to gamble his or her money away. These people are best handled by clinical professionals or 12-step programs. Still, the clinically addicted gamblers make up only a small percentage of all gamblers.

No, the gamblers I am referring to are the ones who go a little too far, so that today they seriously regret what they did yesterday. No casino gambler likes to lose, and all casino gamblers feel bad when they do lose; but it goes with the territory.

However, some gamblers have a tendency to allow the casino gambling experience to get the best of them. They play too long, bet too much, and take losses that they really shouldn't take.

So how can you tell if you have a tendency to go overboard in the casinos? There are 10 telling signs that you have gone over the edge. Keep in mind, I am not talking about addicted gamblers here, just regular players who have taken a leap off a diving board that they shouldn't have.

1. You think to yourself, *The money I am betting could go to my heart operation!* If you think that the money you are wagering could be used for something else, then it *should* be used for something else. This thinking is a way for one part of your mind to tell the other part of your mind to reduce the amounts of your bets or to take a break.

2. You go back to your room (or your home), and your spouse or companion looks stunned and says, "You lost *how* much?" If you can shock someone who knows you so well, then you have obviously gone astray.

3. You go to the ATM or credit-card machine to get more money to play with.

4. You ask for an increase in your casino credit because you used it all up.

5. You borrow money from a friend to play with.

6. You lie about how much you lost.

7. You claim you actually won money instead of lost money.

8. You start to bet more in order to win back everything you lost, hoping to win a few big bets.

9. You start playing a game for which you have no idea of the strategy in order to hit one of that game's big payouts. Slot and video-poker players will also do this by jumping to higher-denomination machines, hoping to hit a few big ones to come back all the way.

10. You want a comp and complain when you don't get the amount you want, using as your reasoning, "But I lost this much!" Comps are not based on how much you lose but on how much you bet and how long you play. You can win and get a comp, and you can lose and not get a comp.

If you fall into any one or more of these categories, you have to rein yourself in. It's no fun playing casino games if doing so causes you to go on tilt.

CHAPTER 36
Letters from Gambling's Mixed Nuts

Harrah's does a survey every year of the American gambler, and the last one I read said there were about 54 million of us—about 30 percent of the adult population, in other words—and that we represent something of a cross-section of American society, although somewhat richer and better educated.

As such, there are probably a decent number of "nuts" among the gambling cross-section as there are in society as a whole. Mind you, I do not mean "nuts" in the mental-illness sense (who are to be helped), just nuts in the...well...*nutty* sense.

I've corresponded with some of these nuts, and here are some of their emails and letters to me, followed by my *sane* and *understanding* responses. All spelling is theirs, but I have punctuated some of them slightly so they are less un-understandable.

Dear So-Called Frank Scoblatte:
So what makes you so smart that you think you are so smart? Nothing that is what it all is nothing at all. Why do you say that there are no trends in gambing when I see trends all the time in everything I do, including my so-called normal things of existance, like shopping and bowling and garding? The so-called editos of this magazine should spunk you on your bittox!
Alex

Dear Alex:

I've never tasted latte, but I hear it is delicious! I am smart enough to know I am not that smart, but I do know one thing about randomness. Trends exist in the past but cannot be accurately predicted for gambling purposes when a casino has an edge on every bet you make. Ultimately trend finding is another name for "loss finding." By the way, what is it you are "garding"?

    So-Called Scoblatte

Dear Fnark:

I been reading your artiocles in *Casino Players* and *Strictly Sluts*, and I have enjoyed mots of them, but some of them are too far over my head that I needed to wtrite to you to tell you to make your ideas more simply instead of trying to be so over my head head. I also think Henry Trombone is too far out too. I want things I can understand and not things I don't' understand.

    Martha J.

Dear Martha:

Being tangibly and intimately involved with Strictly Sluts *generated much analytical excitement in all domains of my head head. Now, as to the existential angst calibrating in your particular head head, I will articulate to Henry Trombone and annunciate to him that he trumpet a different tonality.*

    Sincerely,

    Fnark

Dear "Sobe" Ha! Ha! Ha!

How come on one of your books you wrote King Sobe? What are you, a egomaniacal? When you wrote about gaming, I thought you were writing about hunting and fishing, and you were writing about games in a casino that no one platys except crazy lunatic moroons who want to get rid of all of there money and give it to the wealthy dealers and the one-bombed bandits. We shoud outlaw casnois because it boars, but hunting is okay because I hunt and it is okay.

    George

Dear George:

I sob because you called me "Sobe," because my name on that book was King Scobe, but I don't want to offend you because I don't want to be hunted like a boar! Ha! Ha! Ha! I'm just joking; please believe me when I say that. Now, some bullet points: Those dealers make billions of dollars a year just dealing out cards and paying off craps bets. The executives have to work on tips off a minimum wage and empty those exploding one-bombed bandits. How unfair of the marketplace. The reason casnois are so unfair is that they are owned by the French.

Harken,
King Sobe

Dear Mr. Scoblete:

Let me introduce myself to you by way of introduction. I am a gambling expert looking to have my new book, which I am about to write, published so the world can see what I have developed and discovered, as I have developed a way to beat the game of roulette with a number-charting system based on the concepts inherited in quantum physics, which shows that a ball spinning will have an equal and opposite spin too, which will come to rest at a point of design that can be predicted mostly accurately by analyzing the opposite spin and trajectory thereoff and concept of propulsion of a small round object, which is what a roulette ball is, as we all know concerning roulette. Would you be interested in publishing my book or giving me a recommendation to a big publisher, not some little publisher, who could handle my profound breakthrough gambling conceptions? This book will sell millions.

Thanks in advance for helping me.
Edward W. W.

Dear Edward W.W.:
Huh?
Mr. Scoblete

Dear Frankie Boy:

You state that there is a way to beat carps with a controlled ice throw, and we all know this is a wrong idea, or all the casinos would be broke by now and turned into Burger King stories, and are they? No! I know that someone like Rainman could beat blackjack, but all of us aren't geniuses like Dusting Hoffman, but at least there is some speculation that blackjack has a way to be beated. Why do you carry on this dumb idea that you can beat craps, because craps players are a bunch of superstitions and you have to be caregful with them, as many are crasy, to put it moldly. I hate carps because of all the dirty old men who plague it!!!!!

Wake up and smell the roses!!!

Katherine

Dear Katy Girl:

I agree that many of the crasy old men who plague craps are moldy, and that is because they have carps in their pockets that smell. Have you used Dusting Hoffman to clean your house? I heard he does a great job, a great job, a great job. Craps can be beaten with a controlled throw, and you can see just such unedited throws in my new DVD. Your eyes will convince you. Carps can also be beaten with a stick. But carps get very mushy when you clobber them repeatedly.

More blackjacks to you,

Frankie Boy

Dear Frank:

You are wrong about your thinking in the slot machine area about how to judge a hot or cold machine. There are such things as those of us who play the machines know without a doubt concerning these machines. A hot machine can be determined by watching when others play and if they haven't won, that machine is going to get hot, because what follows cold? Logically what follows cold is hot, as anyone who has studied physicals knows.

So once a machine has been cold, it must get hot, as that is as old as a law of nature. How hot it stays for how long it stays hot, I don't know, so you have to be careful not to keep playing it if you start losing it. I know because I lost it a lot in the past by staying too long when a hot machine cold off and I just kept playing. So that is a caution I caution about to people who don't know how to play.

You should inform your readers about this because mostly magazines give the same old wrong advise about slot machines, and that advise is wrong, all wrong, over and over being wrong.

Please take my words seriously because I have played slots for a long time, and I know what works and what doesn't. I just have to get the discipline to leave machines that have gone from hot to cold sooner than after I have been leaving before.

Otherwise good wok.

Mary T.

Dear Mary T.:
Hey, you like Chinese food too! Great! Yes, hot and cold are relative terms, and I just had my yearly physical, so thanks for thinking of me. Sorry you keep losing at slots; your hot/cold system sounds intriguing.
Stay hot,
Frank

Dear Mr. Scobolete:
I have read each and every one of your books, and I enjoyed them each one. You are one fined writer, if I do say so myself. But I have one thing I don't like, and that is your insistence that math is the most important thing in casino gambling when even a fool knows that short-term luck is what makes you a winner. Without luck, players can't win and casinos can't win ether. Why don't you understand how luck works? It is not hard to understand. When things are going good you bet more and when things are going bad you bet less. How hard is that to understand? It isn't hard. But you and your fellow gambling wriers don't seem to understand this simple idea. Why don't you understand it? How hard is it to understand? Are the casinos paying you to lie to us about how to really win at the games because they are afraid of losing all of their money? That is what I think is really happening. I think gambling writers are being bribed!!! I am never buying another book of yours again!!!!!

Carter M.

Dear Carter:
I fell asleep in a casino, and I guess it is because they were lucky and won some ether. You were only hot in the past, you are not being hot. The next decision isn't influenced by what just happened in the past, except if you are counting cards at blackjack. These hot and cold ideas are a fallacy. I am very sorry that you got so angry at the end of your letter and have said you will never buy another book of mine. But that frees me to say...jump off a mountain, you cheap creep!
    Honestly yours,
    Mr. Scobolete

Dear Mr. Sclobetty:
Herd you on the radio and I an now decideding on a carear in gamling writtening because of you and I woul dlike your help. Mayby if we meet and you could infirm me some gelp that wool be okay dokay with myself. I no I haff the tal;ent I juts need the brakes. Can we hafe diner together?
    Your triuly
    Godfrey

Dear Godfrey:
It looks to me that you have the goods to be a journalist. But I have an even better idea—get involved in television news. I hear that MSNBC is looking for a new anchor.
    Yours turdly,
    Mr. Sclobetty

Dear Frank:
I bought a system to beet the casino games and the slots machines but I have lost even with this ssytem, which costs me over one hundred dollars. I sent the papers back to the cellar and guessed what happened? He never returned my money and his post office box sent all my mail back because he closed it. How do I get my money back and can I sue him and the casinos for my loses? He promised me I could buy an idland with what I won, and I have won nothing. Isn't this false misrepresentation?
    Billy

Dear Billy:
Stay in your cellar, eat beets, and never buy systems through the mail that promise you can buy an idland or even an island with your winnings.
Frank

Dear Mister Frank Scobelette:
I fellow the advice of if you see a horn you bet a horn at craps. I think this is good advixe since a horn is a horn is a horn if you didn't know it Mr. Frank Scobelette. You can't blow your money on a horn because this thing repeats itself all over the game and when it comes up you have to jump on it to make a lot of money. Haven't you see this with your own eyes if you supposedly play craps?

That is what is all about craps the repeating numbers, which is against all randomness, so when you see a horn you should bet a horn because randomness has vanished from that game right than and there, and I don't undertand why you go against this idea in your books and articles. It makes perfect sense to me even though it don't to you.

Do you know anything about playing craps and the other casino gams? I think you don't know anything if something so simple as see a horn beat a horn is not on your radar scream. I can't believe you are considered a big time gambling author Mr. Frank Scobelette and you don't even know nothing of this thing!
Evan

Dear Evan:
"See a horn, beat a horn" is an idea whose time has went and, in fact, has never was—got it? The saying was probably promulgated by some ploppy who has won substantial amounts of debt by playing this way. Okay, heck, do what you want. Since the casinos need people to lose their money in fat wads, you shall become one of their beloved.
See a horn, bet you'll lose,
Mister Frank Scobelette

There they are—a bowl of mixed casino nuts. Naturally, most casino players I meet are nothing like the individuals above. The biggest cross-section of casino players actually make slightly more money, donate slightly more money to charity, travel more, and have a more upscale lifestyle than the rest of the country's populace. But sometimes it's fun to dig into a bowl of mixed nuts and see what you get!

Glossary

401(g) Account: A bank account or money-market fund in which a player keeps his gambling bankroll. The *G* stands for *gambling*.

5-Count: The Captain's method for eliminating 57 percent of the random rolls in craps. Players who use the 5-Count will only bet on 43 percent of random rolls. In terms of comping, most 5-Counters have found they get the same comps for less risk because their body time is counted, not their risk time.

Ace: In blackjack an ace can count as a 1 or 11. In baccarat an ace counts as 1.

Action: The amount of money being bet at a table or the amount of money an individual bets.

Action Player: A player who bets a lot of money.

Ada from Decatur: The 8.

Advantage Player: A player who can get a real, mathematical edge over the casinos.

Anchor Player: The player seated in third base and the last to act before the dealer acts on his hand.

Any Craps: A one-roll bet on the numbers 2, 3, and 12.

Any Seven: A one-roll bet on the 7. Also known as "Big Red."

Arm, The: The woman considered by many to be the greatest dice controller of all time.

Automatic-Shuffle Machine: A machine used to preshuffle a separate shoe of cards so that it is ready to be used after the current shoe is exhausted.

Average Bet: The average of the total amount of a player's wagers per round.

Axis: Think of the dice glued next to each other with a stick going through the middle of both of them. The stick represents the axis around which the dice spin. Whenever we set the dice, there is an invisible axis going through the middle of them.

Axis Control: The ability to keep the dice on axis more than probability indicates.

Back Counting: Playing technique in which a player stands behind a table and counts the cards as a spectator with the intent of entering the game once the count becomes positive.

Backed Off: When a casino supervisor asks you to stop playing while you are playing blackjack. Generally when you are backed off, you are not read the trespass act or barred.

Backline: Old term for Don't Pass.

Back Wall: Sides of the table covered with foam-rubber pyramids that should be hit with each shot. These are there to randomize dice rolls.

Bank: A bet in baccarat.

Bankroll: The money you use to gamble.

Bar: Refers to a tie bet on the Come-Out roll for darkside players. The 12 will not win or lose for the Don't player. Some casinos will bar the 2 instead of the 12.

Barber Pole: Bets made with various colored chips, often not arranged in denomination order, high on bottom, low on top.

Barring: When a casino supervisor tells you that you are permanently prohibited from playing in the casino or playing a certain game in a casino, he is barring you.

Basic Strategy: The mathematically optimum way to play your hand based solely on the player's first two cards and the dealer's up-card. Good basic strategy minimizes the casino's edge over the player.

Below Random: The mistaken idea that something can be less than random. A dice throw is either random or controlled. There is no such thing as less than random or more than random.

Bet-All Players: Players who bet on every roll of the dice or on all shooters from the beginning of their rolls.

Bet Sizing: Scaling the size of your bet in relation to your mathematical advantage over the casino.

Bet Spread: The range between a player's minimum and maximum bets.

Betting Spot: Also called the "betting circle" or "square," it's the designated area on the layout in front of a player on which the player places his bet.

Betting Systems: Methods of manipulating bets in the mistaken belief that such a system can overcome the house edge.

Beveled Dice: Fixed dice.

Biased Dice: Dice that are fixed to favor certain dice faces over others. Also called "fixed dice."

Big 6: Even-money bet in the bottom corners of some craps tables.

Big 8: Even-money bet in the bottom corners of some craps tables.

Big Dick: The number 10.

Big Red: A one-roll bet on the 7. Also known as "Any Seven."

Blackjack: When the player's initial two cards consists of an ace and a 10-value card. Also called a "21."

Blackjack Counter/Card Counter: A player who monitors the dealt cards in some fashion that indicates who has an advantage (the casino or player) and by how much. Counters can use one of many different count systems, which all come down to measuring the disproportionate distribution of remaining cards. Depending on the count and the advantage it indicates, the player will bet more or less money.

Blacks: Chips usually worth $100.

Blues: Chips usually worth $1.

Body Time: How long a player stays at a table. Bets are not necessarily or always at risk during the player's body time at the table.

Bones: Another name for dice. Original dice were probably made from the bones of animals and perhaps people.

Bowl: Where the dice are kept in front of the stickman.

Boxcars: A 6:6 combination of the dice equaling the number 12.

Box Numbers: The 4, 5, 6, 8, 9, and 10, which appear in boxes at the top of the craps layout. Also know as "Point numbers."

Box Person: Individual who sits between the dealers at craps. He is responsible for cashing in players' money, counting out chips, and making sure payouts are correct. He also settles most of the disputes at the table.

Boys, The: Synonym for dealers.

Browns: Chips usually worth $5,000.

Buffalo: A bet on all the Hardways and on the Any Seven.

Burn Card(s): After the dealer shuffles the cards and they are cut, it's the top card removed from play. Any cards removed from play at the beginning or at any time during play.

Bust: When a blackjack player or dealer's hand totals more than 21.

Buy Bet: Paying a commission to get true odds, as opposed to house odds, on certain Place Bets at craps.

Buying a Player's Don't Bet: Paying a small fee to take over a Don't bet when the darkside player wishes to take down that bet. This can give the "buyer" an edge over the game.

Buy-in (n.)/Buy In (v.): The exchange of player's cash for casino chips.

Call Bet: Making a bet without any money or chips showing in one's hand. Usually not accepted.

Camouflage: Techniques to disguise the fact you are card counting or have an advantage at any game.

Capped Dice: Biased or fixed dice.

Captain, The: The world's greatest craps player and thinker. He is the developer of the 5-Count and of controlled shooting, also known as "rhythmic rolling" and "dice influence."

Card Counting: Keeping track of the relationship of high cards to low cards. Speed Count is an example of card counting that is extremely easy to learn.

Casino Cage or Cage: The "bank" of the casino, where players can cash in their chips, receive markers for slot play, and cash in some coupons or checks.

Casino Hold: For table games, the hold is a percentage of the player's buy-in that is won by the casino.

Charting/Charting Tables: Checking to see what trends are happening at a given table or with a given shooter. If the game is random, all charting is a waste of time.

Checks or Cheques: Another name for chips.

Chicken Feeders: Another name for random rollers. Coined because some shooters throw the dice in a way that looks as if they are feeding chickens.

Chip Counting: The ability to count the value of the chips of your fellow players, usually done in a tournament.

Chip Tray: Holds chips. Often called "rail" in craps.

Chips: Tokens used in place of money at casino table games.

Cocked Dice: Dice that land against a chip or against the wall in a slanted manner. The stickman will make the call based on what number would come up if the die or dice had continued in the direction they were going.

Color Up or Color: Player hands in chips at the table when finished with play to get higher-denomination chips.

Come Bet: After a shooter's Point is established, a bet that can be made during the Point Cycle of the game. The first placement of a bet will win on the 7 or 11 and lose on the 2, 3, or 12. Once up on a Box number, the bet wins if the number is hit and loses if a 7 is thrown.

Come-Out Roll: The shooter's first roll(s) before establishing a Point. Wins on the 7 or 11 and loses on the 2, 3, or 12. If the shooter makes his Point, the Come-Out Roll occurs again. If the shooter sevens out, he gives up the dice, and the next shooter gets them.

Comps or Complimentary: Casino gifts to the players, such as food, drink, free or discounted hotel rooms, parties, presents, and tickets to sporting or special events. Comps are based on the casino's analysis of what types of losses the player is expected to have. These are known as "theoretical losses."

Continuous-Shuffle Machine (CSM): A shuffling machine that randomly mixes the discards from each round with the undealt cards. Card counting does not work against a CSM, as cards are reintegrated into the shoe after each round.

Contract Bets: Pass Line Point number and Come bets that cannot be taken down or called off once on a number. These are two-part bets. Part one (Come-Out or first Come placement) favors the players and part two (the Point or Box number) favors the casinos. For the casinos to make money they must be able to have part two favor them in order to overcome the players' edge in part one.

Controlled Shooters: People who can change the probabilities of the game by their throw of the dice. Also known as "rhythmic rollers" and "dice influencers," among others.

Count: The value of the Speed Count. Also used to refer to the value of the counting metric with any count system.

Crapless Craps: The 2, 3, 11, and 12 can be Points. There are no Don't bets.

Crapping Out: Rolling a 2, 3, or 12 on the Come-Out roll. It is *not* a term for sevening out.

Craps Numbers: The 2, 3, and 12.

Crazy Crapper Bets: High-house-edge bets. Most of these are in the center of the layout.

Crossroader: A cheat or thief.

Cut Card: A colored plastic card inserted by the player into the shuffled decks of cards to determine where the dealer will cut the decks. When the cut card appears during a round, the round is completed, and then the decks are shuffled.

Cutoff: The unplayed cards remaining in the shoe after the cut card appears.

Darkside or Darksider: The Don't bets. A darksider is a person who makes Don't bets.

DAS: Double after pair-splitting. Conversely, NoDAS means that doubling after splitting is not allowed. DAS in an advantageous rule for the player.

Dead Table: A table at which no one is playing or a table where shooters have had a series of early seven-outs.

Dependent Trial Game: A game where what happened before has an impact on what happens next. An example is blackjack: If all aces have come out, no one can get a blackjack.

Devil, The: A term for the 7.

Dice Influencing: The ability to change the probabilities of the game by a player's throw of the dice. Also known as "rhythmic rolling" and "controlled shooting," among other terms.

Dice Set: A specific arrangement of dice before a shooter throws them.

Discard Tray: A clear plastic device that holds the dealt cards during play.

Discards: The cards that are removed from a round of play and placed in the discard tray.

Do and Do Players: Betting with the number (or Point) and against the 7. A player who bets the Pass Line, Come bet, Place bets, and Crazy Crapper bets, for which a player is rooting for the number to appear. Also known as "lightside" or "rightside" and as "right betting."

Doey-Don't: Betting both the Pass Line and Don't Pass simultaneously. Betting both the Come and Don't Come simultaneously.

Don't Come: Bet placed after shooter's point is established. First placement wins on the 2 or 3, loses on the 7 or 11, and pushes on the 12 (sometimes the 2 and 12 are substituted for each other). Once up on a number, bet wins if shooter rolls a 7, and the bet loses if the shooter rolls the number.

Don't Pass: Opposite of the Pass Line. On the Come-Out roll, player wins if a 2 or 3 is rolled; he loses if a 7 or 11 is rolled; he ties if a 12 is rolled (sometimes the 2 and 12 are substituted for each other). Once the Point is established, a 7 wins for the Don't Pass, and the appearance of the Point loses for the Don't Pass.

Don't Place: A Place bet against a number, where a 7 wins and the number loses.

Double Down: After a player receives his initial two cards, he has the option to make one secondary bet up to the amount of the initial bet and receive exactly one extra dealt card. The money for doubles can equal or be less than the original bet.

Double Odds: A game that offers 2X Odds behind the Pass Line, Don't Pass, Come, and Don't Come.

Down: Bet is taken off the number and is given back to the player. Can be done with all Place bets but not with the contract bets of the Pass Line or Come.

Down Behind: A dealer announces that a darksider's Don't bet has lost.

Down-Card: Dealer's hole card or any card that is dealt facedown.

Down with Odds: A player's Place number hits and his Come bet goes to the number. This means the Odds are put on the Come, and the rest of the Place bet is given back.

Drop Box: Where the player's money is put when he cashes into a game to get his chips.

Early Surrender: A player is allowed to surrender his hand before the dealer checks for a blackjack (see Surrender).

Easy Way: Numbers not made with doubles. Also known as "soft way."

Edge: Generally refers to the mathematical advantage as a percentage the casino has over the player or vice versa. The edge is the average amount that you should expect to win or lose in the long run on each and every bet you make.

Emotional Bankroll: An amount of bankroll that allows a player to take naturally occurring and expected losses in stride.

Even Money: A bet that is paid off 1-to-1, such as the Pass Line, Come, Don't Pass, and Don't Come in craps or the red/black, high/low, odd/even at roulette. Also known as "flat bet."

Expected Win Rate or Expected Win: What the math shows you will either win or lose in the long run based upon how you bet.

Exit Strategy: Leaving a blackjack table or not playing rounds when the count is very poor, indicating a high house edge.

Expectation: What the player can expect to win or lose over time, betting the way he bets.

Eye in the Sky: Video surveillance area above the casino floor.

Face-Down Game: The cards are dealt facedown.

Face-Up Game: The player's initial two cards are dealt face up, and the player is not permitted to handle or touch the cards.

Fair Game: A game at which the casino does not have an edge. Paid at correct odds.

Fever: The 5.

Field Bet: Betting on the numbers 2, 3, 4, 9, 10, 11, and 12 at once. If any of these are hit, the bet wins. If the 5, 6, 7, or 8 appear, the bet loses. On layout, the Field is just above the Pass Line.

Fig-Vig: Buy bets that collect a commission (also called the "vig" or "vigorish") only on winning bets.

Fire Bet: A bet that the shooter will establish and make each number as his Point during his turn with the dice.

First Base: The player's seat located on the far right of the blackjack table that is dealt to first (dealer's left side).

Fixed Dice: Dice that are biased either by design or by accident.

Fixing the Dice: Antiquated term for setting the dice.

Flags: Red, white, and blue chips worth $5,000.

Flat Bet: Bet paid off at even money.

Floor Person: Individual who stands behind one or more box persons in a pit and is in charge of making sure everything is run smoothly. Can also be the person who gives out some comps.

Gaff or Gaffed Game: A rigged gaming device, such as dice.

Gambler's Fallacy: The belief that if deviations from expected behaviors are observed in some random process, these deviations are likely to be evened out by opposite deviations in the future.

George: A player who tips. A player who is easy to deal with.

Giving Odds: The same as Laying odds. Taking the long end of a bet.

Gold: Chips usually worth $5,000.

Golden Touch Craps: The premier school for learning dice control.

Grays: Chips usually worth $5,000.

Greens: Chips usually worth $25.

Grind Joint: A low-level casino that shuns high-roller action.

H17: Dealer must hit on a soft 17. Conversely, S17, when dealer must stand on soft 17, is a favorable and preferable rule for the player.

Hand Spreading: Increasing the number of hands one plays if the count has gone positive.

Hard Hand: Any hand that either does not contain an ace, or, if it does, the ace must count as 1.

Hardway: A number that comes up in doubles: 1:1, 2:2, 3:3, 4:4, 5:5, and 6:6.

Hardway Set: A set with Hardway Box numbers all around it: 2:2, 3:3, 4:4, and 5:5, with the 6-spot and the 1-spot on the axis. These doubles are called "hard numbers."

Heads Up: Playing alone with the dealer.

Heat: When casino executives scrutinize a player very carefully while he plays.

Hedging Bets: Using one or more bets to offset the impact of one or more other bets.

High-Low: Betting the 12 and the 2 at the same time. Betting the high or low numbers in roulette, which is an even-money bet.

Hi-Lo: Traditional card-counting method.

High Roller: Big bettor.

Hit: When a player requests another card or when, by the rules, a dealer must draw another card at blackjack or baccarat. Or, a number that has been rolled at craps or a number that has been decided at roulette.

Holding Pattern: During the 5-Count process, if no Box number is rolled after the 4-count, the 5-Count can't be completed yet and is said to be at "4-count and holding."

Hole Card: The dealer's card that is dealt facedown; also known as the "down-card."

Hook or Corner: Where the craps table turns. Area of pyramids under the hook is considered the Mixing Bowl, where the dice tend to be randomized even for controlled shooters.

Hop Bet or Hopping Bet: One-roll bet that a certain number will come up, usually in a certain way, such as an 8 with 5:3 or a 10 with 6:4.

Horn Bet and Horn-High Bet: Multinumber bet, in units of $4, that the 2, 3, 11, or 12 will be rolled. A $5 variation allows a $2 bet on any of the four numbers. This is called a Horn-High bet.

Host: A casino employee who caters to casino players who wager a significant amount in the casino.

House Edge: The percentage of each bet that the house keeps. The house does this by winning more bets than the player or by taxing the players' wins by not paying off at true odds.

In and In For: How much the player has cashed in for.

In Control of Tip: Player puts down a tip for the dealers and says, "I control it." This means when the bet wins, the dealers can only take down the winning portion, not the original bet.

Independent Trial Game: All the previous decisions at the game have no influence or bearing on what is coming up next.

Inside Numbers: The 5, 6, 8, and 9.

Insurance: A bet the player can make when the dealer is showing an ace. The player puts half his bet or less in the insurance area. If the dealer has a blackjack, the player wins 2-to-1 on the insurance bet.

ISC: Initial Speed Count, or the value of the Speed Count at the start of a new shoe.

Jimmy Hicks: The number 6.

Juice: Another term for casino edge. Also a term for a high-rolling player who gets what he wants.

Juice Joint: A casino that cheats.

Kelly Criterion: Betting a percentage of your total bankroll based on the percent of your edge at any given time in a game.

Lay or Lay Bet: To bet against a number and for the 7 at craps. Player pays long end of the Odds on such bets.

Laying Odds: When the darkside bet is up on the number, the player may put Odds on the bet. Player puts long end of the Odds, because he is betting that the 7 will show. The 7 has an edge against every number and is the favorite to show.

Lightside and Lightsiders: The overwhelming majority of craps players bet with the Pass Line at the game. The Pass Line is a lightside bet. Lightside players bet with the numbers and against the 7 during the Point Cycle of the game. Also called "rightside" players.

Little Joe or Little Joe from Kokomo: The number 4.

Live One: A player who tips.

Lock the Chips: Bets or extraneous chips that no one claims are taken by the casino.

Low Roller: Small bettor.

Markers: Casino credit. Is essentially a check to the casinos for borrowed money and has a specific time frame in which to be repaid.

Martingale: Betting increasingly more money when you are losing, to make up for previous losses. Also known as a "negative progression." Most players will double their bets after losses, thinking, *I have to win at least one bet.*

Maximum Bets or Table Maximum: The most a player can wager on one bet at a given table.

Midnight: The 12.

Midshoe Entry: A big question in blackjack is what happens if you place a bet on the felt in the middle of a shoe. Some casinos will not allow you to make a bet if you have not been betting since the start of the shoe. This restriction is designed to hamper card counters from betting only when the count is favorable.

Mini-Baccarat: A version of baccarat played on a blackjack type of table. Players do not get to deal at this game, and it is a very, very fast game.

Minimum Bets or Table Minimum: The least a player can wager on one bet at a given table.

Mixing Bowl: Where the craps table turns and where the dice tend to be randomized even for controlled shooters.

Monetary Edge: The player's expectation in the game coupled with comps gives the player more money than he loses.

Money Management: How much you bet based on how much money you give yourself to gamble.

Money Player: A player who wagers with actual currency instead of chips. Also a big bettor.

Money Plays: A call made by the dealer indicating that a player is playing with real money instead of chips. Not allowed in most casinos anymore.

Monster Roll: A long roll.

Nailing a Player: Catching a player cheating.

Natural: A 7 or 11 on the Come-Out roll or on the initial placement of a Come bet. Also, another name for a blackjack hand or a 9 or 8 at baccarat.

Negative Count: A count that favors the casinos.

Negative Progressions: Betting increasingly more money when you are losing to make up for previous losses. Also called "martingale."

Nickel: A $5 bet.

Nina Ross and the Bucking Horse: The number 9.

Ninety Days: The number 9.

No Bet: A late bet that is not accepted by the dealers.

No Hole Card: In some games the dealer waits until the players have played their hands before giving himself a hole card.

No Roll: A roll in craps that does not count.

Odds: The likelihood of something happening against the likelihood of that same thing not happening. The 7 will come up six times for every three times the 4 will come up. The odds are 6-to-3, or 2-to-1. The Odds bet in craps can be placed on Pass Line, Don't Pass, Come, and Don't Come bets and is paid off at its true value. For example, a 4 would pay 2-to-1 on the Pass Line, and on the Don't Pass it would pay 1-to-2.

Odds Working: On the Come-Out roll the Odds can work on all Come and Don't Come bets if the player desires.

Off: Odds and Place bets can be turned off, which means the bet is not working and can neither be won nor lost.

Opposition Stance: Right-handed shooters standing at stick right; left-handed shooters standing at stick left.

Optimum Basic Strategy (OBS): A hand-playing strategy that is used by a player who uses Speed Count.

Outside Numbers: The 4, 5, 9, and 10.

Over Seven or Under Seven: The craps player can bet that the next roll will either be higher than 7 or lower than 7. If a 7 is hit, the bet loses.

Pair-Splitting: Splitting your pairs to make two hands. You must bet the same amount on second hand as you did on the first.

Parlay: Letting the win and the initial bet ride on the next decision.

Pass and Passers: The shooter is making his Pass Line Points. The term for a shooter who makes his Pass Line Points.

Passing the Dice: Player prefers not to shoot the dice and passes them to the next player.

Pass Line: Player is betting that the 7 or 11 will win on the Come-Out roll and that the shooter's point will be made before the 7 is rolled.

Past Posting: Making a bet after the decision has been called. This is the most common form of cheating.

Pay Behind: Dealer call to pay off Don't bets.

PC: Abbreviation for *percentage*.

Peek: When the dealer is dealt an ace or 10 up-card and manually checks the hole card to determine if he has a blackjack. Insurance is offered prior to the peek if the up-card is an ace. If the hand is a blackjack, the dealer flips the hand, and the round is done.

Pendulum Swing: Right-handers standing at stick left; left-handers standing at stick right. The swing looks like a pendulum as it takes place.

Penetration: The percentage of cards that are dealt before the shuffle.

Phoebe or Little Phoebe: The number 3.

Pinks: Chips usually worth $2.50.

Pig Vig: Buy bets on which the commission (vig) must be paid on all wagers, whether they win or lose. The house edge is much higher on these than on Fig-Vig Buy bets, on which commission is only taken out of winning bets.

Pips: White dots or spots on the sides of the dice.

Pit: A group of table games looked over by a pit boss.

Pit Boss: The executive in charge of supervising table games in a given pit.

Pitch: A method used by the dealer to deal the cards to players, usually in single- and double-deck games.

Pivot Point: The value of the Speed Count when the player's expectation turns from negative to positive.

Place Bets or Placing Numbers: Going right up on a number without using the Pass Line, Come, Don't Pass, or Don't Come bets. The casino takes a higher percentage of money from the players for such bets.

Place Odds: Payment of Place bets at "house odds," which means they do not pay off at the true odds of the bet.

Play Variation: A deviation from the basic playing strategy used by advanced card counters, based upon the count.

Player: A bet at baccarat.

Ploppy: Multifaceted term that describes foolish, stupid, idiotic, and pathetic dopes and dingbats, and also those who look these parts. Not a compliment. *Ploppy* can be used to describe players, gambling writers, and casino personnel...and even people who never go near a casino.

Point: The number the shooter establishes that he must hit before the appearance of the 7 in order for the Pass Line bet to win.

Point Cycle: The part of the craps game during which the shooter is looking to make his Point on the Pass Line and avoid the 7.

Point Numbers: Also known as Box numbers. The 4, 5, 6, 8, 9, and 10.

Positive Count: A count that favors the players. In Speed Count, it is 31.

Positive Progression: Increasing your bets when you are winning.

Post Holes: The Hard 8.

Power of the Pen: Casino employee has it if he can write comps for the players.

Press: Increasing one's bet. Usually by doubling it, but the increase can be in any amount.

Pressure: Increasing one's bet.

Primary Hit: Hitting the numbers that your dice are set for. On the Hardway Sets these would be the Hard 4, Hard 6, Hard 8, and Hard 10.

Probability: The likelihood that an event or decision will occur.

Progressive Betting: Increasing or decreasing one's bet based on past decisions.

Proposition Bets: High-house-edge bets. Also known as Crazy Crapper bets.

Puck: A black (*off*)/white (*on*) disk that shows whether game is on Come-Out roll or which Point number has been established by the shooter.

Pumpkins: Orange chips, usually worth $1,000.

Puppy Paws: Another name for a Hard 10.

Purples: Chips usually worth $500.

Push: A tie.

Pushing the House: Getting a better game from the casino than it advertises.

Put Bets: Placing of a Pass Line or Come bet with Odds without going through the Come-Out or initial bet on the Come.

Pyramids: Foam-rubber pyramids at the back of the table (also known as the "back wall") that players' dice must hit with each throw. These are used to help randomize dice throws.

Quarter Chips: Worth $25, usually green in color.

Quarter Player: A player who wagers a minimum of $25 on each hand.

Rail: Term in craps for the area in which a player's chips are held.

Railbird: A criminal who steals players' chips from their rails, usually when they are shooting or watching the game and not paying attention to their chips.

Random Rollers: Shooters who have no dice-control skills and shoot the dice with results being determined by randomness. One type of these shooters is called a "chicken feeder."

Random Rolls: Dice rolls that are determined by randomness and exhibit no control whatsoever.

Rat-Hole: Putting chips in your pocket, usually to prevent the casino from knowing how much was won.

Rating: A method used by the pit to keep track of the amount of money wagered by a player for the purpose of establishing a comp value.

Reds: Chips usually worth $5.

Resplits: Allowing a player to resplit a pair, usually limited to three or four hands.

RFB: Stands for "Room, Food, and Beverage" and is a term used for high rollers in the casinos. These players get most or all of their expenses comped.

Rhythmic Rollers: Shooters who take care with the dice and with their throw. Early term for dice control, dice influence, and controlled shooting.

Rightside and Right Player: Betting with the point and against the 7 during the Point Cycle of the game on Pass Line, Come, and Place bets. Also known as "lightside."

Risk Time: The amount of time a player's money is at risk.

RLFB: Stands for "Room, Limited Food and Beverages" (usually non-gourmet). The comp step that is just under RFB.

S17: Dealer must stand on all 17s (including soft 17). This rule is advantageous for the player.

Same Dice: Many shooters will ask for the same dice when one or both of their dice go off the table. The superstition is that when dice go off the table and the shooter is given new dice, he will seven out.

Save the Odds: When a 7 is rolled on the Come-Out and the Come bet Odds are not working, these will be returned to the player.

Savvy Players: Smart players who make the best bets at the table.

Scoreboard/Scorecard: Keeping track of the numbers that have hit at roulette or other games. Electronic scoreboards are now found on almost all roulette tables and at some craps tables. Trend bettors like to use these to decide what bets to make.

Secondary Hit: The dice hit a number you are not specifically setting for but which contains one or two of the numbers whose faces are a part of the initial set.

Session: Amount of time a player spends at a table from cashing in to completion.

Session Stake: The total amount of money a player gives himself to play for a certain period of time.

Seven Out: Call made by the stickman indicating that the Pass Line bet lost and that the dice go to the next shooter, as well as an expression that your roll ended.

Shift: Usually a period of eight work hours.

Shift Boss or Shift Manager: The executive in charge of a given shift.

Shill: A casino worker who plays games with casino money in order to entice others to play that game.

Shoe: Device used to hold the undealt cards, usually when four or more decks of cards are used.

Skinny Dugan: The number 7.

Sleeper: Money left on the table that the player has forgotten about.

Smart Player: Players who use the best possible strategies at the games they play.

SmartCraps: A software program composed of three tests to gauge the axis control of a shooter.

Snake Eyes: A 1:1 combination of the dice equaling the number 2.

Soft Hand: A hand containing an ace.

Soft Way or Soft Bets: Dice combinations not made with doubles.

Speed Count: A new and novel card-counting method that tracks the ratio of 2s through 6s played per hand.

Split House: A casino at which dealers pool their tips.

Splitting: A player choice available only when your first two cards are a pair, or two 10-value cards. A new card is dealt to each original card, creating a new hand, and the player adds a new bet for the second hand. Each hand is then played separately (including more splits if applicable). Dissimilar face cards and 10s may be split as well, although it is not generally to the player's advantage to split 10-value cards and is rarely done.

SRR: Seven-to-rolls ratio. A random dice roll averages six 7s for every 36 rolls in the long run. The SRR is therefore 1:6. An SRR above 1:6 or below 1:6 over an extended period of time would probably mean the shooter is influencing the dice.

Stand: The player's decision not to receive any more cards (or the dealer requirement that he not draw any more cards).

Standard Deviation: A reflection of the variability of win or loss, or risk. A higher standard deviation means you will have more fluctuation in your bankroll as you play.

Stick or Stickman: Individual who uses the stick to move the dice to and from the shooter. Individual who calls the numbers when rolled and indicates which Proposition bets have won. Sometimes called "stick person."

Stick Left (SL): On the left-hand side of the stickman.

Stick Right (SR): On the right-hand side of the stickman.

Stiff: A player who doesn't tip.

Stiff Hand: A hard hand that totals 12 through 16. These are poor hands.

Suits: Those working the pits who wear suits. Generally a negative connotation.

Surrender (AKA Late Surrender): A playing option whereby a player can forfeit half of his bet and the right to complete his hand. You can only surrender after you receive your initial two cards and after the dealer checks if he has a blackjack.

Sweat: Casino personnel who get upset when they lose money or have to deal with savvy players.

Table Dumping: A table that is losing money.

Tabletop Throw: Shooting the dice from the tabletop before lifting them. Requires more muscle action than a pendulum throw.

Taking Odds: On the Pass or Come, putting extra money in play when the number is established. This extra money is called "Odds" or "Free Odds."

Testes Tanking: When a male who is shooting for the first time sevens out quickly.

Texas Sunflowers: The Hard 10.

Theoretical Loss: How much a player can expect to lose in the long run betting as he does. This "loss" is the baseline used for comps.

Third Base: The playing seat located to the far left of the blackjack table, dealt to last before the dealer (to the right of the dealer).

Tie: A specific bet at baccarat. Also, no decision on a bet or a "push."

Tip: A gratuity.

Toke: A tip specifically given to a dealer.

Too Tall to Call: When a die or both dice land on the chip rail. Also, "In the wood, no good!"

Trend(s): Recent streaks in numbers. In a random game, these decisions are meaningless for future decisions.

Trend Systems: Betting either with or against a recent trend, thinking it will continue or end.

Trip Bankroll: An amount of bankroll required for a trip (consisting of more than one playing session).

True Bounce: Bounce that comes from a 45-degree angle on a traditional table.

True Odds: The correct payout based upon the real odds of a bet.

Tub Table: Small, one-dealer craps table that resembles a tub. Players sit to play the game.

Two Ways: Same bet for both the player and the dealer.

Unit or Units: The minimum bet a player makes. If a player's minimum bet is $5, a bet of $10 for him would be a two-unit bet.

Up-Card: The dealer's card (of the two initial cards) that is dealt face up for the players to see.

Variance: The ups and downs and swings of a game.

Vig or Vigorish: Another name for the casino edge.

Virgin Principle: The superstition that a woman who has never rolled the dice before will have a good roll.

Watermelon: Chips worth $25,000.

Whirl or World Bet: A wager that the 2, 3, 7, 11, or 12 will be rolled.

Whites: Chips usually worth $1.

Working Bets: Bets that can be won or lost. Player can have his bets on the various numbers can work on the Come-Out roll as can one-roll proposition bets.

Wrong Side and Wrong Bettor: The wrong side of a craps game is rooting for the 7 instead of the Point during the Point Cycle of the game. During Come-Out roll, the wrong bettor is rooting for the 2 or 3 for a win but does not want a losing 7 or 11 to be rolled. Also called "darkside" or "darksider."

Yo: Another term for the 11.